Liberty,
Equality,
Fraternity

JACK R. CENSER AND LYNN HUNT

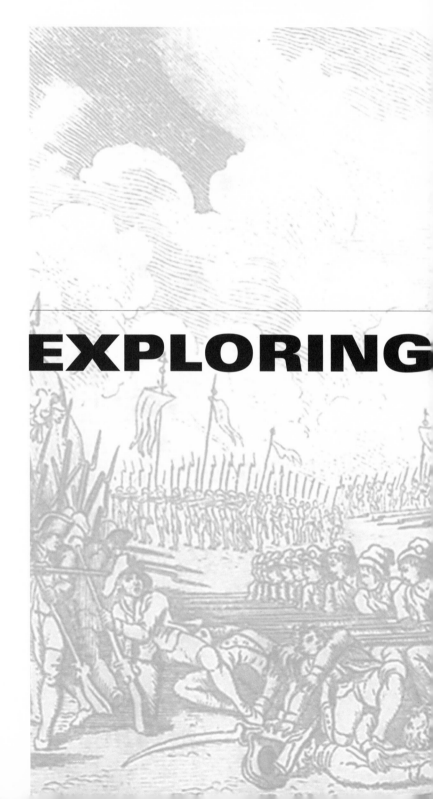

EXPLORING

Liberty, Equality, Fraternity

THE FRENCH REVOLUTION

The Pennsylvania State University Press
University Park, Pennsylvania

The CD-ROM included with this book was prepared with the support of the Center for History and New Media at George Mason University and of the American Social History Project at City University of New York. Copyright © 2001 American Social History Productions, Inc.

Library of Congress Cataloging-in-Publication Data

Censer, Jack Richard.
  Liberty, equality, fraternity : exploring the French Revolution / Jack R. Censer and Lynn Hunt.
     p.   cm.
  Includes bibliographical references and index.
  ISBN 0-271-02087-3 (alk. paper)—ISBN 0-271-02088-1 (pbk. : alk. paper)
  1. France—History—Revolution, 1789–1799. I. Hunt, Lynn Avery. II. Title.
  DC148.C388 2001
  944.04—dc21

Second printing, 2001

It is the policy of The Pennsylvania State University Press to use acid-free paper for the first printing of all clothbound books. Publications on uncoated stock satisfy the minimum requirements of American National Standard for Information Sciences—Permanence of Paper for Printed Library Materials, ANSI Z39.48–1992.

CONTENTS

LIST OF IMAGES

STUDY IN IMAGES, FOLLOWING PAGE 82

STUDY IN IMAGES (cont'd)

LIST OF DOCUMENTS

PREFACE

Another study of the French Revolution! Few historical subjects have received such exhaustive treatment by scholars and other writers. In fact, the number of monographic as well as synthetic works on this topic occupies substantial space even in small libraries. Larger collections contain many of the tens of thousands of primary and secondary sources available. And historians have responded to this tremendous outpouring of scholarship with a steady flow of surveys of the Revolution that try to master its complexity for the reader.

This book and the CD-ROM included with it add important new dimensions for those interested in the French Revolution. The structure of this book differs somewhat from most surveys. Four of its six chapters take up the customary narrative of the Revolution, from its causes through Napoleon. Although no study, especially one as brief as this, could ever be inclusive, we try to follow a wide range of events, including the social and cultural events as well as the military and political ones. Women's history and gender relations, topics that have become especially important in recent years, are not separate but have been integrated into the general story. Furthermore, one chapter focuses on the Revolution as it unwound in the Caribbean colonies, the locale outside France that most radically experienced the effects of the France-based explosion of ideas and actions. In addition, the Caribbean colonies were a crucible in which race was added to the revolutionary mix. Too often general studies ignore this subject, and seldom do they examine how the Revolution embroiled other nations and had important repercussions up to our own time. The last chapter considers the contemporary international reaction and follows nineteenth-century liberals, conservatives, and socialists who fashioned their beliefs around their perceptions of the Revolution. Finally, the book grapples with how several generations of scholars have interpreted the Revolution.

Because the French Revolution is such a complex subject, we have tried to make the text as accessible as possible. Each chapter includes a section containing documents that illuminate points for debate and discussion. Each group of documents focuses on a single important point so that readers can delve more deeply into the issues. These sections not only provide new information and insights but also give the reader some solid foundations to use as a framework for coming to grips with the Revolution. In a sense the issues highlighted in this way provide an outline around which one can more easily organize the plethora of information available.

This book also serves as an introduction to the enclosed CD-ROM, which itself is a substantial archive. (Cross references to the CD-ROM are also noted by icons in the margin, as here.) The CD-ROM contains some 400 documents, more than 250 images, an album's worth of songs, many maps, a time line, a glossary, and plenty of other helpful materials. Although the CD-ROM may be used by itself, readers of this book will be able to maximize their use of its electronic companion. The framework for the CD-ROM is two different layers of material. At the most general level there is a series of multimedia overviews, each consisting of a lecture and appropriate images. These overviews present in summary form the arguments made in this book's six chapters. The numerous materials contained in the CD-ROM are closely organized around the themes of the document sections in the book. The CD-ROM has its own chapters, each of which expands and deepens the issues raised in the documents. The book provides many good starting points for exploring issues raised during the Revolution, among them the tradition of rights, the experience of the Terror, Parisian politics, and the rise and fall of Napoleon. The CD-ROM includes many more details about each of the many issues. Every CD-ROM chapter has as its "spine" an additional essay on the designated subject. At appropriate points, the user may consult relevant documents that prove a point or demonstrate exceptions. The same may be said for the images, maps, and songs, which are also placed along the "spine" of each CD-ROM chapter. Each of those documents has further explanations and introductory material. Supporting all this, on the CD-ROM are a glossary, a time line, and what is perhaps most original, essays on how to "read" images and listen to revolutionary songs. These essays allow readers to gain even more from the material presented here. In addition, the CD-ROM includes information about the Museum of the French Revolution, the institution that provided many of the images published here.

The CD-ROM has some remarkable advantages in addition to the amount of material on it and the multimedia materials it provides: the reader can underline, erase, and re-underline; pages can be dog-eared; and the reader can take notes, which the CD-ROM automatically indexes. The CD-ROM also makes it possible to search by key word or by concept, and has a "notebook" with it for developing longer trains of thought about a topic. Best of all, the materials can be downloaded for the user's own purposes.

The CD-ROM, with its own overviews and introductory material, can stand alone. But used along with this book it will be even more exciting and helpful. Likewise, the book opens the way to further study when combined with its electronic partner. The possibilities such multimedia combinations offer are only just now becoming apparent, and we have found that our effort to bring them into fruitful conjunction intellectually as well as pedagogically has been rewarding. We know you will find that this combination of book and CD-ROM will add valuable approaches to the study and appreciation of the French Revolution.

We wish to thank both Peter Potter, our editor at Penn State Press, for his assistance and insights, and Joan Landes, who read this book for the Press. Her suggestions improved the volume. Research assistants at George Mason University, Jessica Finnefrock and Troy LaChance, helped select the documents and organize them within the sections. Jessica Finnefrock and Lynne Zegeer assisted with the permissions process.

In addition, this book includes and is based on a CD-ROM that was completed by a large team of people and subsidized by various organizations. While a complete list of credits for that project may be found in the CD-ROM itself, it is important to mention here the key contributors. Most of the editorial work on that project was done at the Center for History and New Media, directed by Roy Rosenzweig, at George Mason University. Roy Rosenzweig's advice on both editorial and production matters was essential, and his efforts were instrumental in locating the necessary funding for this project. Key staff included associate editors of the CD-ROM, Greg Brown and Jeff Horn, and Jessica Finnefrock, who served as the manager for the last year of the project. The American Social History Project (City University of New York) provided the site, expertise, and personnel for production activities. Led by Steve Brier and Josh Brown, the American Social History Project (ASHP) has pioneered the development of multimedia projects in historical studies. Without them, this project would not have been feasible. Josh Brown and Pennee Bender organized and supervised the completion of the CD-ROM at the ASHP offices in New York City. The work of everyone involved was generously supported by the National Endowment for the Humanities and the Florence Gould Foundation. We are very grateful to them.

I

France on the Eve of 1789: A Society in Crisis?

THERE IS BESIDES SOMETHING SPECIAL IN THIS MALADY OF THE FRENCH REVOLUTION THAT I FEEL WITHOUT BEING ABLE TO DESCRIBE IT WELL OR TO ANALYZE ITS CAUSES. IT IS A *VIRUS* OF A NEW AND UNKNOWN KIND. THERE WERE VIOLENT REVOLUTIONS IN THE WORLD, BUT THE IMMODERATE, VIOLENT, RADICAL, DESPERATE, AUDACIOUS, ALMOST MAD, AND NONETHELESS POWERFUL AND EFFECTIVE CHARACTER OF THESE REVOLUTIONARIES IS WITHOUT PRECEDENT, IT SEEMS TO ME, IN THE GREAT SOCIAL AGITATIONS OF PAST CENTURIES. FROM WHENCE CAME THIS NEW RACE? WHAT PRODUCED IT? WHAT MADE IT SO EFFECTIVE? WHAT IS PERPETUATING IT?

—ALEXIS DE TOCQUEVILLE (1858)

(CD-ROM p. 167)

The French Revolution transformed French society and politics and threatened the entire established order of Europe. French revolutionaries granted equal rights to religious minorities, suppressed serfdom and the remaining feudal obligations, abolished the nobility, reorganized the Catholic church, installed a republican form of government, executed the king, and started a war that would eventually engulf much of Europe, the Caribbean, and the Near East. They also executed 40,000 supposed counterrevolutionaries and arrested 300,000 suspects for political crimes. Some 250,000 people died in civil wars fought within France; many hundreds of thousands died in the wars with foreign powers. By the end of 1799 France had tried out four different constitutions at home and imposed new constitutions on conquered territories in the Netherlands, Italy, and Switzerland. The French aimed to revolutionize all of Europe; as might be expected, the European monarchs did everything they could to hold back this seemingly irresistible tide.

After the decade of revolutionary upheaval, 1789–99, came fifteen years of rule by Napoleon Bonaparte, a minor Corsican nobleman who rose to become emperor of the French nation. Between 1799 and 1815, Napoleon recast France in a more authoritarian mold and at the same time continued to impose revolutionary reforms on the rest of Europe. By 1810 Napoleon controlled most of Europe west of Vienna, but his invasion of Russia in 1812 spelled the beginning of his decline. Though he won most of the battles, he lost his army to the cold and to the rigors of withdrawal. In 1814 his own government deposed him, and after a brief attempt to regain his position the united European allies defeated him definitively at Waterloo in 1815. The victors sent Napoleon into permanent exile, where he died in 1821. The rulers of Europe finally breathed a collective sigh of relief.

Twenty-five years of constant turmoil and upheaval seem to require equally dramatic origins. As the French aristocrat and social commentator Alexis de Tocqueville observed in the letter excerpted above, "the immoderate, violent, radical, desperate, audacious, almost mad, and nonetheless powerful and effective character of these revolutionaries is without precedent." Tocqueville devoted many years of his life to assessing the causes of the French Revolution, and yet even he confessed that he never entirely penetrated its secrets. How could the most populous country in western Europe, one with a history of centuries of monarchical rule, become the home of modern revolution? Did revolution arise out of particularly oppressive social conditions? Was French society in crisis on the eve of 1789? Or was the Revolution an accident of history? Tocqueville was only one of many who have argued about the same questions since 1789.

The origins of the French Revolution can be divided into three major categories: society, monarchy, and new ideas. French society did not experience more tensions and conflicts than other European societies. The French monarchy did not oppress its subjects more than the other European rulers did. And the ideas of the movement known as the Enlightenment affected other countries and not just France. Nevertheless, the interaction of social tensions, monarchical failures, and new ideas was explosive in France. It is the task of the next few pages to explain how this could be so.

Society and Social Tensions

The best way to understand French society as a whole is to compare it with the societies of its nearest powerful neighbors, Great Britain and Prussia (a leading German state). On a scale ranging from most capitalist to most feudal, France ranked just about in the middle, with Great Britain on the capitalist end and Prussia on the feudal end. By 1789, Great Britain had long been free of the remnants of serfdom or feudalism. All land was freely owned and exchanged on the market, nobles enjoyed no meaningful legal privileges, and the middle classes were growing in numbers, wealth, and self-confidence. In contrast, France still lived with the vestiges of a feudal or seigneurial regime.[1] There were between 140,000 and 1,500,000 serfs, depending on how strictly serfdom is defined, and almost every peasant paid seigneurial dues to his noble landlord. Dues ranged from required labor on the lord's estate to fees for baking in his lord's oven or using his wine or olive press. (Document 1.3 includes several examples of seigneurial dues.) French nobles enjoyed various legal privileges, including exemptions from some forms of taxation. Yet the French middle classes, like their English counterparts, were growing in number (tripling in the eighteenth century), due to an explosive increase in overseas commerce and domestic manufacturing. French peasants owned about 50 percent of the land in the country. Prussia, on the other end of the scale, was much more caught up in the coils of feudalism or seigneurialism than France. Prussian nobles dominated their serfs on the land and occupied all the important positions in the army and the bureaucracy. Prussian nobles did not just enjoy legal privileges; they controlled both the army and the state administration. Few Prussian peasants owned the land they worked, and the middle classes were still small in number and relatively timid in political outlook. In other words, French society was a kind of hybrid, neither entirely free of the feudal past nor entirely caught up in it. As the quote from Abbé Emmanuel

> It is not sufficient to show that privileged persons, far from being useful to the nation, cannot but enfeeble and injure it; it is necessary to prove further that the noble order does not enter at all into the social organization; that it may indeed be a burden upon the nation, but that it cannot of itself constitute a nation.
> —Emmanuel Sieyès, *What Is the Third Estate?* (1789) (CD-ROM p. 41)

---

1. *Feudal* regime and *feudalism* were terms used by the French revolutionaries to denounce those aspects of landholding that they considered backward. Historians now prefer the terms *seigneurial* and *seigneurialism*, labels derived from the French word *seigneur* for lord, because feudalism had virtually disappeared in France by the end of the sixteenth century. In the Middle Ages, lords of the manor exercised almost total control over the lives of their serfs. As serfdom disappeared in France, landowners who could claim titles as lords continued to insist on their rights to forced labor and payment of dues even from "free" peasants. These rights were considered feudal or seigneurial and denounced as such by the revolutionaries.

Sieyès demonstrates, many commoners deeply resented the privileges claimed by the nobles.

In 1789 France, excluding overseas colonies, had some 26,000,000 inhabitants. In theory, they were divided into three orders or estates: the clergy (the First Estate, those who prayed), the nobility (the Second Estate, those who fought), and the Third Estate (everyone else, those who worked). The First Estate included 130,000 Catholic priests, monks, and nuns, who ministered to a largely Catholic population. Yet at least 250,000 Calvinists lived in southern France, and 200,000 Lutherans resided in eastern France. Eastern France was home as well to 30,000 Jews, and smaller communities of Jews lived in various southwestern French cities and in Paris. The Catholic church owned about 10 percent of the land in the kingdom. The church paid no taxes, though it negotiated a voluntary payment to the government every five years in return for its monopoly of public worship, public charity, and education. It levied its own tax in the form of the tithe, or tenth tax, often collected in goods directly in the fields during the harvest. Ordinary people admired their parish priest, but they resented the taxes levied by the Catholic church, especially since one-quarter of church revenues ended up in the pockets of noble clergymen.

The Second Estate comprised some 300,000 nobles (just over one percent of the population). Nobles owned as much as 30 percent of the land, yet they were exempt from the major land tax known as the *taille*. Although they paid other kinds of taxes, nobles enjoyed not only seigneurial rights but also a variety of privileges, from the right to carry swords to the right to death by decapitation rather than hanging if they were convicted of a capital crime. Nobles held most of the high positions in the church, the judiciary, the army, and government administration. All the bishops of the Catholic church in 1789 were nobles. (Sieyès, author of the antinoble pamphlet quoted above, was a nonnoble clergyman.) The highest positions in the army officer corps were reserved to nobles who could prove that their families had been nobles for four generations.

The Third Estate, because it included everyone not in the First or Second Estates, consisted of a wide variety of people from different stations in life. The middle classes accounted for about 5 percent of the French population, and the lower classes in the cities and towns made up about 10 percent of the population. Peasants were the vast majority—80 percent—of the population. Less than half the French people could read and write; more men were literate than women, and more city dwellers were literate than peasants. Public affairs therefore usually had limited resonance; they attracted the attention of educated city folk who had access to newspapers, reading clubs, and other places where people might meet and learn about current events.

Historians have long debated the social origins of the French Revolution. Did hatred of the nobility fuel the Revolution? The quote from Abbé Sieyès seems to support the view that resentment of noble domination lay behind the revolutionary outbreak. According to Sieyès, nobles were parasites and should be excluded from the revolutionary nation. Evidence for hatred of the nobility is quite extensive. The playwright

Fig. 1.1 The People Under the Old Regime

This image shows "the people" as a chained and blindfolded man being crushed under the weight of the clergy and nobility. Such a perspective on the period before 1789 purposely exaggerates social divisions and would have found few proponents before the Revolution, but the caricature does reveal the social clash felt so intensely by the revolutionaries.

le Peuple Sous l'ancien Regime

Beaumarchais (Document 1.2) put strong words of denunciation into the mouth of his central character in *The Marriage of Figaro* (1784): "What have you [nobles] done to deserve so much? You went to the trouble of being born—nothing more!" It was not just fictional characters who expressed strong sentiments. When asked for their views in 1789, peasants railed against "the thousands of abuses" heaped on them by their noble landlords (Document 1.3).

After the Revolution began in 1789, some newspapers and pamphlets quickly took up the antinoble theme; they vehemently denounced the nobles as degenerate, corrupt, and ridden with venereal disease—a "rotten carcass" that threatened the health of the nation (see Fig. 1.1). The revolutionaries abolished the legal privileges of the nobles and all their titles and sent many nobles to the guillotine as enemies of the new nation. A few aristocrats fell victim to crowd violence, often being mutilated in the process. The most notorious incident, no doubt, was the murder of the Princess of Lamballe, a close friend of the queen, Marie-Antoinette. On 3 September 1792 an enraged mob dragged Lamballe out of an improvised courtroom and hacked her to death. Her head—and some said her genitals too—was paraded on a pike outside the window of the queen's residence. "Aristocrat" became a common smear; for many it was synonymous with "conspirator" and "counterrevolutionary" and merited death.

Nobles inspired resentment and retaliation because they claimed that their political and social distinctions derived from their high birth; they insisted that their family lineages justified their legal status and privileges. In the eighteenth century, moreover, monarchy and nobility went hand in hand, as they had since the Middle Ages. The king ranked first among the nobles, and many believed that nobles constituted a separate "race" from the common people. Noble blood and birth supposedly made them natural leaders of a society based on deference to one's betters. Wealth often accompanied this elevated status. In some regions a few noble families owned as much as 50 percent of the land. The wealthiest nobles at court enjoyed fortunes worth 2 to 4 million livres a year, while ordinary workers earned a measly 300 livres. It is not surprising that critics of the regime seized upon the theme of inequality (Document 1.1).

Although it is true that the Revolution brought antinoble sentiments to the surface, such feelings had lain largely dormant for generations. Before 1789 no one imagined that noble titles and privileges would be abolished, just as no one dreamed that the king would be deposed and executed. Only a major upheaval could galvanize people to act upon their feelings of resentment. Scholars disagree about whether the nobility was rising or declining in wealth and influence in the eighteenth century. The evidence is inconclusive. Some nobles took up modern farming techniques and invested in overseas commerce in order to secure their wealth; others did not. Yet many people, like Sieyès, concluded that something had gone wrong in French society, and they pointed first and foremost to noble privileges as the cause. Nobles were not the only ones who enjoyed special privileges and exemptions, however. Privilege extended beyond the so-called "privileged orders" (the clergy and the nobility) down to the lowliest positions among the common people. Some regions paid much lower taxes than others did; in Brittany, for example, the rate of taxation was only one-fifth that of the Paris region. Regions, towns, artisanal guilds, and individual officeholders laid claim to or even bought exemptions from taxes.

In many ways, France was not one unified country, but rather a patchwork of special privileges. From the top to the bottom of the social hierarchy, individuals and groups tenaciously defended whatever privileges they managed to acquire. Conflicts over status and privilege even pitted nobles against one another. Great nobles derided the ambitions of those who had only recently acquired noble status. Rich men could buy noble status directly, or they could buy one of the 3,750 judicial and administrative offices that conferred nobility after a specified time in office. Between one-quarter and one-third of all noble families in 1789 had only become noble during the eighteenth century. Animosity between new and old noble families incited many of the political disputes of the eighteenth century.

Although nobles towered over the social hierarchy, every group sought to distinguish itself from those below it on the social ladder and tried to become more like

Map 1 The Old Regime Provinces

The King of France ruled over a kind of federation of provinces. In the provinces surrounding Paris he exerted the most direct rule, but farther away, especially in the southern half of the country, provinces often had their own institutions, known as provincial estates, which controlled the levy of taxation, public works, and administration. The king had the final word everywhere, but he had to work through local officeholders and institutions. Languedoc and Brittany had the strongest provincial estates.

those on the rung above. Rich merchants and high-ranking royal officials emulated the habits of the nobility and dreamed of amassing enough wealth to move up the social scale. Such middle-class people considered the lower classes inferior because they worked with their hands; property owners, doctors, lawyers, government officials, and merchants prided themselves on using mental skills to make their living and considered tailors, butchers, and weavers—not to mention peasants—lower in status because they relied on manual labor in their work. Respectable artisans and shopkeepers kept their distance from their journeymen, apprentices, and servants; for them independence rather than manual labor was the key variable. Master artisans and shopkeepers depended only on themselves, whereas their journeymen, apprentices, and servants depended on them for room and board and wages. Lowest of all were the utterly dependent: the unemployed, the poor, and anyone who relied on charity. Official parades, the order of seating in the parish church, the number of bells rung at a funeral, the clothes one wore and especially the material they were made of, the size of one's house and its location—these were all markers of social distinction. Privilege and hierarchy shaped the whole society, not just its highest reaches. As Voltaire pronounced in his usual acerbic tones, "Equality is therefore both the most natural of things, as well as the most unreal" (Document 1.1).

Hierarchy may have been most pronounced among the peasantry. At the top were the big farmers, who owned some land of their own but mainly farmed large estates as tenants. A big farmer and his wife might have as many as fifty people working for them, and because of their relative wealth such farmers controlled the village council and decisions made in the parish. In French such men were known as "the cock of the village." More than half the peasants had no land of their own and either worked as agricultural laborers or farmed small plots as tenant farmers or sharecroppers. The wives of landless peasants and small farmers helped make ends meet by spinning cotton, silk, or wool at home. In the eighteenth century, this home industry expanded dramatically, employing hundreds of thousands of women as spinners. As the textile industry expanded, many rural families moved to the towns and cities, where the men worked as weavers and their wives and children assisted them. These new sources of work did not provide a living for everyone. At the bottom of rural society were hundreds of thousands of paupers and beggars forced to roam the roads in search of work or charity. The unexpected death of a father, a series of crop failures, or even a season of bad weather could ruin whole families.

The lower reaches of French society certainly lived in a state of nearly perpetual crisis, but French society as a whole seemed to be in a relatively buoyant state in the eighteenth century. Huge sums of money flowed back to France from the expanding trade in African slaves and the stunning growth of production of sugar, coffee, indigo, and cotton in the Caribbean colonies. At home, the textile industry expanded dramatically, prices for grain and other staples increased steadily, the population grew, and wages increased, though not always keeping up with prices. This general prosperity made the economic downturn of 1786–89 seem all the more distressing. Ordinary people had come to expect constant improvement. In 1786 a free-trade treaty with Great Britain opened the floodgates to cheaper British textiles and revealed the dangers of overexpansion in the French industry; in some towns unemployment among weavers and spinners soared to 50 percent or more. In 1787 the silk harvest failed, and in 1788 a mammoth hailstorm cut a swath through the major grain-growing regions. By the spring of 1789 massive unemployment and rising grain prices threatened many with starvation. It was in this atmosphere that political events now unfolded.

The Monarchy and Its Critics

The kings of France ruled over a disparate collection of lands that except for the colonies were geographically contiguous but separated by language, custom, and history. People in the central heartland around Paris spoke French, but elsewhere people spoke Breton, Basque, German, or various local dialects. There was no one national law code; the southern half of the country relied on versions of Roman law, whereas the northern half used customary or common law, which varied from region to region. Royal officials governed most directly in provinces near Paris; farther away from the capital many regions enjoyed virtual autonomy, at least in questions of taxation. These regions were known collectively as "the country of estates," because they had their own "provincial estates" to represent their interests to the king. The king and his officials had to negotiate new taxes with the provincial estates. When the crown acquired colonies in North America and the Caribbean, and trading outposts in Africa and India, all of them months away by ship, the challenge of ruling from Paris only increased.

In theory, the king of France exercised "absolute" power—that is, no person or institution could block his initiatives. Unlike Great Britain, France did not have a functioning national parliament; the equivalent in France, the Estates General, had not met since 1614. In practice, however, the king depended on nobles, local elites, and royal officials to make his rule effective; he relied on them to carry out his will. The king's control over his own bureaucracy was limited by the fact that royal offices had been bought and sold as personal property since the late Middle Ages. The 50,000 royal officials who owned their offices paid a yearly tax to the crown in exchange

Liberty is without doubt the principle of all actions. It lies at the core of each Estate. . . . Sire, your subjects are divided into as many different bodies as there are Estates in the kingdom: the clergy, the nobility, the high courts and lower tribunals, the officers attached to these tribunals, the universities and academies, the banks and commercial companies. In every part of the state there are bodies that can be seen as links in a great chain, the first link of which is in the hands of Your Majesty as head and sovereign administrator of all that constitutes the body of the nation. The very idea of destroying this precious chain should be appalling.

—Argument of the Parlement of Paris against the Edict Suppressing the Guilds, presented to the King, 12 March 1776 (CD-ROM p. 26)

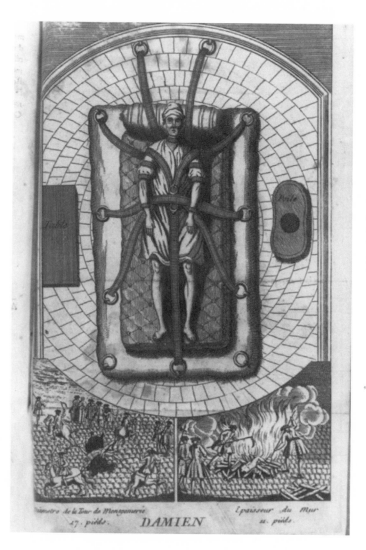

Fig. 1.2 Damiens Being Broken on the Wheel

These three depictions of Damiens narrate his fate. Placed on a flat bed, he had to submit to physical torture, including the shattering of his legs. Below left, one sees him drawn and quartered, though his limbs had to be hacked to assist the horses. Below right, the executioner burns the dismembered body.

for being able to pass on the offices as inheritable property. They consequently enjoyed a certain autonomy, though the king and his ministers could send office-holders into exile for refusing to cooperate, change their functions or the fee rates paid for official services, or suppress the offices altogether. The exercise of monarchical power therefore required a subtle balancing act between insistence on the king's right to rule unhindered by any interference, and compromise aimed at shoring up support from nobles, officeholders, and local elites.

From the middle of the eighteenth century onward, the French monarchy faced a succession of constitutional and fiscal crises. The threats could be very personal. In 1750, rumors circulated that King Louis XV (ruled 1715–74) suffered from leprosy and was kidnapping children off the streets of Paris in order to cure himself by bathing in their blood. In 1757 Robert-François Damiens tried to assassinate Louis XV with a dagger. He narrowly missed killing the king, and he paid a horrible price for his effrontery: after breaking his limbs on the wheel, the executioner poured molten lead and boiling oil on them; horses then dismembered his body, and the parts were burned at the stake (Document 1.10; see Fig. 1.2).

The assassination and its aftermath revealed the political and religious fault lines in monarchical government. The assassination attempt came in the midst of a bitter campaign waged by the Parlement of Paris (high court) against clerical influence on the king. In 1750 the archbishop of Paris, with Louis XV's encouragement, had organized a new campaign against Catholics known as Jansenists. Jansenists supposedly followed the doctrines of the seventeenth-century Flemish theologian Cornelius Jansen, whose 1641 publication, *Augustinus,* had been condemned by the pope. Jansenists argued for reform of the Catholic church and for more ascetic and individual forms of worship. They insisted, for example, that parishioners take Communion only when they felt true contrition. Louis XIV had tried to suppress the Jansenists in the seventeenth century, but they had won many followers among lawyers, judges, and even bishops. After 1750 the archbishop of Paris encouraged parish priests to refuse the last sacraments (last rites) to anyone who refused to sign a written statement of support for the church's official position against Jansenism. The Parlement of Paris roundly condemned this denial of the sacraments and denounced "the power of the clerics." They urged the king "to stop ceding your authority to the clerics who abuse and compromise it." (CD-ROM p. 24) Because the parlement had taken such a vociferous position, some concluded that it directly inspired the action Damiens took. Supporters of the parlement insisted that the Catholic clergy were behind the plot (Document 1.7). During his interrogation Damiens seemed to take the side of the parlement, insisting that he acted because of the archbishop's refusal of sacraments (Document 1.8).

The Damiens Affair showed that the parlement had become more aggressive in the assertion of its constitutional powers; though the judges insisted on their "poignant love for Your Majesty's sacred person," they also claimed now to speak for "the people" and their "liberty," challenging the king's exclusive hold on power (Document 1.6). The Parlement of Paris and its counterparts in the provinces aimed to take the place of the defunct Estates General and represent the people's interests to the king. The conflict also opened the way to the expression of unpredictable popular resentments. During the Damiens Affair posters pasted on the walls of Paris sometimes violently criticized the king himself.

The parlementary magistrates did not want to be revolutionaries. As the argument quoted at the beginning of this section demonstrates, they claimed to be preserving the fundamental nature of the monarchy. They resisted any effort, whether by the clergy or by the monarchy itself, to break the great chain linking the king down through his officials to the lowliest subjects in the land. What this really meant, however, was that any attempt at reform inevitably failed. Again and again between the 1760s and the 1780s, the king and his ministers tried to standardize taxation, eliminate abuses, and modernize the French government. But the parlements denounced all such measures as examples of ministerial despotism and tyranny. These conflicts gave them the chance to enhance their reputation as guardians of the fundamental constitution of the kingdom. The parlements countenanced change only when they authored it themselves, and their proposals always reinforced local autonomy rather than fostering national reform.

When the Seven Years' War ended in 1763, the French monarchy faced enormous deficits as well as a disastrous loss of face. The French armies fought to a stalemate against the Prussians on the continent but lost decisively to Great Britain overseas. By the terms of the peace, France ceded Canada to Great Britain and withdrew from India. From this moment forward, the French crown would ceaselessly seek new sources of revenue. When King Louis XV doubled and even tripled some forms of taxation during the war, the parlements objected. Although they could not prevent the new levies, they continued to protest through the 1760s. In 1771 the king's reform-minded chief minister abolished the troublesome parlements. At first the new courts that replaced them functioned well and the bold stroke seemed to have succeeded. But when Louis XV died in 1774, his successor Louis XVI (ruled 1774–92) restored the parlements to curry favor with public opinion.

Other efforts at reform from above also failed. Louis XVI tried to implement his own ambitious program of reform in 1774. It aimed at modernizing the economy, which not coincidentally would enhance tax collection. The king ordered the establishment of free trade in grain, the suppression of guilds that controlled access to manual trades (the subject of the protest excerpted above), and the conversion of forced labor by peasants into a money tax payable by all landowners. He also planned to introduce elected local assemblies to make government more representative. Riots against rising grain prices, and widespread resistance led by the parlements, convinced Louis to dismiss the minister in charge and withdraw the measures in 1776. The crown's efforts at reform succeeded only in fostering the expression of new forms of dissent. As one court argued in 1775 in opposing the reforms, "Why can Your Majesty not abandon today those fatal maxims of government, or just that policy introduced a century ago by jealous ministers, which has reduced all the Orders [Estates] of the State to silence with the sole exception of the Magistracy? Why is it not possible for the nation to speak for itself about its most cherished interests?" (CD-ROM p. 27)

In 1778 France took the side of the British North American colonists in their war for independence from Great Britain. The French government supported the Americans in order to exact revenge against the British for its defeats in the Seven Years' War twenty years earlier, but though the Americans gained their independence, the French crown succeeded mostly in adding to its fiscal woes. During the years of its participation in the war (1778–83), the French spent as much as five times their usual navy budget. In the early 1780s, as a result, taxes had to be increased dramatically once again. To inflict a blow against its enemy Great Britain, France found itself supporting a revolution dedicated to defending liberty and rights. Scores of young French aristocrats reported back home about the new republican hero, George Washington, and in Paris Benjamin Franklin electrified gatherings when he appeared dressed as a rustic American wearing a beaver cap. Mobbed whenever he left his house (Franklin lived in Paris between 1776 and 1785), Franklin soon found his likeness on every conceivable consumer item from snuffboxes to popular prints. This mania for things American allowed returning aristocratic officers and their ordinary soldiers to talk in new heartfelt ways about freedom in action.

In the 1780s, government deficits became the subject of public discussion. As one minister gave way to another in the frantic search for new sources of revenue and short-term loans, each one published his own competing version of the national budget. This, in itself, marked a major change in the monarchical regime: the crown and its officials now had to respond to public opinion. Public opinion had become increasingly important in the aftermath of the Damiens Affair. In the 1760s and 1770s, as the parlements portrayed themselves as defenders of the country's fundamental constitution (there was no written constitution as such, just a combination of legal tradition, judicial precedent, and custom), the crown had been forced to develop its own counterargument. In 1773, for example, a spokesman for the crown published a book on the "lessons of morality, politics and law" for the instruction of the crown prince. In it he argued, "After examining the nature of the Government throughout our history, you will then look for the one that should always exist so that Kings are powerful and Peoples free and happy." By entering into debate with the parlements in this fashion and speaking the same language of liberty, the crown had implicitly altered the monarchical style of rule; while still insisting that he ruled by divine right as the lieutenant of God himself, the king now simultaneously argued that he protected the interests of the people and responded to the requirements of public opinion. All sides now invoked the public, a new factor in French politics. As the recently fired finance minister Jacques Necker argued in 1781 when he published his account of the budget, "This report would also allow each of the people—who are part of YOUR MAJESTY's Councils—to study and follow the situation of the Finances. . . . Such an institution could have the greatest influence on public confidence." Lawyers now published their briefs defending their clients and appealed directly to public opinion in part to stake out their own independence. The growing importance on all sides of public opinion meant that before 1789 the constitution of the kingdom was already in transition.

Behind the scenes of this subtle transformation in national politics lay a hidden world of underground publishing that devoted much of its attention to increasingly scurrilous attacks on the monarchy. Both Louis XV and Louis XVI devoted great effort and money to ferreting out the writers and publishers of this scandal literature, which began to appear in the 1770s and reached tens of thousands of readers in the 1780s. The juiciest target of attack was Louis XV, notorious for his string of mistresses and insatiable sexual appetites. One such publication of 1775, *Anecdotes on the Countess du Barry*, laid out what were soon to be the usual charges against the lascivious king, recently deceased. He had kept a veritable harem of young virgins, and married them off to his officials when he tired of their attentions. Most notorious of all was the so-called Countess du Barry, a low-born courtesan who had "what it takes to revive even the most worn-out partner," even "a jaded lover such as the aged King." (CD-ROM p. 28) After the accession of Louis XVI, the scandal sheets linked the new king's Austrian wife, Marie-Antoinette, to du Barry: "The same debauchery and agitation of passions were observed in Marie-Antoinette's life. Men, women, everything was as she liked." (CD-ROM p. 28) Various courtiers, from Louis XVI's brother to the Princess of Lamballe, were linked erotically with the queen in these publications. The scandal sheets got added spice from the well-known fact that Louis XVI had at first been unable to consummate his marriage. It was easy to imagine that a king whose only passions were hunting and lock-making might inspire little feeling in his wife. This underground literature, which proliferated despite police surveillance, may well have tainted the reputation of the monarchy and contributed to its eventual downfall.

New Ideas

The time has come when it is no longer acceptable for a law to overtly overrule the rights of humanity that are very well known all over the world.

—Jean-Paul Rabaut Saint-Etienne, a Protestant pastor, commenting on the Edict of Toleration for Protestants, 1787

Nobles might have maintained their dominance of society, and the crown might have weathered the storm of criticism of its policies, if new ideas associated with the intellectual movement known as the Enlightenment had not profoundly influenced the expectations of most educated people in France. The writers of the Enlightenment wanted to apply reason and science to improve society. They aimed, in the words of the editors of *The Encyclopedia* (published 1751–72), the manifesto of the movement, to "overturn the barriers that reason never erected" and "give back to the arts and sciences the liberty that is so precious to them." Contrary to the impression given by its name, *The Encyclopedia* provided not only a compendium of knowledge but also the principles for attacking despotism, superstition, and intolerance, the major targets of the Enlightenment. Freedom of the press, freedom of religion, and the freedom to pursue knowledge unfettered by government restriction—these were the leading goals of the Enlightenment. The pursuit of such freedoms inevitably brought Enlightenment writers into conflict with both church and state, yet by 1787, as the quote opening this section illustrates, talk of "the rights of humanity" had become widespread in France.

The Enlightenment did not immediately precede the French Revolution. It began as a low rumble in 1685 when France's King Louis XIV revoked the rights of French Protestants, forcing hundreds of thousands of them into exile in the Dutch Republic, Great Britain, and Prussia. In exile the French Protestants began to publish works that were much more critical of the French monarchy than anything allowed past the French censors. At the same time, new breakthroughs in science by Isaac Newton gave scientific method—and reason in general—an enormous boost in prestige. In the 1720s and 1730s a few hardy souls began to write critical works from within France itself. Charles-Louis de Secondat, Baron of Montesquieu, published his *Persian Letters* in 1721. Although himself a judge in a provincial parlement, Montesquieu used his fictional correspondence between two Persians to satirize French politics at the end of the reign of Louis XIV (d. 1715). In 1733 Voltaire (the pen name for François-Marie Arouet) published his *Letters Concerning the English Nation.* He praised the work of Newton and compared French laws and customs with those in Great Britain, always to the disadvantage of the French, especially in questions of religion. The British Bill of Rights of 1689 (Document 1.11) had guaranteed freedom of speech and granted freedom of religion to all the Protestant sects. Voltaire wanted the same for France (he neglected to mention that Catholics had no rights in Great Britain), and he ridiculed those who opposed him as ignorant fanatics. Montesquieu published his book anonymously, and Voltaire published his first in English, but the books nonetheless made their authors celebrities in France.

By the 1750s the Enlightenment had moved into high gear as leading writers, called *philosophes* (French for "philosophers"), explicitly challenged the intellectual authority of the French Catholic church and the French state and gained an international audience for their efforts. The French government arrested, exiled, or even imprisoned the writers and banned their books, but they were welcomed by intellectuals across Europe, feted by neighboring monarchs, and read by an eager French public willing to buy its books from clandestine sources. In the 1760s the Enlightenment reached its high point when Voltaire and Jean-Jacques Rousseau published their most influential works. The French government and the Catholic church still tried to ban their publications, but the public appetite overcame all forms of censorship and surveillance. By the 1770s even the king's ministers had become devotees of the movement. Clergy from both the Jansenist and anti-Jansenist camps had been influenced by Enlightenment ideas. The Enlightenment had triumphed over its adversaries. Voltaire and Rousseau died in 1778, but by the 1780s all sides to political dispute in France spoke the language of the Enlightenment. Hardly any of the original band of Enlightenment writers remained to greet the revolution that has often been attributed to their influence, and none of them ever explicitly supported the notion of revolutionary change. As Denis Diderot, one of the editors of the *Encyclopedia,* said, "We will speak against senseless laws until they are reformed; and, while we wait, we will abide by them."

If the Enlightenment did not immediately lead to revolution, in what sense did it prepare the way? And if the Enlightenment was not exclusively French, then why did only France have a revolution? These two questions have sparked passionate debate ever since 1789, for as soon as the French Revolution erupted, conservative critics claimed to see in it the nefarious influence of the Enlightenment *philosophes*. These critics often tied the impact of the Enlightenment to the secret designs of two other groups in prerevolutionary France: the Protestants and the freemasons. Masonic lodges had spread from Great Britain across Europe during the eighteenth century. Based on secret rituals of the masons' guilds ("freemasons" were those who had passed through their apprenticeship), the Masonic lodges offered conviviality, philanthropy, and a kind of constitutional discussion. All brothers in the lodge were supposedly equal, and lodges wrote their own constitutions and elected their officers. In the conspiratorial view of some critics, freemasons wanted to install an anti-Christian regime, Protestants wanted revenge against Catholics, and the Enlightenment *philosophes* helped them accomplish their goals by denigrating the Catholic church and destabilizing the French monarchy. Scholars have long since debunked any notion of a plot behind the French Revolution, but they still want to track down the influences that made it possible. Both the Enlightenment and the freemasons usually figure in some way in their accounts.

Enlightenment writers opened a breach in the authority of church and state by persistently questioning official policies. They insisted that reason must be the final judge in all matters, not custom, history, tradition, or Scripture. They wanted to apply a scientific and critical approach to all the problems of society from religious persecution to poverty. They did not limit themselves to works about social problems, however. Voltaire, for example, wrote poetry, plays, a "philosophical" dictionary, and a satirical novel. Rousseau, a Genevan Protestant who lived most of his life in France, wrote a treatise on education, a constitution for Poland, an analysis of the effects of the theater on public morals, a best-selling novel, an opera, and a notorious autobiography, as well as assorted political writings.

These writers did not just vehemently criticize religious intolerance or the lack of freedom of the press; they also offered new ideals for society and government. If reason were applied to the question of the legitimacy of government, Rousseau argued (Document 1.12), people would have to recognize that "the source of right" could only be found in a "social contract" joining all the citizens, not in divine right, historical tradition, or biblical precedent. Although his account might seem too abstract to be threatening, at the time (1762) both the French and the Genevan governments outlawed the book. Rousseau insisted that "there is in the State no fundamental law which cannot be revoked" by the citizens; in effect, he was saying that nothing about the French monarchy was immune to change. Moreover, his very abstraction of argument seemed to undermine the monarchy; he talked only of the "body politic" and the "sovereign," implying that people might choose to express their social contract in a form other than monarchy. Rousseau's formulation of the social contract left open the question of the concrete form of government. This made his work attractive to the revolutionaries, but it also left an ambiguous legacy. Rousseau maintained that "the general will is always right and always tends to the public advantage." His argument opened the way for supporters of extreme revolutionary measures to declare that the government had the right to enforce the general will, even against dissidents.

Rousseau never advocated revolution, but his notion of the social contract had revolutionary implications. In his view, all (adult male) citizens possessed the same rights; there seemed to be no room for the nobility in this vision of the just society. The citizens guaranteed their rights by entering into a social contract; each gave up their individual rights in order to enjoy rights guaranteed by law to everyone. Government therefore gained its legitimacy from protecting rights that applied equally to every citizen. In other words, Rousseau appeared to be arguing for democracy: each man had the same say in determining the social contract. It is not surprising, therefore, that Rousseau displaced all the other Enlightenment figures as the Revolution proceeded. The more radical the Revolution, the more the revolutionaries relied on Rousseau as their guide. As might be expected, then, many opponents of the Revolution blamed the violence and terror on Rousseau.

The Enlightenment might have remained in the realm of ideas if it had not been able to reshape public opinion. More books were published in the eighteenth century than ever before, and more people could read; although illiteracy only dropped from 71 percent in 1700 to 63 percent in 1790, most people could read and write in Paris and other big cities. Even an ordinary Parisian glassworker might be familiar with the ideas—or at least the reputation—of Rousseau. But book reading alone does not explain the influence of the Enlightenment, which depended in large part on new social institutions. Cafés, newspapers, provincial academies, literary societies, and masonic lodges all grew in number toward the end of the eighteenth century. By 1789 Paris alone had about 100 Masonic lodges, which drew men from the upper aristocracy, the military, the parlements, commerce, and even the manual trades. Many freemasons became politically active during the Revolution, but they took no one side during the upheaval. Masons could be radicals, conservatives, or moderates.

The growth of new social institutions gave backbone to the "public" and provided a secular forum for the development of "public opinion." Ordinary people had always gathered in their churches and in church-sponsored organizations, and conflicts over Jansenism had initiated many into political discussion. Now the public had more options, new places to congregate and inevitably to discuss the affairs of the day. In addition to meeting in coffeehouses, lodges, and academies, the public attended the newly established annual art exhibitions in Paris. By 1787, some 10 percent of the Parisian public visited the art exhibitions. Art and theater criticism, newspapers, and such forbidden books as those of Voltaire and Rousseau, or the gutter publications that attacked the court, all helped shape public opinion, which was then reinforced by the social interactions fostered in the new institutions. Enlightenment *philosophes* sometimes joined Masonic lodges (Voltaire became a mason at the end of his life) and certainly frequented cafés, but they also met in private circles called "salons," where under the patronage of leading women of high society they would read their manuscripts and discuss ideas. The salons (French for living room) of Paris drew an international crowd of intellectuals from England, Scotland, Italy, and the German states. They gave such men as Voltaire and Rousseau a launching pad for their attempts to sway public opinion, and they provided women with a way to participate in the Enlightenment. Women also set up Masonic lodges of their own.

Although Voltaire and Rousseau had to flee France more than once to escape prosecution for their books (Voltaire established his permanent residence one mile from the Swiss border), government censorship proved incapable of holding back the floodgates of criticism. Printers in Switzerland and the Dutch Republic were able to make fortunes publishing books banned in France. They smuggled them into France by every means imaginable and often sold them under the counters of the most respectable bookstores. Faced with this losing battle, the French government began to loosen its grip on publishing in the 1760s. As the monarchical government sought ways of modernizing the country's economy through reforms of taxation, freeing-up markets, and lessening burdens on peasants, government officials began to move closer to the positions enunciated by Enlightenment writers.

Conflict between Enlightenment figures and state authorities consequently began to abate in the 1770s. When Voltaire died in 1778 he was celebrated as a national hero. The reform plans of Anne-Robert Turgot, Louis XVI's chief minister from 1774 to 1776, show the impact of Enlightenment thinking on the highest reaches of the French bureaucracy (Document 1.13). A career official, Turgot had secretly contributed to the *Encyclopedia,* frequented the Paris salons, and corresponded with Voltaire. Turgot rejected the old practice of citing precedent, which he called the "example of what our ancestors did in times of ignorance and barbarism." Like a good Enlightenment *philosophe,* he advocated relying on "the rights and interests of men." The Enlightenment had succeeded in putting "natural" or "human" rights on the agenda. By the 1770s most writers, even those supportive of the government, agreed that rights were, as Turgot claimed, "based upon the principles of justice that each of us bears in our heart." Statesmen and Enlightenment reformers did not always agree on just what those rights were or how they would best be guaranteed, but rights had become part of public discourse, and they could be defended in ways that privilege could not.

The American War of Independence gave a big boost to the notion of natural or human rights in France. Many French followed events in the colonies with avid interest because they believed that the Americans were putting Enlightenment ideas into practice in an almost pure form. French translations of the Declaration of

Fig. 1.3 Liberty

Even before the Revolution, the French had used a woman wearing a toga to symbolize liberty. By July 1789 this symbol had become quite common and would become even more familiar over the revolutionary decade. The female Liberty was usually depicted in a statuesque pose to convey calm determination. Belonging to no group and no particular place, she stood for a universal principle based on reason.

La Liberté

Independence and various declarations of rights drafted by the new states appeared almost immediately in French-language newspapers, many of them published outside France's borders but distributed within France. In addition, translated collections of the state constitutions and bills of rights were published in the late 1770s and throughout the 1780s. One of the most influential of these documents was George Mason's Declaration of Rights for the state of Virginia, drafted in 1776 (Document 1.14). Mason's opening statement, "That all men are by nature equally free and independent, and have certain inherent rights" seemed to put Rousseau's social contract into constitutional form. This Declaration later served as a model for those drafting a French Declaration of Rights in July and August 1789 (Document 1.16). The influence of these American documents was enhanced by the correspondence and visits among leading figures on both sides of the Atlantic. Thomas Jefferson's presence in Paris in 1789 made the American influence palpable.

The spread of the language of rights produced concrete reforms by the end of the 1780s. In 1787, the crown granted French Calvinists freedom of religion for the first time since 1685; Calvinists still had no political rights. The Royal Society of Arts and Sciences of the city of Metz in eastern France held an essay contest in 1787 and 1788 on the status of the Jews in France (Document 1.15), and in 1788 the monarchy set up a royal commission to consider the question of Jewish rights. Writings against the slave trade and slavery in the colonies began to increase after 1780, and a group of Enlightenment-inspired Frenchmen set up an abolitionist society in 1788 in Paris. The Society of the Friends of Blacks, as the founders called it, regularly corresponded with abolitionist groups in Great Britain (see Fig. 1.3).

The French were not the only Europeans interested in things American or in natural rights. German, Swedish, Italian, Polish, and English commentators all seized upon American developments to forward their own arguments about "the rights of man." For example, one German wrote in 1777 that American victory in the War of Independence would give "greater scope to the Enlightenment, new keenness to the thinking of peoples and new life to the spirit of liberty." As those words suggest, the Enlightenment echoed not only in France but also in many other places in Europe. The rights of religious minorities, the abolition of slavery, reform of harsh forms of corporal punishment, debates about the use of torture in the legal process, and efforts to alleviate the burdens on peasants occupied statesmen and reformers almost everywhere in western and central Europe.

Given this widespread interest in rights and in the American example, why did revolution occur only in France? Once again, the answer seems to lie in France's intermediate position. Still lacking many of the freedoms (of the press, of religion, and of an elected national parliament) already achieved in Great Britain, the French monarchy nonetheless eventually allowed the dissemination of critical literature and did not prevent the development of new social institutions that helped spread Enlightenment values. In short, the French government was oppressive enough to warrant widespread criticism and not oppressive enough to eliminate its critics.

Although the combination of social tensions, failure of political reform, and increasing influence of Enlightenment ideas goes a long way toward explaining why France was susceptible to revolution, it does not account for the specific timing of its outbreak. Harvest failures, such as the one in 1788–89, occurred periodically under the monarchy without threatening its existence. In fact, Louis XVI's popularity had soared when French forces helped decisively defeat the British at Yorktown in 1781. Yet almost immediately thereafter, French foreign policy faced a series of setbacks. First, the British sank the French fleet in the West Indies. By 1783 the independent United States and Great Britain had patched up their quarrel, leaving France with huge deficits and little else to show for its role in aiding the colonists. In 1787 France stood by while Prussian forces invaded the Dutch Republic to suppress "patriots" there who tried to set up a republic on the American model. The once enthusiastic public mood turned sour.

An escalating series of constitutional crises brought all these tensions to the boiling point. To stave off bankruptcy, Louis XVI first called an Assembly of Notables and then asked the Parlement of Paris for help. Both refused, ultimately forcing the king to convoke the Estates General, which had not met since 1614. The Estates General consisted of deputies from the three Estates or Orders. In 1614 each estate had voted as an estate, allowing the deputies of the clergy or the nobility to veto any proposal for reform that might come from the Third Estate. Under pressure, Louis XVI agreed to double the number of deputies from the Third Estate, making them equal in number to the other two combined. But he left it to the Estates General to decide whether the estates would vote separately (as estates) or by individual head. Voting by order (one vote for each estate) would guarantee the traditional powers of the clergy and the nobility; voting by head would make the Third Estate dominant. Abbé Sieyès wrote his pamphlet *What Is the Third Estate?* to argue for voting by head. (CD-ROM p. 41) It was one of hundreds of pamphlets that now poured off the presses, raising the political temperature. The king invited nearly all adult males to participate in elections of deputies. Just as bread prices began to escalate, an unprecedented political mobilization took place as French men met in their villages and towns to choose deputies and draw up their lists of grievances. Asked to state their complaints, ordinary men found their voices. When the Estates General opened at Versailles on 5 May 1789 the country held its collective breath in anticipation. France had entered new and uncharted territories.

Documents

The Question of Equality

Inequality permeated the fabric of the Old Regime's social structure. Legal as well as economic inequality followed from the widely shared belief in a "Great Chain of Being," a natural ordering principle set up by God in which members of society, layered by function, had different rights and privileges. In this chain, those at the top, the clergy and the nobility, possessed more rights and privileges than those lower down, the commoners. Within this latter group, which comprised more than 95 percent of the population, there were also gradations of rank beginning with the professional classes and descending all the way down to the homeless. Despite these considerable differences, almost everyone possessed privileges and the right to defend them. And even those without any meaningful enumerated privileges of their own lived in a country in which such privileges served to constrain the actions of the government and of social superiors. The superiors on the Great Chain had an obligation to help those lower down.

The system of "orders," based on the legal inequalities created by particular rights and privileges, came under attack in the eighteenth century, most obviously from the Enlightenment. The *philosophes* wanted to substitute talent for birth as the basis for distinctions. They especially criticized the nobility for their tax exemptions. Nobles originally gained tax exemptions in exchange for raising troops for the king and providing protection and justice for their serfs. As kings took charge of raising armies and feudal forms of landholding disappeared, noble privileges came to seem unjustified. When peasants were asked to state their grievances in preparation for the Estates General, such privileges aroused bitter commentary.

During the Revolution, criticism of noble privileges soon boiled over into a general attack on all forms of social inequality. The most radical revolutionaries attacked the rich, arguing that the government should not only control prices but also redistribute property confiscated from counterrevolutionaries to the poor. Gracchus Babeuf advocated a kind of preindustrial communism. Most revolutionaries, however, endorsed only legal equality and refused schemes to enforce economic and social equalizing.

Document 1.1: Voltaire's Understanding of Inequality

This passage from François-Marie Arouet, pen-named Voltaire, perhaps the best-known writer of the eighteenth century, illustrates the spirit of investigation of the Enlightenment. The *philosophes* wanted to understand the rationale behind inequality and were particularly interested in whether there were natural reasons for it or whether inequality came entirely from social conventions. From a well-to-do middle-class background, Voltaire condemned arbitrary inequality and the social conditions that spawned it.

Source: François-Marie Arouet, *Dictionnaire philosophique* (London [Nancy], 1765), 157–60.

> Does a dog need another dog, or a horse, another horse? No animal depends on any other of its species. Man, however, has received that divine inspiration that we call Reason. And what has it wrought? Slavery almost everywhere we turn.
>
> If this world were as good as it seems it could be, if everywhere man could find a livelihood that was easy and assured a climate suitable to his nature, it is clear that it would be impossible for one man to enslave another.
>
> If all men then were without needs, they would thus be necessarily equal. It is the poverty that is a part of our species that subordinates one man to another. It is not inequality, it is dependence that is the real misfortune. It matters very little that this man calls himself "His Highness," or that man "His Holiness." What is hard is to serve them.
>
> In our unhappy world it is impossible for men living in society not to be divided into two classes:
>
> The rich who command, and the poor who serve. These two classes are then subdivided into a thousand, and these thousand have even more subtle differences.
>
> The human race, such as it is, cannot subsist unless there is an endless number of useful men who possess nothing at all. For it is certain that a man who is well off will not leave his own land to come and plow yours, and if you have need of a pair of shoes, it is not the Appellate Judge who will make them for you. Equality is therefore both the most natural of things, as well as the most unreal.
>
> Deep in their hearts, all men have the right to think themselves entirely equal to other men, but it does not follow from this that the cardinal's

cook can order his master to prepare him dinner. But the cook can say: "I am a man like my master, born in tears, as was he. When he dies, it will be with the same fear and the same rituals as I. Both of us perform the same natural functions. If the world was turned upside down, and I became cardinal and my master became the cook, I would take him into my service." This discourse is reasonable and just, but while waiting for the world to turn over, the cook must do his duty or else all human society becomes corrupted.

Document 1.2: Beaumarchais's Understanding of Inequality

Like his predecessors of earlier generations, playwright Pierre-Augustin Caron de Beaumarchais—who became an important figure of the late Enlightenment because of the controversy surrounding his work *The Marriage of Figaro* [1784]—believed that a truly rational society would not tolerate arbitrary inequality.

Source: Pierre-Augustin Caron de Beaumarchais, *La folle journée ou le marriage de Figaro* (Amsterdam, n.p., 1785 [1784]), act 5, scene 3.

Because you are a great lord, you think you are a great genius! . . . Nobility, wealth, rank, position . . . they all make you feel so proud! What have you done to deserve so much? You went to the trouble of being born—nothing more! As for the rest—a rather ordinary man!

And as for me, zounds! Lost among the obscure masses, I have had to use more knowledge and be more calculating just to survive than all the rulers of Spain have needed over the last hundred years! And you want to take me on. . . . Could anything be stranger than a fate such as mine? The son of God-knows-who, kidnapped by bandits, schooled in their ways, they now disgust me and I yearn for an honest job—but everywhere I go, I am turned away. I study chemistry, pharmacology, surgery, and all the money of a great lord could barely get me a job wielding a veterinarian's probe!

A question about the nature of wealth came up, and since it's possible to discuss things one doesn't actually possess, and not having two pennies to rub together, I wrote about the value of money and its net profit. Soon thereafter, from inside a carriage, I see a castle's drawbridge being lowered for me, and as I entered, abandoned any hope and freedom. [He rises.] How I would like to get hold of one of those seven-day wonders—so thoughtless about the evils that they cause—after a healthy misfortune had curbed his pride! I'd tell him . . . that stupidities that appear in print acquire importance only where they are restricted, that without the freedom to criticize, praise has no value, and that only small minds are apprehensive about small notes. [He sits down again.]

Document 1.3: A Grievance List from a Rural District: Attack on Seigneurial Dues

As part of the process of choosing deputies for the Estates General, rural villages drew up lists of grievances. Many of the lists from rural communities decried the abuse of seigneurial dues that peasants owed to lords, in exchange for which they were supposed to receive protection and supervision. By 1789, as these excerpts demonstrate, peasants had come to see their lords (usually but not always nobles) not as protectors but as creditors constantly turning the screws on them for ever more rent or other payments.

Source: Patrick Kessel, *La nuit de 4 août 1789* (Paris: Arthaud, 1967), 307–12.

> Upper Alsace, Bailliage de Belfort
> To His Grace, Monsieur Necker, Minister of Finances
>
> Statement concerning the unjust, onerous, and humiliating dues and other unheard of burdens which the undersigned inhabitants of the seigneury of Montjoye-Vaufrey are made to endure by the Count of Montjoye-Vaufrey. The seigneury of Montjoye-Vaufrey is small with almost inaccessible mountains, covered in large part by forests of beech and fir trees. The soil is naturally barren and produces nothing but brambles and thorn bushes. It is part of Upper Alsace and enclosed by the diocese of Basel, lying on the kingdom's border.
>
> Close to one thousand individuals live in this region, which is almost wild because of its location. There they stagnate, living in misery, crushed beneath the entire weight of the most inhumane and detestable feudal system and the victims of the thousands of abuses that the seigneur of Montjoye heaps upon them. The truth of these statements will be found to be more than convincing once we have outlined the rights that the [seigneur] claims to have over them and the manner in which these rights are exercised.
>
> *The Tithe of the Sixth Sheaf*
> The seigneur demands one of every six sheaves produced on the majority of the lands of the seigneury. The other sheaves are left to the owner, who uses one and a half sheaves for seed because the soil only yields four sheaves for every sheaf planted. The remaining three and a half sheaves constitute his only profit from sowing and are used to feed himself and to pay other seigneurial dues.
>
> *Corvées*
> It would seem that the owners of these same lands should be left to enjoy their produce in peace, obliged as they are to submit to such an outrageous tithe and to the odious exercise of the right of *mortmain* [the lord's right

to claim property on the death of the landholder]. But far from it. In addition, this seigneur requires five days of work from them, and if he obliges them to perform this service in actual labor, he assigns the work when it is convenient for him.

Communal Forests

His greed leads him to appropriate all of the communal forests, selling them for his own profit.

Communal Pasturelands

The seigneur does not allow land to be cleared at all unless one agrees to plant and give him a sixth of what is produced. Otherwise it is forbidden to touch the smallest bramble or thorn.

Beating the Woods

When it pleases him, and as often as it pleases him, he obliges them to beat the woods in order to satisfy his desire to hunt. The farmer who is thus forced to wander through the woods for a whole day receives neither sustenance, nor a bonus, nor payment.

For more than a century, they have taken their seigneur to court in order to oblige him to produce the legal titles which give him the right to oppress them. To thwart these just measures, the predecessors of the current seigneur had the deputies of the leading communities clapped in irons and imprisoned, charging them with insubordination and holding them in custody at the seigneur's will. The current seigneur has again outdone his predecessors. For two months, he has kept . . . an entire family composed of six heads of household in prison, and he has charged each fifteen gold *louis*.

Document 1.4: Manifesto of the Enragés

Jacques Roux, a former priest turned radical revolutionary, became the leading voice for a group known as the "Enraged" because they expressed constant anger at the unfairness shown toward the ordinary, poor people who made up the bulk of the patriotic citizenry and whose plight Roux demanded the government redress by any means necessary. In this speech to the Convention on 25 June 1793, Roux laid out the basic economic demands of this group: more stringent economic measures against the rich, hoarders, speculators, and profiteers, who should be made to justify themselves to the hardworking, honest patriots for whom Roux claimed to speak. Here Roux explains his understanding of equality and trade.

Source: Jacques Roux, *Scripta et acta,* edited by Walter M. Markov (Berlin: Akademie-Verlag, 1969), 140–46. Translated by the Exploring the French Revolution project staff from original documents in French found in John Hardman, *French Revolution Documents, 1792–1795,* vol. 2 (New York: Barnes & Noble, 1973), 136.

> Freedom is but an empty illusion when one class of men can starve another with impunity. Equality is but an empty illusion when the rich, through monopolies, have the decision of life or death over their own kind. The Republic is but an empty illusion when the counterrevolution takes place daily because three-quarters of the citizenry cannot afford the price of basic foodstuffs and no one sheds a tear.
>
> Stopping trade which is nothing short of highway robbery must be clearly distinguished from simple commerce. It will only be by placing the cost of food within reach of the *sans-culottes* (ordinary working people) that you will win them over to the Revolution and its constitutional laws.

Document 1.5: Babeuf's Trial

Long after sans-culottes influence on the government had waned, social conflicts continued to drive some revolutionary events. Throughout 1794 and 1795, urban and rural radicals alike demanded "bread and the constitution of 1793," meaning that the government should feed the people and grant universal male suffrage. One such radical, who took the name Gracchus Babeuf, supposedly organized the "Conspiracy of Equals," a secret group that he hoped to lead in a surprise insurrection to take power and use that power to distribute land equally among all citizens. When the "conspiracy" was betrayed, Babeuf was arrested and tried. Before being sentenced and executed, Babeuf offered a statement of his principles and a defense of his action.

Source: Victor Advielle, *Histoire de Gracchus Babeuf et du Babouvisme,* vol. 1 (Geneva: Slatkine, 1978), 28–30.

> I noticed that after the 13th of Vendémiaire [5 October 1795] the majority of the people were tired of a Revolution whose every fluctuation and movement had had fatal results. The fact that the Revolution had "royalized" them cannot be ignored. In Paris I saw that the ordinary, uneducated masses had really been led by the enemies of the people into a deep contempt for the Republic. . . .
>
> I told myself that, barring a salutary stroke of genius, the Republic was lost. I was certain that the monarchy would not hesitate to seize us once again. I looked around me and saw many demoralized people, even among those patriots who had once been so fervent, so brave, and who had had such success in their efforts to strengthen Liberty. It was a scene of universal discouragement with the people almost totally muzzled (if it can be put that way), and which was followed by witnessing the disbanding and

the stripping away of all the guarantees that the people had once been given against any undertakings by their rulers. Together with the scars left by the chains recently worn by almost all these energetic men, the near conviction (of many people who seemed to me not to have thought through the reasons for their convictions) that the Republic might really be, after all, something other than a blessing, had very nearly brought the people's spirit to a state of total resignation, and everyone seemed ready to bend under the yoke.

I saw now who was in a position to revive the courageous mood of earlier days. And yet, I told myself, the same zealous turbulence and love of mankind still exists. Perhaps there are still ways to keep the Republic from being lost. Let every man gather his strength and do what he can. As for myself, I am going to do all that is within my power.

I vented my words in my *Tribune of the People*. I said to everyone: "Listen: I have to admit that those of you who seem to believe, after this long series of public disasters, that the Republic is worthless and that the Monarchy might be preferable, are right." I made it a banner headline: WE WERE BETTER OFF UNDER THE KINGS THAN UNDER THE REPUBLIC. But you must understand of which Republic I was speaking. A Republic such as the one we see is, without a doubt, totally worthless. But this, my friends, is not a true Republic. A true Republic is something you are not yet familiar with.

The Republic is not a word—or even several words—empty of meaning. The words *Liberty* and *Equality*, which have continuously echoed in your ears, cast a spell over you in the early days of the Revolution because you thought that they would mean something favorable for the People. Now they mean nothing to you at all because you see that they are nothing more than empty statements and the embellishments of deceitful expressions. You must learn once again, however, that these two words can and should stand for something that is very valuable for most people.

People revolt because the injustice of deceitful institutions has pushed the best impulses of a society to the limits such that the majority of its functioning constituents can no longer go on as before. The society then feels uncomfortable in this situation, and feeling the need to change, takes the required actions. And that society is right to do so because the only reason it was instituted in the first place was to make the bulk of its members as happy as possible. The purpose of society is the common well-being. . . .

The aim of the Revolution also is the well-being of the greatest number; therefore, if this goal has not been achieved, if the people have not found the better life that they were seeking, then the Revolution is not over. This is true despite what those who want only to substitute their own rule for somebody else's say, or hope it to be. Otherwise, if the Revolution is really over, then it has been nothing more than a great crime.

THE DAMIENS AFFAIR

Searing the political landscape of mid-century was the 1757 assassination attempt on Louis XV by Robert-François Damiens. Aiming a dagger at the chest of the king, the would-be murderer failed because his short blade was blocked by thick clothing. This attempt and its consequences not only were spectacular events but also clearly reveal the major participants in Old Regime politics.

In theory, the Old Regime had no "politics"—that is, no organized political contention. According to the theory of absolutism, advanced by a series of Bourbon kings for well over a century, all sovereignty was exercised by the king. His decisions were announced in edicts, which allowed for no discussion. Closer examination, however, reveals widespread controversy and debate about political issues.

The 1750s proved to be an especially contentious decade. Indeed, for some scholars it was a crucial turning point because in this period the monarch was not able to suppress debate; in addition, and more important, he lost the ability to dominate it. The hinge on which debate swung was the Catholic movement known as Jansenism. In the 1750s the clergy tried once again to crush Jansenism. Mainly the church tried to deny last rites—and thereby salvation—to those who had not sworn an oath against Jansenism. Allied with the Jansenists were the law courts, especially the parlements. The king vacillated at first and eventually gravitated toward the clergy, earning the enmity of the courts.

The investigators tried to link Damiens's attempted murder to the pro-Jansenist critics of the king. The magistrates denied any connection, but still used the crisis as an opportunity to resume their attacks on the clergy. The investigation of Damiens revealed unsuspected reservoirs of antimonarchical sentiment, yet also showed the continued and somewhat contradictory depth of promonarchical feeling. Damiens suffered a particularly brutal execution as punishment for his attempt.

Document 1.6: Remonstrance by the Parlement Against the Denial of Sacraments in Paris (1753)

As the controversy over the refusal of sacraments came to dominate political and religious discussions in Paris, Versailles, and across the kingdom, the magistrates argued all the more strenuously that the king should compel the archbishop to drop his intolerant attitude toward the Jansenists and allow greater diversity of opinion among French Catholics. The magistrates appealed to the king's sense of obligation—an obligation to uphold the traditions of the French monarchy, including the tradition of conferring with his subjects through the intermediaries of the parlementary courts, and the tradition by which the king, rather than the pope, oversaw the church in France to ensure that it served the interests of French men and women rather than those of Rome.

Source: Jules Flammermont, *Remonstrances du Parlement de Paris au XVIIIe siècle,* vol. 1 (Paris: Imprimerie Nationale, 1888–98), 506–614.

Sire,

The most essential interest of the Sovereign is to know the truth, and your parlement is tasked by the State to bring it to you. . . . Today it is a question of religion and the conservation of the State, both equally threatened by the alarming schism that has aroused our enthusiasm. This schism, too long overlooked, has sunk such deep roots and grows so rapidly each day that soon no barriers will be able to contain it.

Filled with the most poignant love for Your Majesty's sacred person and jealous of increasing in all your subjects the feelings that tie them to you, as if that was possible, your parlement can only fear that which attempts to divide them. In the hands of a Prince as fair, they will always respect the use of his supreme power. But allow us, Sire, to tell you that these sudden and shocking misfortunes, these bursts of dreadful wrath that only cause hardship and that herald nothing but austerity, can only spread terror. And the French, in whom love is the tenet and gauge of fidelity, become alarmed and troubled as soon as they fear their sovereign. If he is gentle with his People, it is more natural for them to feel and state over and over, "May justice and kindness keep the King, and may his throne be strengthened by clemency." Thus they become concerned, Sire, when they see themselves abandoned to the clerics and exposed to the arbitrary application of power mistakenly placed in the hands of the ecclesiastics. The power of the clerics will soon have no limits beyond those of their own organization, and will subjugate the People in a dominion rising from the ruins of their liberty. The clerics are capable of using the People's slavery for whatever purpose they desire. Your subjects see themselves being carried away, so to speak, to a realm so different from yours, and which, in their eyes, offers nothing but risks and uncertainty—being taken to a realm that offers them nothing but a frightful spectacle of citizens already deprived of their legitimate freedom. They see houses desolated by the loss of their most important members, magistrates removed from office, entire families required to go elsewhere to receive asylum from captivity. Shuddering in this disgrace too often takes on the form of resentment and revenge towards one's adversaries! . . .

. . . Innocent Christians find themselves reduced to the cruel alternative of being regarded as indifferent to the sacraments if they do not request them, or undergoing a scandalous and unfair refusal if they do.

Sire, it is time to show these ministers of the Church that they are abusing your indulgence and that your intention is not to authorize the schism that, for the happiness of your People, you have so often condemned.

Document 1.7: "Letter from a Gentleman in Paris to His Friend in London" (1757)

The news of Damiens's attack on the king and of his subsequent trial spread rapidly and generated great interest across France and all of Europe. This pamphlet, published in London, describes for English readers the goings-on in Paris, especially the public outpouring of sympathy for the king and the general hostility toward Damiens. Damiens, even for this English observer, was horrible for having dared to touch, let alone tried to kill, the king—God's anointed representative in France and the guarantor of public order and domestic peace.

Source: "Letter from a Gentleman in Paris to His Friend in London," in *A Particular and Authentic Narration of the Life, Examination, Torture, and Execution of Robert Francis Damien* [*sic*], trans. Thomas Jones (London, 1757).

Of all sorts of madness this appears to be the worst: for, whereas the generality of madmen reason right from wrong principles; these people are for the most part wrong both in their fundamentals and in their deductions from them, representing murder, gun-powder-plots, &c. as innocent under the masque of religion and pious zeal. Hence the enterprize of the fryar, who murdered Henry the third of France; hence *Ravaillac* stabbed *Henry* the fourth, and hence another assassin has made an execrable attempt upon *Lewis* [Louis] the XVth.

The name of this enthusiastical assassin is *Robert Francis Damien,* born in *St. Catherine's* suburb in the city of *Arras.* . . .

He was a very superstitious enthusiastical sort of a man, and therefore a very proper tool or cat's-paw for the Romish priests to work upon. What horrid crimes are committed under the sanction of religion! The artful popish clergy had worked him up to such a pitch of enthusiasm; that, saint-like, he was proud to die in so glorious a cause, imagining his meritorious sufferings would certainly procure him a residence in heaven.

The king was supported by the *counte de Brionne* and the master of the house, who were leading him to his coach, a page of the bed-chamber walked before him with lights; the dauphin was behind him along with the duke *d'Ayen,* captain of the guards in waiting, and several exempts and equerries followed. A footman, named *Selim,* near whom the assassin stood, seeing the king approach, said to the villain, *why don't you take off your hat, don't you see the king?* While he was saying this, the monster struck the king with a knife, which had two blades of different sizes; with one of these blades he wounded the king between the fourth and fifth rib, but the stroke glanced to the right side, and most fortunately did not reach the bowels. The king, who at first had scarce felt any thing, then turning to the footman who had just bid the fellow take off his hat, said, looking at the assassin, *that man has given me a terrible blow;* and clapping his hand to the place where he had been struck, and feeling it warm, he drew back his hand all bloody, and said, *I am wounded, seize him, but do not hurt him.*

Whatever may be the sallies of this monarch's private life, he certainly has publick virtue, and therefore his mind must soon have rested in a conviction that he did not deserve an assault upon his life.

Certainly there appears somewhat providential in the escape the king had from this treasonable design. It happened, that on that day, besides his usual cloathing, he put on a sur-tout of thick velvet, which no doubt greatly obstructed the blow, and hindered the wound from proving mortal.

The execrable assassin, after striking this horrid blow, never stirred from the place, and the duke *d'Ayen* having asked which was the man, the fellow answered with the countenance of a *Ravaillac.* "Tis I." He was seized and led to the guardroom, which stands at the gate from whence he had just come out. There he was stripped to his shirt, and there were found about him the knife, a New Testament, some images, and between thirty and thirty-five *Louis d'Ors.*

The trial of the villain was agreed to be committed to the parliament; and the people in general began to rid themselves of their anxiety, when it was reported abroad, that the stab was no more than a common wound, and that his majesty wanted but a few days to recover his strength, which was somewhat reduced by being bled so plentifully after the wound was given.

Damien appears very resolute; his feet have been scorched, and the calf of his leg pinched with red hot tongs. He shrieked indeed, but confessed nothing. He was afterwards carried to prison, and chained in a dungeon, and guards set over him.

He was asked if he had any accomplices, and answered he had, but was sure they had escaped before this time, but that great care ought to be taken of the dauphin, otherwise the like accident might, perhaps, befall him soon. When he was urged to discover more, he answered, he would speak when it was time; that he was very sensible he deserved death, and begged it might be hastened.

It is reported that there was great commotion in *Paris;* that several religious houses were shut up, to prevent cabals among the clergy, and that the archbishop of *Paris* was publickly accused of being at the bottom of this atrocious design; but these givings out have since totally vanished for want of any kind of confirmation.

But before he parted from *Versailles,* he begged to speak with the king and the dauphin, in hopes that notwithstanding the heinousness of his crime he might still obtain mercy from his majesty's known good nature and lenity. He was much surprized when they put him into a vehicle in order to convey him to the *Conciergerie.* He said he had many things to reveal, but was told he must discover them to his judges.

Document 1.8: Damiens's Testimony to the Parlement

During the course of his trial, Damiens was interrogated over fifty times by the magistrates of the Parlement of Paris and by the king's prosecutors. The interrogators were concerned above all to determine whether Damiens had accomplices and, if so, what group was behind the attack. In this passage Damiens testifies that his action had been prompted by "preachers of the parlementary party," meaning those who criticized the excessive power of the court and the bishops. Attributing his actions to dissatisfaction with the state of the kingdom, Damiens then asks the king to show his concern for the hard-pressed French people by pardoning him.

Source: Anonymous, *Pièces originales et procédures du procès, fait à Robert-François Damiens* (Paris: Pierre Guillaume Simon, 1757).

He said his name is Robert-François Damiens and he is a forty-two-year-old servant living in the City of Paris.

When he was questioned about telling when he had made plans to kill the King, he answered he planned on doing it three years ago and because of the Archbishop's bad behavior.

When asked if somebody had inspired his plan, he said he had been inspired by everybody around him.

When asked if he had told somebody about this project, either in Paris, in Artois, or in a foreign country, he said no. He had wanted to say it but would not say it here.

When asked if any secular or legitimate Priest had inspired this dreadful plan, he answered that nobody had inspired him to it, but he had heard many ecclesiastics talk dangerously.

When asked about the dangerous things these ecclesiastics were talking about, he answered that he heard them saying that the King was risking a lot for not preventing the Archbishop's actions. . . .

When asked what he had understood in this following statement: "What a pity that your Subjects had tendered their resignations, they were the only ones who created this conspiracy," he answered that the conspiracy could not come from the *Parlement,* but from the Archbishop who started it by refusing sacraments. . . .

When he was told that the Archbishop's actions could never have made a man like him commit this crime, he answered that he had nothing else to say except that if the Archbishop had not refused some Sacraments, these things would not have happened.

When asked if he, his family or friends had been refused Sacraments, he answered no.

When asked about the idea he has concerning Religion, he answered that no one should refuse Sacraments to good people who pray in Churches every day, from morning to evening.

When asked if he thinks that Religion allows one to kill Kings, he answered that he had nothing to say about it.

When he was told that his silence proves that he thought that it was allowable for him to kill Kings in some cases, he said he had nothing to say. . . .

After having read all this, the prisoner persisted in saying his answers were real and true, and he also persisted by not wanting to answer, and he signed his name, Damiens.

At this time, the prisoner was tied up.

Document 1.9: *"Letter from a Patriot Claiming to Prove Damiens Had Accomplices"*

This pamphlet was one of the many published in France in response to the news of Damiens's attack on the king. It is written from the standpoint of the so-called patriot party, which opposed the concentration of power in the hands of the king, the royal advisers at court (mostly aristocrats), and the bishops of the church (mostly Jesuits). Patriots instead supported the parlements and the lower clergy as more morally suited to represent the interests of all three orders that composed the French "nation."

Source: Anonymous, *Pièces originales et procédures du procès, fait à Robert-François Damiens* (Paris: Pierre Guillaume Simon, 1757).

Yes sir, no matter how big our misfortunes may have been, I dread that bigger are yet to come. When I think about everything that is happening to us, it could be said that it has been happening against nature . . . everything that should put a stop to our ills, in fact only makes them worse.

First of all, what is really the true source of the problems that beset us? Is it not solely a stubbornness, a spurious point of honor, a spirit of domination and independence found in the bishops and clerics? They, who by their very nature should set an example of the opposite virtues? I have not avoided putting myself at risk to show that the pretext of religion, which they use to cover themselves, is nothing but a mask. I know that you were never fooled by it, and that now no one is fooled anymore. . . .

If our bishops had thought for one instant about the uselessness of these bulls or about the atrocious damage that they cause their clergies and parishes, they would have been the most ardent defenders of this law that condemned them to eternal oblivion. But the true authors of these fateful decrees, and the only people with an interest in maintaining them, knew how to convince our prelates that, after the commitments that they had made, the law that spelled the doom of these decrees was also, inevitably, the same that bestowed their honor and their authority. That is how they came to finally hatch the secret plot of a powerful league against the most important monument of our monarch's wisdom.

Document 1.10: The Sentence Against Damiens (1757)

Having found Damiens guilty, the judges ordered him punished in a gruesome public spectacle, with the intention of repressing symbolically, through his body, the threat to order that the judges perceived in his attack on the king. In the 1760s the *philosophes* began to criticize brutal corporal punishments and the legal use of torture. The revolutionaries aimed to replace them with a painless death by guillotine.

Source: Anonymous, *Pièces originales et procédures du procès, fait à Robert-François Damiens* (Paris: Pierre Guillaume Simon, 1757).

> The Parlement declares "the said Robert-François Damiens has been convicted of having committed a very mean, very terrible, and very dreadful parricidal crime against the King. The said Damiens is sentenced to pay for his crime in front of the main gate of the Church of Paris. He will be taken there in a tipcart naked and will hold a burning wax torch weighing two pounds. There, on his knees, he will say and declare that he had committed a very mean, very terrible and very dreadful parricide, and that he had hurt the King. . . . He will repent and ask God, the King and Justice to forgive him. When this will be done, he will be taken in the same tipcart to the Place de Grève and will be put on a scaffold. Then his breasts, arms, thighs, and legs will be tortured. While holding the knife with which he committed the said Parricide, his right hand will be burnt. On his tortured body parts, melted lead, boiling oil, burning pitch, and melted wax and sulfur will be thrown. Then four horses will pull him apart until he is dismembered. His limbs will be thrown on the stake, and his ashes will be spread. All his belongings, furniture, housings, wherever they are, will be confiscated and given to the King. Before the execution,

the said Damiens will be asked to tell the names of his accomplices. His house will not be demolished, but nothing will be allowed to be built on this same house."

THE UNIVERSALITY OF RIGHTS

The hallmark of the Revolution is the Declaration of Rights of Man and Citizen (1789). Most who favor the revolutionary tradition would ascribe centrality to this document, which makes amazingly assertive claims. As it preceded constitution-making, it posited a range of natural rights against which all laws and arrangements, even constitutions, had to be measured. Nevertheless, the Declaration of Rights of Man and Citizen was not without antecedents. The "rights of Englishmen," dating back centuries, had been reaffirmed and formalized in the 1689 "Bill of Rights." Enlightenment figures such as Jean-Jacques Rousseau argued that individual rights could be guaranteed only by a "social contract" among the citizens, thus suggesting the need for a formal constitution, which neither the English nor the French had. The influence of such thinking can be seen in the reform proposals of Louis XVI's minister Anne-Robert Turgot, who traced France's problems to its lack of a constitution. At about the same time, Americans Thomas Jefferson and George Mason took the notion of rights a step further, insisting that governments could only be based on the constitutional defense of individual rights. By 1789, talk of rights had galvanized both Protestants and Jews in France. Protestants had gained civil but not political rights. Jews had neither, and now they used the language of rights to press their claims. When the French Revolution began, revolutionaries could draw upon a century of interest in new, universally applicable rights.

Document 1.11: The Bill of Rights (1689)

In England, in response to policies that threatened to restore Catholicism in that country, Parliament deposed King James II and called William of Orange from the Dutch Republic and his wife Mary, who was James's Protestant daughter, to replace him. William and Mary agreed to the Bill of Rights presented to them by Parliament, thereby acknowledging that their power came from the legislature rather than from any concept of the "divine right" of kings. The Bill of Rights confirmed traditional English liberties, especially the power of Parliament to make laws and consent to taxation. It also confirmed and guaranteed freedom of speech and denied the legitimacy of cruel and unusual punishments. The Bill of Rights, excerpted below, quickly took its place as a foundation of English constitutionalism and exercised great influence in the British North American colonies during their war for independence.

Source: Guy Carleton Lee, *Source-Book of English History* (London: Henry Holt, 1901), 424–31.

Whereas the Lords Spiritual and Temporal, and Commons, assembled at Westminster, lawfully, fully, and freely representing all the estates of the people of this realm, did, upon the thirteenth day of February, in the year of our Lord one thousand six hundred eighty-eight, present unto their Majesties, then called and known by the names and style of William and Mary, Prince and Princess of Orange, being present in their proper persons, a certain declaration in writing, made by the said Lords and Commons, in the words following; viz:—

Whereas the late King James II, by the assistance of diverse evil counsellors, judges, and ministers employed by him, did endeavour to subvert and extirpate the Protestant religion, and the laws and liberties of this kingdom:—

1. By assuming and exercising a power of dispensing with and suspending of laws, and the execution of laws, without consent of Parliament.

2. By committing and prosecuting divers worthy prelates, for humbly petitioning to be excused from concurring to the same assumed power. . . .

4. By levying money for and to the use of the Crown, by pretence of prerogative, for other time, and in other manner than the same was granted by Parliament.

5. By raising and keeping a standing army within this kingdom in time of peace, without consent of Parliament, and quartering soldiers contrary to law.

6. By causing several good subjects, being Protestants, to be disarmed, at the same time when Papists were both armed and employed contrary to law.

7. By violating the freedom of election of members to serve in Parliament. . . .

11. And excessive fines have been imposed.

12. And illegal and cruel punishments inflicted.

All which are utterly and directly contrary to the known laws and statutes, and freedom of this realm.

And, thereupon the said Lords Spiritual and Temporal, and Commons, pursuant to their respective letters and elections, being now assembled in a full and free representation of this nation, taking into their most serious consideration the best means for attaining the ends aforesaid, do in the first place (as their ancestors in like case have usually done), for the vindicating and asserting their ancient rights and liberties, declare:—

1. That the pretended power of suspending of laws, or the execution of laws, by regal authority, without consent of Parliament, is illegal.

2. That the pretended power of dispensing with laws, or the execution of laws by regal authority, as it hath been assumed and exercised of late, is illegal. . . .

4. That levying money for or to the use of the Crown, by pretence of prerogative, without grant of Parliament, for longer time or in other manner than the same is or shall be granted, is illegal.

5. That it is the right of the subjects to petition the King, and all commitments and prosecutions for such petitioning are illegal.

6. That the raising or keeping a standing army within the kingdom in time of peace, unless it be with consent of Parliament, is against law.

7. That the subjects which are Protestants may have arms for their defence suitable to their conditions, and as allowed by law. . . .

8. That election of members of Parliament ought to be free.

9. That the freedom of speech, and debates or proceedings in Parliament, ought not to be impeached or questioned in any court or place out of Parliament.

10. That excessive bail ought not to be required, nor excessive fines imposed; nor cruel and unusual punishments inflicted.

11. That jurors ought to be duly impanelled and returned, and jurors which pass upon men in trials for high treason ought to be freeholders. . . .

13. And that for redress of all grievances, and for the amending, strengthening, and preserving of laws, Parliaments ought to be held frequently.

Document 1.12: Rousseau's Social Contract (1762)

Jean-Jacques Rousseau was the maverick of the Enlightenment. Born a Protestant in Geneva in 1712 (d. 1778), he had to support himself as a music copyist. Unlike Voltaire and Montesquieu, both of whom came from rich families, Rousseau faced poverty nearly all his life. He wrote on an astounding variety of topics, including a best-selling novel (*Julie, or the New Heloïse,* 1761), a major tract on education (*Émile,* 1762), and the work selected here, *The Social Contract* (1762). Rousseau believed that life in society was essentially corrupting but that men (it is not clear whether women figured in the social contract) could achieve true morality by joining in the social contract and living under laws that they themselves made. Rousseau's concept of the "general will" can be, and has been, interpreted as simultaneously providing the origins of democracy and the origins of totalitarianism. Under the general will everyone is equal, but the government also has unlimited power.

Source: Merrick Whitcomb, ed., *Translations and Reprints from the Original Sources of European History,* vol. 6 (Philadelphia: University of Pennsylvania History Department, 1899), 14–16.

Since no man has any natural authority over his fellow men, and since force is not the source of right, conventions remain as the basis of all lawful authority among men.

Now, as men cannot create any new forces, but only combine and direct those that exist, they have no other means of self-preservation than to form by aggregation a sum of forces which may overcome the resistance, to put them in action by a single motive power, and to make them work in concert.

This sum of forces can be produced only by the combination of many; but the strength and freedom of each man being the chief instruments of his preservation, how can he pledge them without injuring himself, and without neglecting the cares which he owes to himself? This difficulty, applied to my subject, may be expressed in these terms.

"To find a form of association which may defend and protect with the whole force of the community the person and property of every associate, and by means of which each, coalescing with all, may nevertheless obey only himself, and remain as free as before." Such is the fundamental problem of which the social contract furnishes the solution.

If then we set aside what is not of the essence of the social contract, we shall find that it is reducible to the following terms: "Each of us puts in common his person and his whole power under the supreme direction of the general will, and in return we receive every member as an indivisible part of the whole."

But the body politic or sovereign, deriving its existence only from the contract, can never bind itself, even to others, in anything that derogates from the original act, such as alienation of some portion of itself, or submission to another sovereign.

The public force, then, requires a suitable agent to concentrate it and put it in action according to the directions of the general will, to serve as a means of communication between the state and the sovereign, to effect in some manner in the public person what the union of soul and body effects in a man. This is, in the state, the function of government, improperly confounded with the sovereign of which it is only the minister.

What, then, is the government? An intermediate body established between the subjects and the sovereign for their mutual correspondence, charged with the execution of the laws and with the maintenance of liberty both civil and political.

Besides the extraordinary assemblies which unforeseen events may require, it is necessary that there should be fixed and periodical ones which nothing can abolish or prorogue; so that, on the appointed day, the people are rightfully convoked by the law, without needing for that purpose any formal summons.

So soon as the people are lawfully assembled as a sovereign body, the whole jurisdiction of the government ceases, the executive power is suspended, and the person of the meanest citizen is as sacred and inviolable as that of the first magistrate, because where the represented are, there is no longer any representative.

These assemblies, which have as their object the maintenance of the social treaty, ought always to be opened with two propositions, which no one should be able to suppress, and which should pass separately by vote. The first: "Whether it pleases the sovereign to maintain the present form of government." The second: "Whether it pleases the people to leave the administration to those at present entrusted with it."

I presuppose here what I believe I have proved, viz., that there is in the State no fundamental law which cannot be revoked, not even this social compact; for if all the citizens assembled in order to break the compact by a solemn agreement, no one can doubt that it could be quite legitimately broken.

Document 1.13: Turgot's Memorandum on Local Government (1775)

In 1774, on the accession of Louis XVI, Anne-Robert Turgot was named controller general. In this position he became responsible for royal finances, and hence for administrative policies relating to taxation, the economy, and local government. With his recent experience as an *intendant* in mind, Turgot directed his secretary (economist Pierre-Samuel Dupont de Nemours) to draft a long memorandum diagnosing the problems of provincial administration and outlining the plans for national regeneration that the controller general intended to submit to the king. Although this *Mémoire sur les Municipalités* was written in 1775, Turgot fell from power before it could be presented to Louis XVI. But its arguments exercised a powerful influence on administrative thinking in the remaining years of the old regime.

Source: Gustave Schelle, ed., *Oeuvres de Turgot,* 4 vols. (Paris: F. Alcan, 1913–23), 4:568–628.

Sire:

To discover whether it is expedient to establish municipalities in those cantons of France where they do not exist, whether it is necessary to improve or change those already in existence, and how to constitute those it is deemed necessary to create does not involve going back to the origin of municipal administrations, giving an historical account of the vicissitudes they have undergone, or even analyzing in great detail the diverse forms they exhibit today. In deciding what must be done in serious matters, it has been much too frequent a practice to revert to the examination and example of what our ancestors did in times of ignorance and barbarism. This method serves only to lead justice astray in the multiplicity of facts presented as precedents; and it tends to make princes disgusted with their most important functions, by persuading them that it is necessary to be prodigiously learned in order to discharge these functions with success and glory. However, it is really only necessary to understand thoroughly and to weigh carefully the rights and interests of men.

This nation is numerous. That it obey is not everything. It is necessary to make sure that it can be commanded effectively. In order to succeed in this, it would first seem necessary to know, in fairly great detail, the nation's situation, its needs, its capabilities. This knowledge would doubtless be more useful than historical accounts of past positions. . . .

The cause of the evil, Sire, stems from the fact that your nation has no constitution. It is a society composed of different orders badly united, and of a people among whose members there are but very few social ties. In consequence, each individual is occupied only with his own particular, exclusive interest; and almost no one bothers to fulfill his duties or to know his relationship to others. As a result, there is a perpetual war of claims and counterclaims which reason and mutual understanding have never regulated, in which Your Majesty is obliged to decide everything personally or through your agents.

Your realm is made up of provinces. These provinces are composed of cantons or districts which (depending on the province) are called *bailliages, élections, vigueries,* or some other such name. These districts are made up of a certain number of towns and villages, which are in turn inhabited by families. To them belong the lands which yield products, provide for the livelihood of the inhabitants, and furnish the revenues from which salaries are paid to those without land and taxes are levied to meet public expenditures. The families, finally, are composed of individuals, who have many duties to fulfill towards one another and towards society, duties justified in terms of the benefits they have received, and which they continue to receive daily.

But individuals are educated poorly regarding their duties within the family and not at all regarding those which link them to the state.

Families themselves scarcely know that they depend on this state, of which they form a part: they have no idea of the nature of their relationship to it. As a result, everyone seeks to cheat the authorities and to pass social obligations on to his neighbors. Incomes are concealed and can only be discovered very imperfectly by a kind of inquisition which would lead one to say that Your Majesty is at war with your people. And in this type of war which, were it only apparent, would always be destructive and deadly, no one has an interest in taking the government's part, and anyone who did so would be regarded with hostility. There is no public spirit because there is no known and visible common interest.

In order to dissipate this spirit of disunity, which vastly increases the work of your servants and of Your Majesty, and which necessarily and prodigiously diminishes your power; in order to substitute instead a spirit of order and union which would mobilize the forces and means of your nation for the common good, gathering them together in your hand and making them easy to direct, it would be necessary to conceive of a plan that would link individuals to their families, families to the village or town to which they belong, towns and villages to the district of which they form part, districts to their province, and provinces finally to the state. This plan would involve instruction that would be compelling, a common interest, deliberating about it and acting according to it. . . .

Document 1.14: Virginia's Declaration of Rights (1776)

The Declaration of Rights drafted in 1776 by George Mason for the state constitution of Virginia influenced both Jefferson's Declaration of Independence and the French Declaration of the Rights of Man and Citizen. It clearly states that rights are "the basis and foundation of government." The Virginia Declaration of Rights also influenced the drafting of the Bill of Rights that was added to the U.S. Constitution as the first ten amendments.

Source: Kate Mason Rowland, *The Life of George Mason, 1725–1792,* vol. 1 (New York: G. P. Putnam's Sons, 1892), 438–41.

A Declaration of Rights made by the representatives of the good people of Virginia, assembled in full and free Convention; which rights do pertain to them, and their posterity, as the basis and foundation of government.

I. That all men are by nature equally free and independent, and have certain inherent rights, of which, when they enter into a state of society, they cannot, by any compact, deprive or divest their posterity; namely, the enjoyment of life and liberty, with the means of acquiring and possessing property, and pursuing and obtaining happiness and safety.

II. That all power is vested in, and consequently derived from the people; that Magistrates are their trustees and servants, and at all times amenable to them.

III. That government is or ought to be, instituted for the common benefit, protection, and security of the people, nation, or community; of all the various modes and forms of government, that is best, which is capable of producing the greatest degree of happiness and safety, and is most effectually secured against the danger of maladministration; and that when any government shall be found inadequate or contrary to these purposes, a majority of the community hath an indubitable, unalienable, and indefeasible right, to reform, alter, or abolish it, in such manner as shall be judged most conducive to the public weal.

IV. That no man, or set of men, are entitled to exclusive or separate emoluments or privileges from the community, but in consideration of public services; which not being descendible, neither ought the offices of Magistrate, Legislator, or Judge to be hereditary.

V. That the Legislative and Executive powers of the State should be separate and distinct from the Judiciary; and that the members of the two first may be restrained from oppression, by feeling and participating the burthens of the people, they should, at fixed periods, be reduced to a private station, return into that body from which they were originally taken, and the vacancies be supplied by frequent, certain, and regular elections, in which all, or any part of the former members, to be again eligible, or ineligible, as the laws shall direct.

VI. That elections of members to serve as representatives of the people, in Assembly, ought to be free; and that all men having sufficient evidence of permanent common interest with and attachment to, the community, have the right of suffrage, and cannot be taxed or deprived of their property for public uses without their own consent, or that of their representatives so elected, nor bound by any law to which they have not, in like manner, assented for the public good.

VII. That all power of suspending laws, or the execution of laws, by any authority without consent of the representatives of the people, is injurious to their rights and ought not to be exercised. . . .

XI. That in controversies respecting property, and in suits between man and man, the ancient trial by jury is preferable to any other and ought to be held sacred.

XII. That the freedom of the press is one of the great bulwarks of liberty, and can never be restrained but by despotic governments. . . .

XVI. That religion, or the duty which we owe to our Creator, and the manner of discharging it, can be directed only by reason and conviction, not by force or violence, and therefore all men are equally entitled to the free exercise of religion, according to the dictates of conscience; and that it is the mutual duty of all to practise Christian forbearance, love, and charity towards each other.

Document 1.15: *Zalkind Hourwitz,* Vindication of the Jews *(1789)*

In 1789 some 40,000 Jews lived in France, most of them in the eastern provinces of Alsace and Lorraine. In some respects they were better treated than Calvinists under the laws of the monarchy; Jews could legally practice their religion, though their other activities were severely restricted. They had no civil or political rights, except the right to be judged in their own separate courts, and they faced pervasive local prejudice. The major Jewish communities—in the city of Bordeaux in the southwest and in the regions of Alsace and Lorraine in the east—essentially constituted separate "nations" within the French nation (and nations separate from one another, because their status differed in many ways).

In 1787 and 1788 the Royal Society of Arts and Sciences of the city of Metz in eastern France set up an essay competition on the question "Are there means for making the Jews happier and more useful in France?" Its 2,000 Jews gave Metz the single largest Jewish population in the east. Among the three winners declared in 1788 was Zalkind Hourwitz (1738–1812), a Polish Jew. His pamphlet rapidly earned him a reputation in reformist circles, even though by today's standard its language seems moderate, if not excessively apologetic. The excerpt here represents what might be called the "assimilationist" position—that is, that granting rights to the Jews would make them more like the rest of the French. At times the author's own arguments sound anti-Semitic to our ears, because in his concern to counter all the usual stereotypes about the Jews, he repeats many of them and gives them a kind of creditability. As a follower of the Enlightenment, Hourwitz disliked the extensive powers Jewish leaders exercised over their communities, and he even held out the possibility of encouraging conversion to Christianity. The inclusion of such a suggestion, and the defensive tone of the recommendations for improvement, highlight the many difficulties and prejudices faced by the Jews.

Source: The materials listed below appeared originally in *The French Revolution and Human Rights: A Brief Documentary History,* translated, edited, and with an introduction by Lynn Hunt (Boston/New York: Bedford/St. Martin's, 1996), 48–50.

> The means of making the Jews happy and useful? Here it is: stop making them unhappy and unuseful. Accord them, or rather return to them the right of citizens, which you have denied them against all divine and human laws and against your own interests, like a man who thoughtlessly cripples himself. . . .
>
> To be sure, during times of barbarism, there was no shortage of ways of oppressing the Jews. Yet we are hard pressed even in an enlightened century, not to repair all the evils that have been done to them and to compensate them for their unjustly confiscated goods [hardly to be hoped for], but simply to cease being unjust toward them and to leave them peacefully to enjoy the rights of humanity under the protection of general laws. . . .
>
> The simplest means would be therefore to accord them throughout the kingdom the same liberty that they enjoy in [Bordeaux and Bayonne]; nevertheless, however simple this means appears, it is still susceptible to greater perfection, in order to render the Jews not only happier and more useful but even more honest in the following manner.

1. They must be accorded permission to acquire land, which will attach them to the fatherland, where they will no longer regard themselves as foreigners and will increase at the same time the value of the land.

2. They must be permitted to practice all of the liberal and mechanical arts and agriculture, which will diminish the number of merchants among them and in consequence the number of knaves and rogues. . . .

4. To make their merchants more honest, they must be accorded the freedom to exercise every sort of commerce, to keep their stores open, to carry any product, and to live among the other citizens. Then being more closely allied with the other citizens, more at their ease and with their conduct more exposed to the inspection of the police, having moreover to manage their credit, their reputation, and especially their regular customers, they will have in consequence less inclination, less necessity, and less facility in cheating and buying stolen goods.

5. To better diminish this facility in cheating, they must be forbidden, on pain of annulment of the transaction, the use of Hebrew and German [Yiddish] language and characters in their account books and commercial contracts, whether between themselves or with Christians.

6. It is necessary therefore to open the public schools to their children, to teach them French, which will produce a double advantage: it will make it easier to instruct them and to make them familiar from earliest infancy with Christians. They will establish with the Christians bonds of friendship which will be fortified by living near to each other, by the use of the same language and customs, and especially by the recognition of the freedom that they will be accorded; they will learn from these bonds that the Christians worship a Supreme Being like themselves, and as a result the fraud that the Talmud authorizes in dealings with pagans will no longer be permitted.

7. To better facilitate these bonds, their rabbis and leaders must be severely forbidden from claiming the least authority over their co-religionists outside of the synagogue, from prohibiting entry and honors to those who cut their beards, who curl their hair, who dress like Christians, who go to the theater, or who fail to observe some other custom that is irrelevant to their religion and only introduced by superstition in order to distinguish the Jews from other peoples. . . .

We could add that the freedom of the Jews is the best means of converting them to Christianity; for, once putting an end to their captivity, you will render useless the temporal Messiah that they expect, and then they will be obliged to recognize Jesus-Christ as a spiritual Messiah in order not to contradict the Prophets, who predicted the arrival of some kind of Messiah. . . .

Are so many verbiages and citations necessary to prove that a Jew is a man, and that it is unjust to punish him from his birth onward for real or supposed vices that one reproaches in other men with whom he has nothing in common but religious belief? And what would the French say if the Academy of Stockholm had proposed, twelve years ago, the following question: "Are there means for making Catholics more useful and happier in Sweden?"

Document 1.16: Declaration of the Rights of Man and Citizen, 26 August 1789

The Declaration promised liberty and legal equality to all citizens. It synthesized in one document the notions of natural rights, social contract, and the need for constitutional guarantees. Rights in the Old Regime had simply enumerated individual privileges that grew out of custom or explicit royal grants. Now rights were supposedly universal. In fact, however, liberty and equality proved difficult to realize even in the details of the Declaration itself. A glaring example can be found right in the midst of articles that define law as extremely limited (articles 5–9): "citizens summoned or seized by virtue of the law should obey instantly, and render themselves guilty by resistance." In effect, the very resistance that made the Revolution and that the Declaration also guaranteed (article 2) would become utterly impossible. Equally ambiguous was the principle guaranteeing religious toleration. This freedom is protected only if it "does not trouble public order" (article 10). For all its limitations, however, the Declaration marked a stunning expansion on all previous French notions of rights.

Source: The materials listed below originally appeared in *The French Revolution and Human Rights: A Brief Documentary History,* translated, edited, and with an introduction by Lynn Hunt (Boston/New York: Bedford/St. Martin's, 1996), 77–79.

The representatives of the French people, constituted as a National Assembly, and considering that ignorance, neglect, or contempt of the rights of man are the sole causes of public misfortunes and governmental corruption, have resolved to set forth in a solemn declaration the natural, inalienable and sacred rights of man: so that by being constantly present to all the members of the social body this declaration may always remind them of their rights and duties; so that by being liable at every moment to comparison with the aim of any and all political institutions the acts of the legislative and executive powers may be the more fully respected; and so that by being founded henceforward on simple and incontestable principles the demands of the citizens may always tend toward maintaining the constitution and the general welfare.

In consequence, the National Assembly recognizes and declares, in the presence and under the auspices of the Supreme Being, the following rights of man and the citizen:

1. Men are born and remain free and equal in rights. Social distinctions may be based only on common utility.

2. The purpose of all political association is the preservation of the natural and imprescriptible rights of man. These rights are liberty, property, security, and resistance to oppression.

3. The principle of all sovereignty rests essentially in the nation. No body and no individual may exercise authority which does not emanate expressly from the nation.

4. Liberty consists in the ability to do whatever does not harm another; hence the exercise of the natural rights of each man has no other limits than those which assure to other members of society the enjoyment of the same rights. These limits can only be determined by the law.

5. The law only has the right to prohibit those actions which are injurious to society. No hindrance should be put in the way of anything not prohibited by the law, nor may any one be forced to do what the law does not require.

6. The law is the expression of the general will. All citizens have the right to take part, in person or by their representatives, in its formation. It must be the same for everyone whether it protects or penalizes. All citizens being equal in its eyes are equally admissible to all public dignities, offices, and employments, according to their ability, and with no other distinction than that of their virtues and talents.

7. No man may be indicted, arrested, or detained except in cases determined by the law and according to the forms which it has prescribed. Those who seek, expedite, execute, or cause to be executed arbitrary orders should be punished; but citizens summoned or seized by virtue of the law should obey instantly, and render themselves guilty by resistance.

8. Only strictly and obviously necessary punishments may be established by the law, and no one may be punished except by virtue of a law established and promulgated before the time of the offense, and legally applied.

9. Every man being presumed innocent until judged guilty, if it is deemed indispensable to arrest him, all rigor unnecessary to securing his person should be severely repressed by the law.

10. No one should be disturbed for his opinions, even in religion, provided that their manifestation does not trouble public order as established by law.

11. The free communication of thoughts and opinions is one of the most precious of the rights of man. Every citizen may therefore speak, write, and print freely, if he accepts his own responsibility for any abuse of this liberty in the cases set by the law.

12. The safeguard of the rights of man and the citizen requires public powers. These powers are therefore instituted for the advantage of all, and not for the private benefit of those to whom they are entrusted.

13. For maintenance of public authority and for expenses of administration, common taxation is indispensable. It should be apportioned equally among all the citizens according to their capacity to pay.

14. All citizens have the right, by themselves or through their representatives, to have demonstrated to them the necessity of public taxes, to consent to them freely, to follow the use made of the proceeds, and to determine the means of apportionment, assessment, and collection, and the duration of them.

15. Society has the right to hold accountable every public agent of the administration.

16. Any society in which the guarantee of rights is not assured or the separation of powers not settled has no constitution.

17. Property being an inviolable and sacred right, no one may be deprived of it except when public necessity, certified by law, obviously requires it, and on the condition of a just compensation in advance.

2

From Constitutional to Democratic Revolution 1789-January 1793

MEN ARE BORN AND REMAIN FREE AND EQUAL IN RIGHTS. SOCIAL DISTINCTIONS MAY BE BASED ONLY ON COMMON UTILITY.

—ARTICLE I, DECLARATION OF THE RIGHTS OF MAN AND CITIZEN, AUGUST 1789

(DOCUMENT 1.16)

The French Revolution began as a struggle for constitutional monarchy and only gradually turned into a democratic movement. In its first days it brought almost everyone together. Even though the three estates of the Estates General did not agree on a common method of proceeding, once the logjam had broken, nobles, clergymen, and members of the Third Estate enthusiastically undertook to make their beloved king into a constitutional monarch. No one imagined that this would eventually entail dismantling the entire traditional social and political order. Most believed it was an essential reform, a step in modernization, not a total rupture.

Yet in the opening article of the Declaration of the Rights of Man and Citizen drafted in the first months of the Revolution (Document 1.16), there were clear traces of a fundamentally new vision of French society. If all men "are born and remain free and equal in rights," if "social distinctions may be based only on common utility," then what justified the continued legal privileges and status of the nobility? Did equality of rights mean that all men could vote and hold office? At this time no country in the world allowed all adult men to vote and hold office. And what did "men" mean? Were Protestants and Jews included? They had had no political rights under the monarchy before 1789. Could slavery be justified if all men were born equal in rights? And why were women left out? It took time for these questions to come into the open. Even in 1789, however, many saw that a major political upheaval was threatening the monarchy.

The Revolution Begins

Veteran armies inured to War have never performed greater prodigies of valour than this leaderless multitude of persons belonging to every class.
  —An insurgent describes the fall of the Bastille, 14 July 1789
  (CD-ROM p. 52)

The Estates General opened in May 1789 on a note of uncertainty. Would the nobles and the clergy compromise on the question of voting by head? The deputies of the Third Estate came armed with grievance lists that demanded voting by head. It is not surprising that the grievance lists of the nobles insisted on voting by order. The clergy were about evenly divided between those who wanted to make common cause with the Third Estate and those who did not. The Third Estate simply refused to proceed to any other issue until the deputies resolved this one in their favor. After six weeks of stalemate, on 17 June 1789 the deputies of the Third Estate took unilateral action and declared themselves and whoever would join them "the National Assembly." In the National Assembly, each deputy would vote as an individual (by head) and not as part of an estate. Two days later the clergy decided by a narrow margin to join the new assembly. The decision to create a National Assembly amounted to a constitutional revolution, for now the elected deputies of "the nation" displaced the old estates in which nobles and clergy dominated. The deputies declared that they alone could approve new taxes and only "provisionally" allowed the collection of previous taxes. Barred from their meeting hall on 20 June by order of the king, the deputies swore an oath in a nearby tennis court not to disband until they had given France a constitution that reflected their newly asserted authority. Every day now deputies reported to their constituents on unfolding events; their published letters became the first revolutionary newspapers. The royal government gave up trying to suppress them.

On 23 June, Louis XVI held a royal session to announce his decision about the unfolding events. Behind the scenes his advisers at court had been fighting furiously among themselves over the direction of policy. His brothers insisted that he had to forbid the formation of a national assembly and maintain the distinction between estates at all costs. His chief financial minister, Jacques Necker, rejected this course of action and advised cooperation under the new arrangement. With soldiers surrounding the meeting room, the king announced a hard line: he annulled the "illegal" national assembly and commanded the deputies to return to their separate chambers and deliberate as estates. But when the king swept out of the room, the deputies of the Third Estate refused to budge. Faced with this unheard-of defiance, the king gave in. Still in mourning for his oldest son, who had died unexpectedly on 14 June, Louis XVI rejected his brothers' advice that he remove the deputies by force. His hesitation proved fateful.

At first the king appeared to agree to the new representative assembly; on 27 June he ordered the deputies of the clergy and nobility to join the deputies of the Third Estate for deliberations in common. At the same time, however, he also commanded thousands of soldiers to march to Paris. The deputies who supported the new National Assembly feared a plot by the king and high-ranking nobles to arrest them and disperse the assembly. "Everyone is convinced that the approach of the troops covers some violent design," one deputy wrote home. Some of the troops arriving in Paris and Versailles were Swiss and Germans who were expected to be less susceptible to sympathizing with ordinary French citizens. Fears of a conspiracy were confirmed when on 11 July the king fired Necker, the one high official believed to be sympathetic to the deputies' cause. The king ordered Necker to leave in secret and return to his home in Switzerland.

As news of Necker's dismissal came out on 12 July, ordinary people enjoying their Sunday promenade began to gather together and listen to impromptu orators who denounced this now seemingly sure sign of a conspiracy. They raced off to the theaters and opera and insisted that the performances be canceled. One group rushed into the wax museum and carried out a bust of Necker. Before long, 5,000 to 6,000 people paraded with the bust and black flags as a sign of mourning for their liberty. The crowd took on soldiers in the center of Paris, forcing them to retreat. As fighting broke out, the most daring looted gun shops and disarmed patrols. Around midnight, armed groups began to attack the customs barriers on the edge of the city, burning most of them to the ground. They hoped to lower the price of grain by eliminating the duties

PRISE DE LA BASTILLE
par les Gardes Françaises et les Bourgeois de Paris, le Mardi 14 Juillet 1789.
Delaunay qui en étoit Gouverneur fut pris et trainé à la Place de Grève, ou en arrivant il eut la tête tranchée, étant convaincu de trahison
sa tête et son cœur furent portés en triomphe par toute la Ville.

Fig. 2.1   Taking of the Bastille

This print emphasizes the populace's participation in the storming of the Bastille. The people of Paris are shown under a red banner fighting with muskets, swords, and pikes against the royal soldiers. Stunning images like these—as well as dramatic press reports—contributed to what has become the widespread view that the taking of the Bastille was a spontaneous, brave, and widely popular revolt against royal authority.

---

levied on it. On the morning of 13 July armed mobs attacked a monastery known for its large storehouse of grain. Next to fall were the prisons in the capital. As anarchy threatened, meetings took place to set up a National Guard to both restore order and defend the National Assembly. Many middle-class Parisians were fearful. Restif de la Bretonne, a well-known novelist, claimed that the crowds were made up of bandits and brigands who crowed that "today is the last day of the rich and well-off."

When day dawned on 14 July, rumors swirled around the city. Thousands of soldiers were preparing a counterattack, said one often repeated report. By now the native French troops had gone over to the side of the people of Paris. Barricades popped up to defend neighborhoods. A huge crowd marched to the Invalides, a veterans' hospital and military storehouse, demanding arms. When the crowd broke in, the soldiers defending the spot held their fire. Some 30,000 to 40,000 guns passed into the hands of the crowd, along with twelve cannons. At almost the same time, another mob marched to the Bastille, an imposing fortress-like prison in the center of the working-class district of eastern Paris (see Fig. 2.1). The defenders there fired on the crowd, killing about 100 of the attackers. Faced with this resistance, the insurgents brought in the cannons from the Invalides and shot their way through the main gate of the fortress. The governor of the prison wanted to blow up the storehouse of powder and take with him all the surrounding dwellings, but his officers refused to let him. When he surrendered, the crowd led him off to city hall, where an unemployed cook broke through the lines and stabbed him with a bayonet. Several others piled on with swords and pistols. Once the poor man was dead, someone in the crowd cut off his head and stuck it on a pike. A new and more grisly parade began, echoing the earlier one with Necker's bust. Three other officers and three ordinary soldiers were likewise massacred. A leading city official, viewed by many as a traitor, was shot to death. His head joined the Bastille governor's head on parade. Liberty and violence had become dangerous partners.

Back in his palace at Versailles, twelve miles away, Louis XVI seemed unaware of the events unfolding in his capital city. On 11 July he wrote in his diary: "departure of M. Necker." On 12 July he noted the leave-taking of three other ministers. On 13 and 14 July, he wrote: "Nothing." The Duke of Liancourt reported that he had told the king about the events on the night of 14 July. The king asked him, "Is it a revolt?" The duke supposedly replied, "No, Sire, it is a revolution." Liancourt convinced him to personally appear in front of the deputies of the National Assembly. There Louis agreed to withdraw his troops from the capital. Thomas Jefferson wrote home that he considered this an unconditional surrender on the part of the king. On 16 July, Louis held a private meeting with his advisers in Versailles. They decided that flight was impossible (the queen wanted Louis to move the court to Metz, near the eastern frontier). Louis agreed to recall Necker and ordered all the troops back to their barracks in the provinces. On 17 July, Louis went to Paris in a solemn procession. At the city hall he consented to wear the new tricolor (red, white, and blue) cockade just invented by the insurgents as their symbol of patriotism. Joseph de Maistre, a leading theorist of the counterrevolution, later wrote: "Few battles are lost physically. Battles are almost always lost morally. The true victor, like the true victim, is the one who believes himself to be such." At this crucial moment the king no longer believed in his ability—or perhaps even his right—to impose his will by force.

The fall of the Bastille on 14 July (an event now commemorated as the French national holiday) completely changed the course of events. Even though it had elements of a bread riot and unfolded haphazardly rather than according to a plan to overthrow the government, contemporaries immediately seized upon this event as the central revolutionary act. "Patriot" journalists guaranteed this result when they depicted the fall of the Bastille as a fundamental revolution, not a simple revolt or bread riot. As it turned out, the fall of the Bastille did have revolutionary effects; most important, it marked the entry of the common people on the scene of organized political activity. The deputies in Versailles could make policy, but they were helpless to enforce it without any military power at their command. The common people of Paris had shown that they were willing to arm themselves to support the deputies and foil royalist hopes for an immediate counterrevolution. Those who participated, as the quotation at the beginning of this section illustrates, emphasized the common will and unity of action of all those involved. "The people" saved the nascent revolution— and not just in Paris.

As soon as news of the fall of the Bastille reached the provinces, ordinary folk made their own local revolutions. In Strasbourg an angry crowd attacked the city hall and destroyed everything in the building. In town after town, food riots forced local governments to set up emergency committees and National Guards on the model of Paris. Local officials begged for army reinforcements. In most of the big towns and cities, "patriot" committees replaced the old town councils.

The new National Guards had to calm the peasants in the countryside, who feared that the beggars and vagrants crowding the roads might be part of an aristocratic plot to starve the people by burning crops or barns. In some instances, this Great Fear, as historians have termed it, turned into peasant attacks on aristocrats or on seigneurial records of peasants' dues kept in the lord's château. Everywhere the royal government began to crumble. One of Louis XVI's brothers and many other leading aristocrats fled into exile. In Paris the Marquis de Lafayette, a hero of the American Revolution and a nobleman sympathetic to the French Revolution, became commander of the new National Guard. The Revolution thus had its first victims, its first enemies, and its first heroes.

The Constitutional Revolution

For two years after July 1789 the deputies of the National Assembly strove to establish a constitutional monarchy that would embody Enlightenment reforms. Some observers, like Anglo-Irish politician Edmund Burke, quoted on facing page, immediately expressed their skepticism about the Assembly's aims. Burke insisted that when put into practice the principles of the Enlightenment—"this new conquering empire of light and reason"—would prove fatal. Reason could not found government, he argued; only a long tradition and patient, gradual experimentation produced sound governmental principles. He and other conservatives found the Assembly's course of action rash and ill-considered. Others, on the contrary, waxed enthusiastic about the dawning era of liberty. English poet William Wordsworth recalled that "'twas a time when Europe was rejoiced, / France standing on top of golden hours, / And human nature seeming born again." Everything seemed possible.

The National Assembly included the lawyers and officials who had represented the Third Estate, as well as most of the deputies from the clergy and a substantial number of nobles. The clerical deputies worried about the fate of the Catholic church under the new regime. Some noble deputies quit their posts in disgust at the turn of events, but most bided their time hoping to conserve noble preeminence in a constitutional monarchy. The first goal of the National Assembly was to write a constitution, but more immediate problems demanded attention. In the countryside, peasants refused to pay seigneurial dues to their landlords, and persistence of the Great Fear raised alarms about the potential for a general peasant insurrection.

In response to peasant unrest the National Assembly undertook sweeping reforms. On the night of 4 August 1789, noble deputies announced their willingness to give up their traditional privileges and dues, thereby freeing the peasants from some of their most pressing burdens. By the end of the night, in a kind of spell of self-sacrifice, dozens of deputies had come to the podium to relinquish the tax privileges of their own professional groups, towns, or provinces. The National Assembly decreed the abolition of what they called "the feudal regime"—that is, they freed the remaining serfs and eliminated all tax exemptions, including all seigneurial dues on the land (a few days later the deputies insisted on financial compensation for some of these dues, but most peasants refused to pay). The assembly also mandated equality of opportunity in access to official posts. Talent and merit, rather than birth, were to be the keys to success; nobility no longer guaranteed access to the highest positions. The Assembly had accomplished far more in one night than the monarchy had achieved during decades of futile attempts at reform.

Three weeks later, after intense debate, the Assembly passed the Declaration of the Rights of Man and Citizen, which proclaimed: "Men are born and remain free and equal in rights" (see Fig. 2.2). In other words, the *subjects* of the monarchy became participating *citizens*. In December 1789 the deputies decided that the Declaration applied to Protestants; Protestants now had full political rights for the first time since 1685. In September 1791, all Jews became citizens if they were willing to renounce their special tax and legal exemptions. However, at first only white men who passed a test of wealth could vote or hold office; these were the "active citizens," while all others, including slaves, women, children, and foreigners, were "passive." The deputies drew a distinction between natural and civil rights, and political rights. Women never received the right to vote during the Revolution (and attained it only in 1944). They enjoyed civil rights but not political rights.

> All the pleasing illusions which made power gentle and obedience liberal, which harmonized the different shades of life, and which, by a bland assimilation, incorporated into politics the sentiments which beautify and soften private society, are to be dissolved by this new conquering empire of light and reason. All the decent drapery of life is to be rudely torn off.
>
> —Edmund Burke,
> *Reflections on the Revolution in France* (1790)
> (CD-ROM p. 160)

Fig. 2.2 French Constitution, Rights of Man and Citizen

This image of the Declaration of Rights of Man and Citizen includes a fascinating mix of symbols. By arranging the articles on tablets, the artist clearly meant to associate this document with Moses' Ten Commandments and establish the revolutionaries' handiwork as equivalent to that of God. Reinforcing this is the all-seeing eye located at the top of the tableau. However, this is not the God of biblical revelation but rather the God of the Masonic order, which espoused a deistic vision of a benevolent creator and founder of general laws. This deity was not a worker of miracles. Thus the Declaration results from the actions of humankind, which enjoy the beneficence of the generous deity.

Although only about two-thirds of adult French men met the property requirements for voting under the new system (more in the countryside and fewer in the cities), political participation expanded in unforeseen ways. The National Guard enrolled men of almost every social class, though the requirement to buy one's own uniform limited membership. Newspapers had sprung up in response to the need to recount fast-moving events after the fall of the Bastille, and they exploded in numbers and undoubtedly in subscribers too. Before 1789, France had one daily newspaper, but by the end of 1789, there were more than thirty, with lower prices and increased availability.

Political clubs now appeared for the first time in French history. The first and most significant of the clubs was the Jacobin Club (Document 2.1), which got its name from the monastery where it met in Paris. The Jacobin Club had its origins in informal meetings of deputies to the Third Estate in the spring of 1789 and gradually evolved into a more formal organization with a manifesto, regular procedures, minutes, and eventually an official newspaper. By the end of 1789 about 200 deputies belonged to it. At the beginning it attracted a wide variety of men ranging from the nobles Lafayette and Liancourt to the budding democrat Maximilien Robespierre, a lawyer from northern France. In October 1789 Robespierre made his first impression when he denounced the decision to limit voting to those who paid taxes equivalent to three days' work.

The Jacobin Club and its affiliates in the provinces were the ancestors of modern political parties. They provided their members with places to coordinate policies, try out speeches, and test prevailing opinion. Some revolutionary newspapers called for the creation of popular clubs: "We need clubs for the people," editorialized one. "Let every street in every town, let every hamlet have one" (Document 2.2). In fact, some had already responded to the example of the Jacobins. In April 1790 a group of journalists and political activists formed the Cordeliers Club in Paris (also named after its meeting place). It soon trumpeted the democratic line and attracted artisans and shopkeepers to its meetings. In many towns and cities, popular clubs soon competed with local Jacobin Clubs. Meeting in neighborhoods and charging minimal dues, the popular clubs sometimes boasted thousands of members who attended speeches and joined in demonstrations when the occasion demanded. By September 1791 the political clubs had become a source of controversy. Some deputies wanted to keep them from publishing any kind of political opinion, but others, notably Robespierre, defended the people's right to meet and discuss policy. "Is there a more legitimate or more worthy concern for a free people?" he asked (Document 2.3). The popular clubs would prove to be an important source of the democratic movement that gathered steam between 1791 and 1794.

Women did not always meekly accept their exclusion from political rights. In October 1789, ordinary women in Paris spontaneously formed one of the largest demonstrations of the Revolution. As tensions mounted over the rising price of bread, rumors spread that officers guarding the king at his palace in Versailles had stomped in drunken fury on the red-white-and-blue cockades worn by supporters of the Revolution. On 5 October 1789, outraged at this insult and determined to get the king's help in securing more grain, a crowd of several thousand women marched in a drenching rain twelve miles from the center of Paris to Versailles. One observer described how they came "armed with broomsticks, lances, pitchforks, swords, pistols, and muskets" (Document 2.7). As soon as they arrived in Versailles, they sent a delegation to the king and demanded an audience with the deputies of the National Assembly (see Fig. 2.3). Before the evening was over, thousands of men had marched from Paris to reinforce the women. The atmosphere turned ominous as the crowd camped out all night near the palace.

Early the next morning, thousands of men and women forced their way into the palace grounds at Versailles and broke into the royal family's private apartments. To prevent further bloodshed—two of the royal bodyguards had already been killed and their heads mounted on pikes—the king agreed to move his family and his government back

JOURNÉE MEMORABLE DE VERSAILLES le jeudi 5 Octobre 1789.

. . . . Nos Modernes Amazones glorieuses de leurs Victoire reviennent a Cheval sur les Canons, avec plusieurs Officiers de la Garde . . tionale, tenant des branches de Peupliers au bruit des cris reiterés de Vive la Nation. Vive le Roi .

Fig. 2.3 Memorable Day at Versailles, 5 October 1789

At first, Louis XVI refused to sign the Declaration of the Rights of Man and Citizen. As political tensions as well as the price of bread mounted, Parisian women in the market decided to force matters. The National Guard initially tried to restrain them, but then its members too joined the march. Under such pressure the king acceded. This engraving marks success and reconciliation among revolutionaries, as men and women as well as soldiers and civilians relax together.

to Paris. A huge procession started out, led by the "baker, the baker's wife, and the baker's son." In the view of the lower classes, the king was obligated to make sure his people were fed, and who did this more effectively than bakers? In his account of the parade of the "royal captives," Burke luridly depicted "the horrid yells, and shrilling screams, and frantic dances . . . and all the unutterable abominations of the furies of hell, in the abused shape of the vilest of women." The same ordinary women had been able to enforce their will and directly influence the course of events. Once in Paris, the king had much less room to maneuver. He could not help but listen to popular demands, or so many hoped.

In addition to joining the march to Versailles, women wrote petitions and published tracts. Newspapers had to admit: "Many women have complained to us about the revolution" (Document 2.8). Some women—and their male supporters—now openly demanded political rights. In 1791, Olympe de Gouges, a self-educated butcher's daughter and published playwright, offered a Declaration of the Rights of Women modeled on the official declaration. In article I she announced, "Woman is born free and lives equal to man in her rights." She also insisted that since "woman has the right to mount the scaffold," she must "equally have the right to mount the rostrum." (CD-ROM p. 74) Gouges would herself mount the scaffold in 1793 when she was tried and judged guilty of counterrevolutionary activity.

Women attended the meetings of all-male clubs, such as those of the Jacobins and the Cordeliers, joined mixed-sex clubs, and eventually set up their own women's clubs as well. The most remarkable of the women's clubs was the Society of Revolutionary Republican Women founded in May 1793. Most women's clubs, like the Society, devoted themselves to general political issues, such as the denunciation of counter-revolutionary activity and demands for more government severity toward traitors, speculators, and "egotistical merchants" (Document 2.4). Food continued high on the list of women's concerns, and women appeared prominently in demonstrations and riots over food prices (Document 2.9). Sometimes women also agitated for more legal rights, including the right to divorce (passed into law in September 1792) and equal rights to inheritance (passed into law in March 1793). Women organized about sixty clubs in provincial towns and cities; they concentrated on charity work, local festivals, and support for revolutionary measures.

Although the new constitution drafted by the National Assembly limited the right to vote to men who paid a specified level of taxation (and therefore owned property), it nonetheless produced fundamental changes. In an Enlightenment-inspired effort to standardize and modernize government, the deputies abolished all the old administrative divisions of the provinces and replaced them with a uniform national system of eighty-three departments with identical administrative and legal structures. All officials were elected; no offices could be bought and sold as they were under the monarchy in the past. The assembly abolished the old taxes and replaced them with new ones that were supposed to be uniformly levied. The government had difficulty

Map 2 The Departments of France (1798)

The National Assembly voted on 11 November 1789 to abolish the provinces and establish departments in their place. The decision galvanized hundreds of French towns and cities, each of which hoped to become the headquarters of the local department. Two months later, on 15 January 1790, the deputies approved the new administrative division with its eighty-three departments, a number that steadily increased as France annexed new territories. The departments, unlike the provinces, were to be roughly equal in size with absolutely identical administrations, levels of taxation, and judicial institutions. The names of the departments reflected this desire for standardization: rather than employing traditional names, the new departments were named after geographical references (most often to rivers or mountains).

collecting taxes, because many people had expected a substantial cut in the tax rate. The new administrative system survived, however, and the departments are still the basic units of French government today. This sudden break with the past had an impact on everyday language: the pre-Revolutionary monarchy now became known as the *ancien régime,* French for "old" or "former" regime.

Because the new regime assumed the debts of the monarchy, it had to find additional sources of revenue to balance the budget. As the financial situation worsened, the deputies could not resist the prospect of confiscating the substantial properties of the Catholic church. In November 1789 they nationalized all church property; they abolished the tithe (the Catholic church's levy of one-tenth of everyone's income) soon after. The nationalized property served as a guarantee for the new paper money (*assignats*) the government issued. To raise cash, the government began to sell church lands to the highest bidders in state auctions, thereby increasing the holdings of wealthy city-dwellers and prosperous peasants but diminishing the value of the government's paper money. By the end of December 1791 the value of the paper money had declined 25 percent.

Convinced that monastic life encouraged idleness and a decline in the nation's population, the deputies outlawed any future monastic vows and encouraged monks and nuns to return to private life on state pensions. Many monks took the opportunity, but few nuns did. Because Enlightenment philosophers had so often attacked the abuses of monastic orders, one deputy concluded: "Much of what is happening today has been influenced by the old quarrels between the sect of [Enlightenment] philosophers and the clergy."

To formalize church reorganization, the National Assembly passed a Civil Constitution of the Clergy in July 1790. It set pay scales for the clergy and provided that the voters elect their own parish priests and bishops just as they elected other officials. Many Catholics objected because Protestants and Jews could vote for Catholic priests and bishops. Because some bishops had emigrated and others had denounced even the Declaration of Rights, the National Assembly voted in November 1790 to require all clergy to swear an oath of loyalty to the Civil Constitution of the Clergy. Pope Pius VI in Rome condemned this constitution, and half of the French clergy refused to take the oath. The oath of allegiance permanently divided the Catholic population, which had to choose between loyalty to the old church and commitment to the Revolution with its own "constitutional" church. The government lost many supporters by passing laws against the clergy who refused the oath and by forcing them into exile, deporting them forcibly, or executing them as traitors. Riots and hostile demonstrations led by women greeted many of the oath-taking priests who showed up to replace those who refused.

Even while debating the Civil Constitution of the Clergy the deputies did not overlook the nobility. On 19 June 1790 the National Assembly voted to suppress hereditary nobility, the defining feature along with royalty of monarchy as a form of government. The Jacobins and popular clubs had first proposed this course of action, but when it was put forward on the floor of the Assembly several liberal nobles leaped forward to sacrifice their titles, coats of arms, liveries for servants, special ecclesiastical rites, and names based on feudal properties. Conservative nobles objected on the spot but were drowned out by the cheers of spectators. "So we have revenge at last for all the humiliations we have had to endure from these arrogant little counts," exulted one commoner deputy. Calmer heads reasoned, however, that the nobles would now become irreconcilable enemies of the Revolution.

The Fall of the Monarchy

It is impossible to reign in innocence. The folly of that is all too evident. All Kings are rebels and usurpers.
—Louis-Antoine Saint-Just, on the trial of Louis XVI (13 November 1792) (CD-ROM p. 100) 📖

Having once ruled in theory by divine right with few restrictions on his will, Louis XVI deeply resented the fundamental changes undertaken by the National Assembly. Unknown to the deputies, he had written a letter in July 1789 to the king of Spain denying responsibility for anything that he might be forced to consent to in the future. As the National Assembly drew up the new constitution in 1790 and 1791, Louis chafed at the limitations put on his power. As chief executive, he could exercise a "suspensive" and not an absolute veto, holding up legislation only through the first two votes on a measure. In most matters the king shared power with the legislature, a previously unheard of arrangement in France. Louis especially resented the reorganization of the Catholic church.

Before the Assembly put the final touches on the new constitution, Louis took matters into his own hands. On 20 June 1791, the royal family escaped in disguise from the Tuileries palace in Paris and fled to the eastern frontier, where they hoped to gather support to overturn the Revolution. The plans went awry when a postmaster recognized the king from his portrait on the new paper money, and the royal family was arrested by the National Guard at Varennes, forty miles from the border. The deputies faced a dilemma. They had already decided to establish a constitutional monarchy, but the monarch had tried to flee. To remove him from office would open the floodgates holding back an increasingly radical popular movement in Paris. To counter the pressure of popular clubs and newspapers, the National Assembly tried to depict this "flight to Varennes" as a kidnapping.

Few were convinced by the maneuver. Cartoons circulated showing the royal family as animals being returned "to the stable." The king had been transformed from a beloved fatherly figure into an object of derision and hostility. (See "Study in Images: 'Down with the King!'") The Cordeliers Club openly demanded the king's removal. On 17 July 1791 thousands of Parisians joined in a demonstration to present petitions for a trial of the king. The National Guard opened fire on them and at least fifty died.

The National Assembly ordered the arrest of popular leaders and the temporary closing of the Cordeliers Club (Document 2.3). Many radical journalists, even the boldly militant Jean-Paul Marat, editor of the notoriously hard-hitting *Friend of the People*, went into hiding. But the tide had turned against the king.

Voters elected a new Legislative Assembly in late August and early September 1791. In a rare act of self-denial, the deputies of the National Assembly declared themselves ineligible for the new assembly, thus opening the door to men with no previous experience in national politics. The status of the king might have remained uncertain if war had not intervened, but by early 1792 everyone seemed intent on war with Austria. The Austrian emperor, Leopold II, was the brother of Queen Marie-Antoinette. Thousands of aristocrats, including two-thirds of the army officer corps, had already emigrated from France, including both the king's brothers, and they were gathering on France's eastern border in territories of Leopold's Holy Roman Empire waiting to join a counterrevolutionary army. Louis and his wife hoped that war would lead to the definitive defeat of the Revolution, whereas deputies inclined toward republicanism hoped war would reveal the king's treachery and lead to his downfall. On 20 April 1792 the Legislative Assembly voted overwhelmingly to declare war on Leopold. Prussia immediately entered on the Austrian side.

When fighting broke out in 1792, all the powers expected a brief and relatively contained war. Instead, it continued despite brief interruptions for the next twenty-three years. In 1792 the French were woefully unprepared for war, and in the first battles the Austrians promptly routed the French armies. As the French frantically reorganized their armies, many suspected that conspirators hoped to overthrow the Revolution. The value of paper money plummeted, and grain prices rose again. In the south of France, some National Guard units joined with their neighbors in attacking noble castles and burning them to the ground. When Louis XVI refused to sign a law directing deportation of priests who failed to take the loyalty oath, an armed demonstration of Parisians invaded the hall of the Legislative Assembly on 20 June 1792 and threatened the royal family. In response, Lafayette left his command on the eastern front and came to Paris to insist on punishing the demonstrators. He appeared before the Assembly to demand the suppression of the Jacobin Clubs. His conduct only fueled distrust of the army commanders, which increased to a fever pitch when the Prussians crossed the border and advanced on Paris. The Prussian commander, the Duke of Brunswick, issued a manifesto—the Brunswick Manifesto—announcing that Paris would be totally destroyed if the royal family suffered any violence.

Faced with this threat of retaliation and growing fears of counterrevolutionary plots, on 10 August 1792 leaders of the local neighborhood governments of Paris (called *sections*) organized an insurrection and attacked the Tuileries palace, where the king resided. The king and his family had to escape into the meeting room of the Legislative Assembly. The Swiss guards of the king fired on the Parisian National Guardsmen and the armed insurgents from the sections. When the Swiss laid down their arms on command from Louis XVI, they were massacred, their bodies mutilated and stripped of every stitch of clothing. Some 600 Swiss soldiers died in the bloodbath. The terrified deputies ordered elections for a National Convention that would write a new constitution. Voting this time would be by universal manhood suffrage; there were no property requirements for voting or holding office. After failing to raise an army to march against Paris, Lafayette fled to the Austrian Netherlands.

Violence exploded again even before the National Convention met for the first time. Early in September 1792, as the Prussians approached Paris, hysterical mobs that included some National Guardsmen dragged inmates out of their cells in the prisons and killed them either on the spot or after kangaroo court trials. A few extremist newspapers, including Marat's, had urged the common people to take vengeance in this way on supposed conspirators and traitors. Over five days from 2–7 September, half the prison population in Paris, between 1,100 and 1,400 people, were killed, including many ordinary and completely innocent people. The Princess of Lamballe, one of the queen's closest friends, died in the carnage. These "September massacres" showed the dark side of popular revolution, in which the common people demanded instant revenge on presumed enemies and conspirators.

When the National Convention convened in Paris two weeks later, it abolished the monarchy and on 22 September 1792 established the first republic in French history. The Republic would answer only to the people, not to royal authority. The situation was dire. The deputies were supposed to draft a new constitution even while fighting a war with external enemies and confronting increasing resistance to the Revolution at home. The experience of the previous three years had divided the population; for some the Revolution had not gone far enough toward providing food, land, and retribution against enemies; for others it had gone too far by dismantling the church, the nobility, and the monarchy. The French people had never known any government other than monarchy. Because less than half the population could read, symbolic actions became very important. Any public sign of monarchy was at risk, and revolutionaries soon pulled down statues of kings and burned reminders of the former regime. As one deputy explained, "It is necessary to destroy this word *king*, which is still a talisman whose magical force can serve to stupefy many men."

The fate of Louis XVI and the future direction of the Republic divided the deputies even though they came from very similar social backgrounds and shared many political beliefs. Most of them were middle-class lawyers and professionals who had developed their republican beliefs in the national network of Jacobin Clubs. They wanted a democratic republic that would be responsive to the needs of the common people. With elections now based on universal manhood suffrage, France had become the most democratic country in the world. After the fall of the monarchy in August 1792, however, the Jacobins divided into two factions that differed over how best to achieve a truly democratic republic: the Girondins (named after one of the departments, the Gironde, which provided some of its leading orators) and the Mountain (so-called because its deputies sat in the highest seats). The Girondins appealed to the

Fig. 2.4   The Good Sans-Culotte

The good sans-culotte (see documents below) embodies frugality, thrift, hard work, and, above all, honest devotion. This is a positive image of a typical lower-class supporter of the Mountain.

Le bon sans Culotte

Fig. 2.5   President of a Revolutionary Committee Distracting Himself

The shoemaker shown here is president of his neighborhood revolutionary committee. Although this engraving does not portray a specific political activity, the caricature evokes hostility toward laborers and artisans who involved themselves in politics. The president hardly seems presidential.

Président d'un Comité Révolutionaire s'amusant de son.

people living outside of Paris; they resented the growing power of Parisian militants over national policy decisions and believed that "the people" meant citizens of all of France. Some Girondins had served as ministers in the royal government of 1792. The Mountain, in contrast, took the side of the Parisian militants who, after all, had saved the Revolution in 1789 and precipitated the fall of the king in 1792. The Parisian militants, known as *sans-culottes* (without knee-breeches) because they wore long trousers instead of knee-breeches (see Figs. 2.4 and 2.5), wanted a much more repressive government that would establish price controls and promptly arrest and execute opponents of the Republic (Documents 2.5 and 2.6).

The first showdown between the Girondins and the Mountain occurred over the trial of the king. In his maiden speech, excerpted above, the young deputy of the Mountain, Louis-Antoine Saint-Just, only twenty-five years old, argued that the king should simply be executed by military court-martial rather than be tried. In a republic, he insisted, a king was by definition a "rebel," a "usurper," "an enemy alien." A king had no part in the social contract between citizens of a republic. To try him was to presume the possibility of innocence. Saint-Just did not carry the day, and the trial went forward, but he had made his mark and would soon assume a position of prominence. At his trial in December 1792, Louis XVI stoically denied all the accusations of treason levied against him and insisted on his constitutional inviolability; according to the Constitution of 1791, he argued, he could not be removed from office much less tried for the actions he undertook. The deputies were unmoved, especially since letters had been recently discovered in which Louis had conspired with foreign monarchs, denouncing the constitution as "absurd and detestable." No one voted for acquittal on the basis of innocence.

Although the Girondins agreed that the king was guilty of treason, many of them argued for clemency, exile, or a popular referendum on his fate. The deputies of the Mountain, among them Robespierre, argued that a vote for a popular referendum was a counterrevolutionary ruse. After a long and difficult debate, the Convention supported the Mountain and voted by a very narrow majority to immediately execute the king. Louis XVI went to the guillotine on 21 January 1793. "We have just convinced ourselves that a king is only a man," wrote one newspaper, "and that no man is above the law." Outside France, however, the execution profoundly shocked most people. William Pitt, prime minister of the British government, called it "the foulest and most atrocious act the world has ever seen." By the end of March 1793 France was at war with Great Britain, the Dutch Republic, Spain and Portugal in addition to Austria and Prussia. The new republic's problems had only just begun.

Documents

Political Clubs

The people of Paris provided much of the force for radical action in the French Revolution. One of the most effective means of organizing them were clubs that, though unofficial, could exert political pressure. At first, clubs were basically the preserve of the well educated. The Jacobins, "The Friends of the Constitution," were the most important of the clubs. The Paris Jacobin Club always included many deputies among its members, who used the club meetings as a forum for policy discussions. The Paris Jacobin Club kept up regular correspondence with affiliates all over France—indeed, all over Europe.

From early in the Revolution, activists wanted to create clubs for the working people too. The most important club that attracted members outside the middle class was the Cordeliers Club. Founded in 1789, the Cordeliers endeavored to champion the goals of the poor, though its leadership hailed from the educated groups. The increasing influence of the sans-culottes could be seen in calls for violence against counter-revolutionaries and demands for price and wage controls.

Although some deputies worried that clubs constituted a threat to the power of elected authorities, they survived all challenges until the end of 1794. Women's clubs joined with the Jacobins and Cordeliers to press for rigorous measures in defense of the Revolution. Yet clubs were not the only means of organization. Each district (*section*) of Paris had its revolutionary committees that worked in liaison with the city and national governments. The committees and clubs gave ordinary people a direct experience of politics.

Document 2.1: Activities of the Jacobins

The Englishman Arthur Young, who was in France during the early stages of the Revolution, recorded his observations. In this letter from mid-January 1790, he describes a Jacobin club meeting, which he depicts as being highly procedural in nature as it elects new leaders.

Source: Arthur Young, *Travels in France and Italy* (London: J. M. Dent & Sons, 1934), 320–21.

> At night, Monsieur Decretot and Monsieur Blin carried me to the revolution club at the *Jacobins*. . . . There were above one hundred deputies present, with a president in the chair; I was handed to him, and announced as the author of the *Arithmetique Politique;* the president standing up repeated my name to the company and demanded if there were any objections—None; and this is all the ceremony, not merely of an introduction but an election: for I was told that now I was free to be present when I pleased, being a foreigner. Ten or a dozen other elections were made. In this club the business that is to be brought into the National Assembly is regularly debated; the motions are read that are intended to be made there, and rejected or corrected and approved. When these have been fully agreed to, the whole party are engaged to support them. Plans of conduct are there determined; proper persons nominated for being of committees, and presidents of the Assembly named. And I may add that such is the

majority of numbers, that whatever passes in this club is almost sure to pass in the Assembly.

ARTHUR YOUNG.
[17 JANUARY 1790]

Document 2.2: Clubs for the People

By creating a fictional man named Jacques who must go to his workshop every day so he can support his family, yet who also wants to do his patriotic duty by following political events, the *Révolutions de Paris,* in this article that appeared in late 1790, calls upon the government to create and to subsidize popular political clubs. The purpose is to ensure that the most patriotic elements of the "people" (and not just wealthy and well-educated professionals) can have their say in the course of the Revolution.

Source: Les Révolutions de Paris, no. 73 (27 November–4 December 1790), 401–6.

Jacques's little stall is situated almost across from the house of the Jacobins in the Rue St.-Honoré. He has noticed the crowds of people who arrive there around dusk. He asked what everyone was doing in that house, and at that particular time, three or four times a week. This is what he was told:

Three or four times a week, twelve to fifteen hundred citizens make a point of meeting in the library of the former convent. There, for four or five hours, they discuss, think, absorb sound principles, and take precautions against pseudo-patriots . . . in a word they make themselves worthy of the liberty which we have won.

Jacques, who has both spirit and good sense, then said to himself, "How fortunate they are in there, to be able to set aside three or four hours out of their day to better themselves! What have I done that I should be condemned to a job which takes up all my time? I feel that I could become, like anyone else, not a better patriot (for I am as good a patriot as any of them) but more enlightened, less easily fooled. Alas! I can't think about that. My first duty is to my children. Looking after them is the chain which binds me to this wall. I must waste my talents on a monotonous and thankless task. My whole life will thus pass in the shadow of ignorance while every day I see the light of education pass before my eyes without ever shining upon me. When I hear about the events that trouble my country I become excited and impassioned. Taken in by rumors and exaggerated stories I take the side of this or that person because I have neither the time nor the guidance necessary to amend my ideas and channel my patriotism. I must blindly follow those who represent me, and for this reason they get their own way with their constituents, three-quarters of whom are no better educated than I am. How cruel it is not to be able to fruitfully enjoy the blessing of liberty without taking advantage of it. That liberty in which I played no small role on 14 July!". . .

We need clubs for the people. Let every street in every town, let every hamlet have one. The primary assemblies [elections] are too formal and too infrequent to take their place. The people need clubs that are fixed and free, where there are not too many people, and where they can be at ease. These clubs should be without regulations or titled officials, because such things detract from liberty in a way, waste too much time, and engender the feeling that the group comes before the country. . . .

The Jacobin club is already very useful. Clubs for the people's use, simply organized and unpretentious, would be of the greatest benefit. Let an honest artisan call together some of his neighbors to his house. Let him read the decrees of the National Assembly by the light of a lamp paid for by all those present. Let him add his own reflections to the reading, or those of some of his attentive neighbors. At the end of the meeting listen as he cheers up his audience, startled by one of Marat's articles, by a reading spiced with the patriotic swear-words of the Père Duchesne. . . .

It is most surprising that some wealthy citizens cannot be found who are good enough patriots to offer their houses as a place to which the people of the district could come on Sundays and holidays, instead of wasting their time in taverns. In this way they could catch up on events and make themselves familiar with the principles of the Constitution. If private houses are not available, couldn't the people take over some of these churches that the suppression of the religious orders and canons have made vacant? It is said that a working-class club has already been formed in the house of the Capucins in the Rue St.-Honoré. It is a club such as this that should be set up in every section of the big cities. In the country, the porches of the parish churches, or even the churches themselves, could be devoted to this. These buildings could only become more respectable.

Document 2.3: National Assembly Debate on Clubs (20 September 1791)

The "Champ de Mars Massacre" inaugurated a brief period of political repression directed at the popular movement and dramatized the growing tension between the claims of political activism and the desire of moderates to bring the Revolution to an orderly close. This issue was foremost in the minds of the representatives in the very last days of the Constituent Assembly, as they debated a proposal for a new decree limiting the political role of clubs. The decree was adopted but never implemented.

Source: M. J. Mavidal and M. E. Laurent, eds., *Archives parlementaires de 1787 à 1860,* première série (1787–99), 2nd ed., 82 vols. (Paris: Dupont, 1879–1913), 31:617–23.

[Le Chapelier spoke on behalf of the constitutional committee:] We are going to speak to you about these organizations formed from an enthusiasm for liberty, and to which they owe their prompt establishment. We speak of those organizations which, during stormy periods, had the fortunate result of rallying public morale, providing centers for similar views, and showing the opposing minority the enormous size of the majority that wanted to exterminate the abuses, reverse the prejudices, and establish a free constitution.

But like all spontaneous institutions created from the purest of motives, due to considerable changes in circumstances and various other causes, they soon deviate from their goal and end up taking on a kind of political role that they should not.

As long as the Revolution lasted, this state of affairs was almost always more useful than harmful. When a nation changes its form of government, every citizen becomes a magistrate. Everyone deliberates, and should deliberate, on the State, and everything that expedites, everything that ensures, everything that speeds a Revolution, must be put to use. It is a momentary agitation that must be sustained and even increased so that the Revolution leaves no doubt in the minds of its opponents, encounters fewer obstacles, and reaches its end more quickly.

But when the Revolution is over and the constitution of the State has been decided, when all public powers have been delegated and all the authorities called up, then everything must be restored to the most perfect order to ensure the security of that constitution. Then, nothing must hinder the actions of the constituted authorities, and deliberation and the power to act must be located where the constitution has placed them and nowhere else. Everyone must also recognize his own rights and responsibilities as a citizen, never exceeding the former nor violating the latter.

The Societies of Friends of the Constitution have done too many favors for the State, and they are driven by excessive patriotism, so normally it is necessary to do no more than just warn their members of the dangers that these organizations pose to the State. They are dragged into illegal actions by men who cultivate them only to stir them up. . . .

All citizens have the right to peaceful assembly. In a free country, where a constitution, founded on the rights of man, has created a homeland, an intense and profound feeling attaches all inhabitants to the State. They feel the need to take care of it and discuss it. Far from extinguishing or restricting this sacred fire, all social institutions must help to sustain it.

But, in addition to this general interest, this deep affection created by the existence of a homeland, and the free use of citizen's rights, the maxims of public order and representative government must be in evidence.

There is no power except that constituted by the will of the People and expressed through their representatives. There are no authorities except those delegated by the People, and there can be no actions except those of its representatives who have been entrusted with public duties.

It is to preserve this principle, in all its purity, that the constitution has abolished all corporations, from one end of the state to another, and henceforth recognizes only society as a whole, and individuals.

A necessary consequence of this principle is the prohibition of any petition or poster issued in the name of a group.

Organizations, peaceful assemblies of citizens, and clubs; all go unnoticed in the State. Should they abandon the private status granted them by the constitution, they rise up against the constitution, thereby destroying it instead of defending it. From that point on the invaluable rallying cry— "Friends of the Constitution"—seems nothing more than a cry of agitation designed to upset the legitimate exercise of authority.

Robespierre: Praise has been lavished on the Societies of Friends of the Constitution, but in truth this is done only to gain the right to denigrate them, and to make extremely vague allegations that are far from proven and absolutely slanderous. But it doesn't matter, because at least the good that cannot be denied has been said—which is nothing less than acknowledging their services since the beginning of the Revolution in the name of liberty and the nation. It seems to me that this consideration alone would have given the constitutional committee reason not to hasten to restrict societies which, by its own admission, have been so useful. But they say we no longer need these organizations because the Revolution is over and it is time to break the tool that has served us so well. [Applause from the galleries] . . .

The Revolution is finished. I would certainly like to join you in assuming this to be true, although I am not entirely clear of the meaning you attach to this proposition that I have heard repeated with such affectation. But assuming this to be the case, is it less necessary now to propagate the knowledge, the constitutional principles, and the public spirit without which the constitution cannot exist? Is it less useful now to form assemblies in which citizens can concern themselves with these matters which are the most important interests of their country, in the most effective manner? Is there a more legitimate or more worthy concern for a free people? To be able to truly say that the Revolution is finished, it requires that the Constitution be firmly consolidated, for its destruction or weakening would necessarily prolong the Revolution, which is nothing more than the nation's efforts to preserve or attain liberty. How then can it be proposed that the most powerful means of consolidating the constitution, that which the committee's spokesman has himself acknowledged to have been generally recognized as necessary until now, be rendered invalid and without influence?

Document 2.4: Women at the Cordeliers

Popular clubs in Paris, unlike electoral assemblies, were not limited to men, at least in the early months of the Republic. One of the most active and radical clubs composed entirely of women, the Society of Revolutionary Republican Women, collaborated with the Cordeliers and Jacobins in petitioning for aggressive action by the government against what they called "enemies of the Republic," meaning Girondin deputies, "aristocratic" landowners, "hoarding" peasants, and unpatriotic "speculators," all of whom were accused of placing short-term personal interest and profit over the general good of all citizens. Exploiting its members' earlier affiliations with the Cordeliers Club, delegates from the women's club joined forces with members of the Cordeliers and formed a joint deputation to the all-powerful Jacobin Club. In this way, nine days after its formation, the women's club was able to publicize its petition recapitulating the tactics and goals of terror.

Source: From *Women in Revolutionary Paris, 1789–1795,* edited and translated by Darlene Gay Levy, Harriet Branson Applewhite, and Mary Durham Johnson. Copyright 1979 by the Board of Trustees of the University of Illinois. Used with the permission of the University of Illinois Press, 150–51.

Session of Sunday, 19 May 1793.

A deputation from the Cordeliers Club and the *citoyennes* (women citizens) of the Revolutionary Society of Women is admitted. The *orator* announces a petition drawn up by the members of these two societies joined together and reads this petition, the substance of which is as follows:

"Representatives of the people, the country is in the most imminent danger; if you want to save it, the most energetic measures must be taken. . . ." (Noise).

"I demand," the orator cries out, "the fullest attention."

Calm is restored.

He continues: If not, the people will save themselves. You are not unaware that the conspirators are awaiting only the departure of the volunteers, who are going to fight our enemies in the Vendée, to immolate the patriots and everything they cherish most. To prevent the execution of these horrible projects, hasten to decree that suspect men will be placed under arrest immediately, that Revolutionary Tribunals will be set up in all the Departments and in the Sections of Paris.

Legislators, strike out at the speculators, the hoarders, and the egotistical merchants. A horrible plot exists to cause the people to die of hunger by setting an enormous price on goods. At the head of this plot is the mercantile aristocracy of an insolent caste, which wants to assimilate itself to royalty and to hoard all riches by forcing up the price of goods of prime necessity in order to satisfy its cupidity. Exterminate all these scoundrels; the Fatherland will be rich enough if it is left with the sans-culotttes and their virtues. Legislators! Come to the aid of all unfortunate people. This is the call of nature; this is the vow of true patriots. Our heart is torn by the spectacle of public misery. Our intention is to raise men up again; we do not want a single unfortunate person in the Republic. Purify the Executive Council; expel a Gohier, a Garat, a Le Brun, etc.; renew the directory of the postal service and all corrupted administrations, etc.

Document 2.5: The Law of Suspects

This law, passed on 17 September 1793, authorized the creation of Revolutionary Tribunals to try those suspected of treason against the Republic and to punish those convicted with death. This legislation in effect made the penal justice system into the enforcement arm of the revolutionary government, which would now set as its primary responsibility not only the maintenance of public order but also the much more difficult and controversial task of identifying internal enemies of the Republic—such as "profiteers" who violated the Maximum—and then removing them from the citizenry, where they might subvert the general will.

Source: Jean-Baptiste Duvergier, *Collection complète des lois, décrets, ordonnances, règlements, avis du conseil d'état . . . de 1788 à 1830 . . .* , 2nd ed., 110 vols. (Paris, 1834–1906), 6:172–73.

1. Immediately after the publication of the present decree, all suspects within the territory of the Republic and still at large, shall be placed in custody.

2. The following are deemed suspects:

1—those who, by their conduct, associations, comments, or writings have shown themselves partisans of tyranny or federalism and enemies of liberty;

2—those who are unable to justify, in the manner prescribed by the decree of 21 March, their means of existence and the performance of their civic duties;

3—those to whom certificates of patriotism have been refused;

4—civil servants suspended or dismissed from their positions by the National Convention or by its commissioners, and not reinstated, especially those who have been or are to be dismissed by virtue of the decree of 14 August;

5—those former nobles, together with husbands, wives, fathers, mothers, sons or daughters, brothers or sisters, and agents of the *émigrés,* who have not constantly demonstrated their devotion to the Revolution;

6—those who have emigrated between 1 July 1789, and the publication of the decree of 30 March (8 April 1792), even though they may have returned to France within the period established by said decree or prior thereto.

Document 2.6: The Maximum

In September 1793 the Convention furthered its role as the guarantor of the basic right to subsistence of all citizens by instituting price maximums on all essential consumer goods, especially foodstuffs, and on wages paid in the production of those goods. The Maximum was to remain in effect, at least theoretically, until the end of 1794 and thereafter would remain for historians evidence that the "revolutionary government" was concerned with more than merely executions, but with enlarging the meanings of "virtue" and "fraternity" to include a concern for the material well-being as well as political rights of all citizens. Yet the gradual abandonment of price controls, as politicians faced pressure from producers, suggested hypocrisy to many contemporaries.

Source: John Hall Stewart, *A Documentary Survey of the French Revolution* (New York: Macmillan, 1951), 499–500.

29 September 1793

1. The articles which the National Convention has deemed essential, and the maximum or highest price of which it has believed it should establish, are: fresh meat, salt meat and bacon, butter, sweet oil, cattle, salt fish, wine, brandy, vinegar, cider, beer, firewood, charcoal, coal, candles, lamp oil, salt, soda, sugar, honey, white paper, hides, iron, cast iron, lead, steel, copper, hemp, linens, woolens, stuffs, canvases, the raw materials which are used for fabrics, wooden shoes, turnips, coats and rape [a forage crop], soap, potash, and tobacco. . . .

7. All persons who sell or purchase the merchandise specified in article 1 for more than the maximum price stated and posted in each department shall pay, jointly and severally, through the municipal police, a fine of double the value of the article sold, and payable to the informer; they shall be inscribed upon the list of suspected persons, and treated as such. The purchaser shall not be subject to the penalty provided above if he denounces

the contravention of the seller; and every merchant shall be required to have a list bearing the maximum or highest price of his merchandise visible in his shop.

8. The maximum or highest figure for salaries, wages, manual labor, and days of labor in every place shall be established, dating from the publication of the present law until the month of September next, by the general councils of the communes, at the same rate as in 1790, plus one-half.

9. The municipalities may put in requisition and punish, according to circumstances, with three days' imprisonment, workmen, manufacturers, and diverse laborers who refuse, without legitimate grounds, to do their usual work. . . .

17. During the war, all exportation of essential merchandise or commodities is prohibited on all frontiers, under any name or commission whatsoever, with the exception of salt.

WOMEN AND THE REVOLUTION: ORDINARY WOMEN POLITICIZED

Women had never been entirely excluded from public or even political activities. Under the Old Regime, they frequently took the lead in riots and disturbances over the price of bread, the most important staple in lower-class diets. Price increases in times of shortage led directly to hunger and often to popular action to seize a stock and sell it at a "fair" or "just" price. Because of their special role in feeding families, women most often took the lead in these efforts. Ironically, it was their private or domestic role that induced them to take public action. They mainly targeted the purveyors of bread—merchants, bakers, and the like—leaving authorities to sort out the consequences.

The new and potent revolutionary rhetoric of popular participation encouraged even more direct action by women. The dramatic example of the exertion of female power was the rising of 5–6 October 1789, when women marched to Versailles and made the royal family and the National Assembly come to Paris. Frustrated by rising bread prices and determined to thwart counterrevolutionary forces, the women marched, some 20,000 strong, to ensure reasonable prices and to rescue the Revolution, and similar protests continued through 1795, though with less spectacular results.

The documents presented here give insight into the motives of these women in the capital. They show both strength and determination, and they indicate the resentment of male politicians and journalists. Furthermore, even though they focus on women, they provide insights into the Parisian working classes. One can feel the vitality. Although the focus is often on the grand ideas, the heroes, the politicians, and the generals, these texts take us into the experience of the Revolution felt by many Parisian laborers.

Document 2.7: Stanislas Maillard Describes the Women's March to Versailles (5 October 1789)

Stanislas Maillard was a national guardsman known for having taken a leading role in the attack on the Bastille. In 1790 he testified before a commission established by the court in Paris to investigate the events of October 1789. He exaggerates his role in the events but gives a vivid account of the women's march, especially their insistence on petitioning the deputies in the National Assembly.

Source: From *Women in Revolutionary Paris, 1789–1795,* edited and translated by Darlene Gay Levy, Harriet Branson Applewhite, and Mary Durham Johnson. Copyright 1979 by the Board of Trustees of the University of Illinois. Used with the permission of the University of Illinois Press, 36–42.

But as he went down the steps of the building, he was stopped by five or six women, who made him go up again, shouting to their comrades that he was a Bastille Volunteer and that there was nothing to fear from him. After this, having mingled with the women, he found some forcing the downstairs doors and others snatching papers in the offices, saying that that was all the city council had done since the Revolution began and that they would burn them. Supported by a certain Richard Dupin, he urged them to keep calm, but these women kept saying that the men were not strong enough to be revenged on their enemies and that they (the women) would do better. While he was in the courtyard, he looked around and saw a large number of men go up, armed with pikes, lances, pitchforks, and other weapons, having compelled the women to let them in. They then flung themselves on the doors that the women had begun to beat, broke them down with great hammers that they had with them and with crowbars that they found in the City Hall, and took all the arms they could find and gave some to the women. He then received word that a number of women had arrived with torches to burn the papers in the building, so he dashed out [and] flung himself upon them (there were but two) as they approached the City Hall, each bearing a lighted torch; he snatched the torches from their hands, which nearly cost him his life, as they were intent on carrying out their design. He prayed them to send a deputation to the council to demand justice and to describe their plight, as they were all in need of bread, but they replied that the whole council was composed of bad citizens who deserved to be hanged from lamp posts, M. Bailly and M. de Lafayette first of all. . . .

M. Maillard . . . continuing his evidence, said that to avert the danger and misfortune that threatened both M. de Lafayette and M. Bailly and the City Hall, he thought it best to go once more to staff headquarters, where he only found present M. Derminy, M. de Gouvion's aide. Where-upon he (the witness) told M. Derminy that these women would not lis-ten to reason and that, having destroyed the City Hall, they intended to proceed to the National Assembly in order to learn all that had been done and decreed up to the present date. He told these ladies that the National Assembly owed them no reckoning and that if they went there, they would cause a disturbance and would prevent the deputies from paying serious attention to the important business arising from the present situa-tion. As the women persisted in their plans, he thought it wise to repair once more to M. Derminy and acquaint him with their resolution, adding that if the latter thought fit, he would accompany them to Versailles in order to prevent and to apprise them of the danger to which they were exposing themselves by embarking on so rash a venture

The witness now seized a drum at the entrance to the City Hall, where the women were already assembled in very large numbers; detachments went off into different districts to recruit other women, who were instructed to meet them at the Place Louis XV. . . . But as the people were assembled in great numbers, and this square was no longer suited as a place of meeting, they decided to proceed to the Place d'Armes, in the middle of the Champs Elysées, whence he saw detachments of women coming up from every direction, armed with broomsticks, lances, pitch-forks, swords, pistols, and muskets. As they had no ammunition, they wanted to compel him to go with a detachment of them to the arsenal to fetch powder, but . . . now by means of prayers and protestations he suc-ceeded in persuading the women to lay down their arms, with the excep-tion of a few who refused, but whom wiser heads among them compelled to yield.

Meanwhile, he had acquired the confidence of these women to the extent that they all said unanimously that they would have only him to lead them. A score of them left the ranks to compel all the other men to march behind them, and so they took the road to Versailles with eight or ten drums at their head.

[Several of the men having been left behind at Sèvres,] he and the women continued on their journey to Versailles. Past Viroflay they met a number of individuals on horseback who appeared to be bourgeois and wore black cockades in their hats. The women stopped them and made as if to commit violence against them, saying that they must die as punish-ment for having insulted, and for insulting, the national cockade; one they struck and pulled off his horse, tearing off his black cockade, which one of the women handed to him (the witness). He ordered the other women to halt . . . and came to the aid of the man whom they were ill-using; he obtained his release on condition that he should surrender his horse, that he should march behind them, and that at the first place they came to he should be made to carry on his back a placard proclaiming that he had insulted the national cockade. . . . [The same treatment having been meted out to two other passersby, and two of the women having mounted their horses,] he drew the women up (as far as it was in his power to do so) in three ranks and made them form a circle and told them that the two cannons that they had with them must be removed from the head of their procession; that although they had no ammunition, they might be suspected of evil intentions; that they would do better to give an air of gaiety than to occasion a riot in Versailles; and that as the city had not been warned of their proceedings, its inhabitants might mistake their purpose, and they might become the victims of their own zeal. They consented to do as he wished; consequently, the cannons were placed behind them, and he invited the women to chant "Long live Henry IV!" as they entered Versailles and to cry "Long live the king!"—a cry which they did not cease to repeat in the midst of the citizens awaiting them, who greeted them with cries of "Long live our Parisiennes!" So they arrived at the door of the National Assembly, where he told them that it would be imprudent for more than five or six of them to appear. They refused, all wanting to go in, whereupon a guards' officer, on duty at the National Assembly, joined him and urged that not more than twelve of the women should enter. . . .

After much discussion among the women, fifteen were chosen to appear with him at the bar of the National Assembly; of these fifteen he only knew the woman Lavarenne, who has just been awarded a medal by the Paris city council. Entering the assembly, he urged the women to be silent and to leave to him the task of communicating to the assembly their demands, as they had explained them to him on the way; to this they consented. He then asked the president's leave to speak. M. Mounier, who was then president, granted him leave. . . .

He (the witness) now once more addressed the assembly and said that to restore calm, allay public disquiet, and avert disaster, he begged the gentlemen of the assembly to appoint a deputation to go to the Life-Guards in order to enjoin them to adopt the national cockade and make amends for the injury they were said to have done to it. Several members raised their voices and said it was false that the Life-Guards had ever insulted the national cockade, that all who wished to be citizens could be so freely, and that no one could be forced to be so. Speaking again and displaying three black cockades (the same that were spoken of earlier), he said that, on the contrary, there should be no person who did not take pride in being so and that if there were within this august assembly any members that felt dishonored by this title, they should be excluded immediately. Many applauded these words, and the hall rang with cries of "Yes, all should be so and we are all citizens." In the midst of this applause he was handed a national cockade, sent in by the Life-Guards, which he showed to all the women as a proof of their submission, and all the women cried, "Long live the king and the Life-Guards!" He once more asked leave to speak and said that it was essential also, in order to avert misfortune and to allay the suspicions that had been spread in the capital concerning the arrival of the Flanders Regiment at Versailles, to withdraw this regiment, because the citizens feared it might start a revolution.

At eight o'clock in the evening the president returned with his deputation from their audience with the king. He repeated the king's words before the assembly; the women listened respectfully, as their intent was to restore calm among his people. Then the president read aloud five papers relative to the demands addressed by the Parisian National Guard to the National Assembly and to the king concerning the food supply. His Majesty had commanded that two officers should accompany him (the witness) back to Paris, but the women objected to this, and all said that they alone should escort him. . . .

Document 2.8: Prudhomme, "On the Influence of the Revolution on Women" (12 February 1791)

Louis-Marie Prudhomme founded the *Révolutions of Paris,* one of the best-known radical newspapers of the French Revolution. In this editorial, he responds to women's criticisms of the Revolution and outlines a theory of women's "natural" domesticity. He stopped publication of his paper in 1794 in response to the growing violence of the Terror.

Source: The materials listed below appeared originally in *The French Revolution and Human Rights: A Brief Documentary History,* translated, edited, and with an introduction by Lynn Hunt (Boston/New York: Bedford/St. Martin's, 1996), 129–31.

Many women have complained to us about the revolution. In numerous letters they report to us that for two years now it seems there is but one sex in France. In the primary assemblies [for voting], in the sections, in the clubs, etc., there is no longer any discussion about women, as if they no longer existed. They are accorded, as if by grace, a few benches for listening to the sessions of the National Assembly. Two or three women have appeared at the bar [spoken to the Assembly], but the audience was short, and the Assembly quickly passed on to the order of the day. Can the French people, some ask, not become free without ceasing to be gallant?

Long ago, in the time of the Gauls, our good ancestors, women had a deliberative vote in the Estates of the nation; they voted just like men, and things did not go so badly. . . .

The reign of the courtesans precipitated the ruin of the nation; the empire of queens consummated it. We saw a prince [Louis XV], too quickly loved by the people, degrade his character in the arms of several women [his mistresses, one of which Prudhomme names in a footnote: Madame du Barry] without modesty, and become, following the example of Nebuchadnezzar [King of Babylonia, 605–562 B.C.], a brute who wallowed with a disgusting cynicism in the filth of the dirtiest pleasures. We saw his successor [Louis XVI] share with the public his infatuation with a young, lively, and frivolous princess [Marie-Antoinette], who began by shaking off the yoke of etiquette as if practicing for one day shattering that of the laws. Soon following the lessons of her mother [Maria-Theresa, empress of Austria], she profited from her ascendancy over little things to interfere in great ones and to influence the destiny of an entire people. . . .

Solemn publicists [in a footnote, Prudhomme cites "M. Condorcet, among others, in a number of the journal of the club of 1789"] have seriously proposed taking the road of conciliation; they have maintained that women enjoy the rights of citizenship like men and should have entry to all public assemblies, even to those that constitute or legislate for the nation. They have claimed that women have the right to speak as much as men.

No doubt, and this power has never been denied them. But nature, from which society should not depart except in spite of itself, has prescribed to each sex its respective functions; a household should never remain deserted for a single instant. When the father of a family leaves to defend or lay claim to the rights of property, security, equality, or liberty in a public assembly, the mother of the family, focused on her domestic duties, must make order and cleanliness, ease and peace reign at home.

Women have never shown this sustained and strongly pronounced taste for civil and political independence, this ardor to which everything cedes, which inspires in men so many great deeds, so many heroic actions. This is because civil and political liberty is in a manner of speaking useless to women and in consequence must be foreign to them. Destined to pass all their lives confined under the paternal roof or in the house of their marriage; born to a perpetual dependence from the first moment of their existence until that of their decease, they have only been endowed with private virtues. The tumult of camps, the storms of public places, the agitations of the tribunals are not at all suitable for the second sex. To keep her mother company, soften the worries of a spouse, nourish and care for her children, these are the only occupations and true duties of a woman. A woman is only comfortable, is only in her place in her family or in her household. She need only know what her parents or her husband judge appropriate to teach her about everything that takes place outside her home.

Women! . . . The liberty of a people has for its basis good morals and education, and you are its guardians and first dispensers. . . . Appear in the midst of our national festivals with all the brilliance of your virtues and your charms! When the voice of the public acclaims the heroism and wisdom of a young citizen, then a mother rises and leads her young, beautiful and modest daughter to the tribunal where crowns are distributed; the young virgin seizes one of them and goes herself to set it on the forehead of the acclaimed citizen. . . .

Citizenesses of all ages and all stations! Leave your homes all at the same time; rally from door to door and march toward city hall. . . . Armed with burning torches, present yourselves at the gates of the palace of your tyrants and demand reparation. . . . If the enemy, victorious thanks to disagreements between patriots, insists upon putting his plan of counterrevolution into action . . . you must avail yourself of every means, bravery and ruses, arms and poison; contaminate the fountains, the foodstuffs; let the atmosphere be charged with the seeds of death. . . . Once the country is purged of all these hired brigands, citizenesses! We will see you return to your dwellings to take up once again the accustomed yoke of domestic duties.

Document 2.9: Police Reports on Disturbances over Food Supplies (February 1793)

The reports of the Paris police provide firsthand information about conditions in the city and about the leading role of women in food disturbances.

Source: From *Women in Revolutionary Paris, 1789–1795*, edited and translated by Darlene Gay Levy, Harriet Branson Applewhite, and Mary Durham Johnson. Copyright 1979 by the Board of Trustees of the University of Illinois. Used with the permission of the University of Illinois Press, 137–41.

And the following day, the twenty-fifth of the same month, same year, at 7 A.M., we went, still assisted by the citizen-secretary-registrar, to the doors of the bakers in our Section to see whether bread deliveries were being made without incident and to take remedial action, if possible. We had the satisfaction of seeing that the measures we had taken the night before, in joint action with the Committee, had produced the full effect we were hoping for. Consequently, we returned to the Committee to find out whether there wasn't some new order, and finding none, we returned to our arrondissement.

There wasn't what you would call a tumult, but [rather] small group-ings of citizens and *citoyennes* at intervals. In some [of these groups] it was being said, "The bakers were rascals and deserved to be worked over." In others, "The grocers deserved the same, because they were hoarders," and finally, in others, "The majority of those who were directing the Republic were also rascals." And among others [there was] a drunk citizen who made himself conspicuous by saying, "We used to have only one king, and now there are thirty or forty of them." We did everything we could to restore calm in these groups. We succeeded in some; it was impossible in others; and lastly, it was folly in still others. All this [was happening] with-out our being able to arrest any of the leaders, who were absolutely unknown to us and not from this Section.

We returned to the Committee at 1 P.M. after having spent the whole morning on the business detailed above.

Document 2.10: Amar on Women's Political Clubs (October 1793)

In the National Convention, Deputy Jean-Baptiste Amar proposed an official decree on 30 October 1793 forbidding women to join together in political clubs. A deputy tried to argue that this notion ran contrary to the right of freedom of association, but he was shouted down by the other deputies.

Source: The materials listed below appeared originally in *The French Revolution and Human Rights: A Brief Documentary History,* translated, edited, and with an intro-duction by Lynn Hunt (Boston/New York: Bedford/St. Martin's, 1996), 136–38.

In the morning at the market and charnel-house [mortuary] of the Inno-cents, several women, so-called women Jacobins, from a club that is sup-posedly revolutionary, walked about wearing trousers and red caps; they sought to force the other citizenesses to adopt the same dress. Several have testified that they were insulted by these women. A mob of some 6,000 women formed. . . .

Your committee believed it must go further in its inquiry. It has posed the following questions: 1) Is it permitted to citizens or to a particular club to force other citizens to do what the law does not command? 2) Should the gatherings of women convened in popular clubs in Paris be allowed? Do not the troubles that these clubs have already occasioned prohibit us from tolerating any longer their existence? These questions are naturally complicated, and their solution must be preceded by two more general questions: . . .

1) Should women exercise political rights and get mixed up in the affairs of government? Governing is ruling public affairs by laws whose making

Study in Images: "Down with the King!"

The downfall of Louis XVI can be traced in engravings, the most widely accessible medium of the era. The monarchy had used engravings to propagate the image of an august, powerful ruler who could also be benevolent and fatherly. Revolutionaries first tried to depict the king fulfilling his new constitutional role, itself already a step down for the dynasty. After his flight to Varennes, the caricatures turned hostile; artists depicted the monarch as a drunkard or barnyard animal, and the Queen was treated as a beast, often as malevolently as possible, even as a serpent. When the king was executed in January 1793, the most zealous republicans provided gruesome reminders of the king's decapitated head and even mocked his presumed arrival in hell. This panoply of images ends with the decapitated king's body used in an English print to condemn the Revolution. Viewed in chronological order, the engravings reveal the changes in attitudes toward the king.

Most striking in these images is the incongruity of the Phrygian cap on the head of the king. Originally a mark of a slave who gained his or her freedom, the Phrygian, or liberty, cap seems out of place on the king's head. In these engravings it seems to signal the revolutionaries' insistence that the king reconcile himself to the new order, for even he had to be freed of the past. As might be expected, the king never looks comfortable wearing the cap.

In one depiction of the 20 June 1792 riot, the cap is raised above Louis's head just before the revolutionaries force him to wear it. In this pose the cap seems to threaten him directly. Surrounded by weaponry, the head covering is poised to descend and crush the hapless Louis. The cap also figures in engravings of the executed king. In the one here, a Phrygian cap hangs on a pike, confronting the king's head as if to say that the king's very existence was incompatible with freedom.

The king rarely exudes majesty in these engravings. Before 1789, monarchs were typically depicted in portraits or in military poses to emphasize determination, power, and glory. In these revolutionary engravings, in contrast, Louis is portrayed in the midst of less exalted activities: traveling to Paris, working on a construction site, repelling attacks by commoners, or being executed. The king has become just a man—and not a very fortunate one. In this way, visual portrayals helped undermine royal authority.

Image 1. Louis XVI.

Here was the "body politic" of the Old Regime. According to royal doctrine, the king was a quasi-divine figure, God's lieutenant on earth. The French people were his subjects, and the geographical parts of France were linked together only through the monarch. Robed and wigged, he was the central emblem of a centuries-old regime.

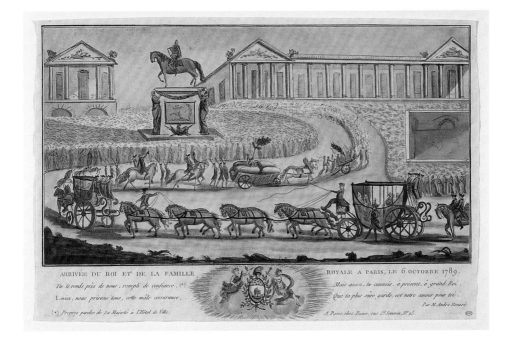

Image 2. Arrival of the Royal Family in Paris on 6 October 1789.

When the revolutionaries, led by thousands of women, marched to Versailles, they triumphantly seized and then brought the king to Paris, where he would live in the midst of his people. Here this image attempts to maintain a perception of royal pomp and grandeur, ignoring the reality that the king was forced against his will. Still, few could fully foresee the ultimate changes under way—that the king had lost much of his sacred aura and was now headed toward an uncertain future.

Image 3. Louis XVI, King of the French.

This fascinating engraving, likely produced before the king's flight from Paris, takes the Louis XVI of the Old Regime and makes him a revolutionary with the addition of the Phrygian cap. While the engraver's precise intention is unknown, contemporaries might have seen this as mocking Louis's new position in the Revolution. Others, less cynical, might have seen an attempt to create a monarch living with the constitution.

LE ROI, prochant au champ de Mars.

Image 4. The King at the Festival of Federation.

Having lived through a tumultuous year, France's political leaders, new and old, perceived the need to foster a sense of unity among the people. The king's more liberal ministers, in particular, hoped to prevent attempts to roll back the changes made since the spring of 1789, while at the same time limiting the momentum for further-reaching challenges to the monarchy. To this end, the Marquis de Lafayette organized a public pageant in Paris to celebrate the "federation" of the different regions and social groups of France. Here Louis XVI helps prepare the construction site, where the festival will take place on 14 July 1790.

NOUVEAU PACTE DE LOUIS XVI.
avec son Peuple le 20. Juin 1792. l'An 4.me de la liberté.

Image 5. Louis as a Drunkard.

This image marks a clear decline in the status of Louis XVI. He wears the dress of a commoner and a Phrygian cap and raises a bottle. This transformation could scarcely have been anticipated in 1789 or even in 1790.

Image 6. Louis as Pig.

After the flight to Varennes in June 1791, critics of the monarchy began to depict the king, the queen, and sometimes the entire royal family as animals. This dehumanizing gesture opened the way to ever more vehement attacks on the king and queen and ultimately to the arrest, imprisonment, trial, and execution of each one.

Image 7. The Attack of 20 June 1792.

After France declared war on Austria in April 1792, the position of the king, who was the brother-in-law of the Austrian emperor, became increasingly untenable. On 20 June 1792 crowds in Paris took matters into their own hands, invading first the Legislative Assembly and then the Tuileries Palace, the residence of the royal family. In this scene, the rioters force the king to don a Phrygian cap and drink a toast to the health of the nation.

Image 8. Marie Antoinette as a Serpent.

The Queen, never popular to begin with in France, also bore the brunt of popular ire in 1792, as seen here. Revolutionaries saw Marie Antoinette as oversexed for a woman. Her exposed breasts give striking evidence of their fear of this sexuality, which they believed was the source of her unnatural dominance of the king and other men.

Image 9. An Exuberant Executioner.

As 80,000 people crowded into the square to watch the execution of Louis XVI, they cannot have been unaware that the guillotine sat in a spot previously occupied by a statue of Louis XV. Here Sanson, the executioner, snatches the detached head of Louis XVI to show to the crowd. He leans forward with approving eagerness. If the head of the king was the most recognizable Old Regime symbol, then the demise of that symbolic system becomes now complete.

Image 10. Louis Arrives in Hell.

In classical mythology, getting to hell involved crossing the river Styx. Revolutionary cartoonists often invoked this image when describing the fate of their enemies. This is no exception. Note the boat on the left with the dog, Cerberus, who was the guardian of the gates of the underworld. Arriving here is the headless Louis, greeted by other previous monarchs. In the right corner is a glade showing a contrasting world in which people dance happily around the liberty pole.

Image 11. Hell Broke Loose, or, The Murder of Louis.

In this English image, as the king's head is about to fall into the executioner's basket, bats out of hell emerge, symbolizing the Revolution. At the same time, God's favor seems to fall on Louis through a shaft of light coming from heaven. From the first, some English, especially Edmund Burke, were skeptical, indeed critical of the Revolution, and the numbers grew over time.

demands extended knowledge, an application and devotion without limit, a severe impassiveness and abnegation of self; governing is ceaselessly directing and rectifying the action of constituted authorities. Are women capable of these required attentions and qualities? We can respond in general no. . . .

2) Secondly, should women gather together in political associations? . . . No, because they will be obliged to sacrifice to them more important cares to which nature calls them. The private functions to which women are destined by nature itself follow from the general order of society. This social order results from the difference between man and woman. Each sex is called to a type of occupation that is appropriate to it. Its action is circumscribed in this circle that it cannot cross over, for nature, which has posed these limits on man, commands imperiously and accepts no other law.

Man is strong, robust, born with a great energy, audacity, and courage; thanks to his constitution, he braves perils and the inclemency of the seasons; he resists all the elements, and he is suited for the arts and difficult labors. And as he is almost exclusively destined to agriculture, commerce, navigation, voyages, war, to everything that requires force, intelligence, and ability, in the same way he alone appears suited for the profound and serious cogitations that require a great exertion of mind and long studies and that women are not given to following. . . .

In general, women are hardly capable of lofty conceptions and serious cogitations. And if, among ancient peoples, their natural timidity and modesty did not permit them to appear outside of their family, do you want in the French Republic to see them coming up to the bar, to the speaker's box, to political assemblies like men, abandoning both the discretion that is the source of all the virtues of this sex and the care of their family?

Decree:

The clubs and popular societies of women, under whatever denomination, are prohibited.

Document 2.11: Police Reports on Women's Discontent (Spring 1795)

Agitation over the shortage of bread reached a breaking point in the spring of 1795. Women played critical roles in these disturbances, as they had before the Revolution.

Source: From *Women in Revolutionary Paris, 1789–1795,* edited and translated by Darlene Gay Levy, Harriet Branson Applewhite, and Mary Durham Johnson. Copyright 1979 by the Board of Trustees of the University of Illinois. Used with the permission of the University of Illinois Press, 287–88.

It has been established from various reports relative to yesterday that groups in the squares, in the streets, and in public places, as well as gatherings at bakers' doors, were as numerous as they were tumultuous and extremely agitated. The women above all, seemed to be playing the principal role there; they were taunting the men, treating them as cowards, and seemed unwilling to be satisfied with the portion that was offered to them. A large number of them wanted to rush into insurrection; even the majority appeared to be determined to attack the constituted authorities, and notably the government Committees, which would have happened were it not for the prudence and firmness of the armed troops. One can easily convince oneself of what has just been reported by glancing attentively and impartially at several reports which bear witness [to this understanding of the situation].

1. In [the report] signed Marceau, who reports having heard it said, "That will make for civil war; that's all we're asking for; is it also possible to live with two ounces of bread? Aren't they doing this on purpose?" he adds that in other gatherings they all said, "The Convention had better put some order into all that; it's about time." He sums up by saying that heads are dangerously inflamed.

2. In [the report] signed Bouillon, here are the phrases, verbatim: "Yesterday a multitude of women from the Section des Piques, after having refused the portion of bread being offered to them, went to the Committee of the Section and from there to the Convention. They stopped all the women they met on their way and forced them to join up with them."

3. Citizen Compere, in his report, confirms the above assertion and adds more alarming occurrences. . . . Surveillance. . . . Bellier reports that at the horse market last night some women were saying that they must go en masse to the Convention to demand a king in order to have bread; the same report states that at 9 P.M., near the Pont Notre Dame, there was a group of two hundred people who were speaking the same language. This inspector was called before the Convention to be reprimanded for his apathy or his carelessness in not having followed the individuals who were making these remarks. A special watch has been set up for this purpose.

SIGNED BEURLIER, DURET

3

Terror, War, and Resistance

TERROR IS NOTHING BUT PROMPT, SEVERE, INFLEXIBLE
JUSTICE; IT IS THEREFORE AN EMANATION OF VIRTUE. . . .
THE GOVERNMENT OF THE REVOLUTION IS THE
DESPOTISM OF LIBERTY AGAINST TYRANNY.

—MAXIMILIEN ROBESPIERRE,

"ON POLITICAL MORALITY," 5 FEBRUARY 1794

(CD-ROM p. 65)

The execution of the king in January 1793 did not end the new republic's problems. The expanding war required even more men and money, and the introduction of a national draft provoked massive resistance. In response to growing pressures, the National Convention set up a highly centralized emergency government designed to provide food, direct the war effort, and punish counterrevolutionaries. Thus began "the Terror," in which the newly invented instrument of capital punishment, the guillotine, came to stand for the suppression of all dissent. The leader of this government, Maximilien Robespierre, aimed to create a "Republic of Virtue," in which the government would teach, or force, citizens to become virtuous republicans through a massive program of political reeducation. These policies only increased divisions, however, and ultimately led to Robespierre's fall from power and to a dismantling of government by terror. Although the Terror lasted only from the summer of 1793 until the summer of 1794, it had its origins in earlier revolutionary policies (Document 3.1), and it had consequences that endured well into the twentieth century. The Terror became the single most controversial episode in the history of the French Revolution.

The Committee of Public Safety

The Republic is but an empty illusion when the counterrevolution takes place daily because three-quarters of the citizenry cannot afford the price of basic foodstuffs and no one sheds a tear.

—Jacques Roux, speech to the National Convention, 25 June 1793 (Document 1.4)

Although the French armies had halted the Prussian advance at the battle of Valmy on 20 September 1792, they faced more foreign enemies in 1793 than before. French forces went on the offensive for the first time, but to continue doing so they needed reinforcements. An attempt to levy 300,000 new men at the end of February 1793 backfired when widespread rioting greeted the recruiters in many places. In western France, the resistance soon turned into a full-scale civil war. As squabbling generals squandered their opportunities in the Austrian Netherlands (Belgium), the French government had to confront resistance, inflation, and refusal to pay taxes at home. Because of the inflation in the value of paper money, grain prices shot up, provoking a demand for price controls. The former priest Jacques Roux explained to the deputies the point of view of the poor (Document 1.4): "Freedom is but an empty illusion when one class of men can starve another."

The deputies of the Mountain could not ignore popular demands for swift action. Consequently, the Convention voted on 10 March 1793 to organize a Revolutionary Tribunal to speed up judgment in cases involving national security. On 21 March 1793 they approved the election of revolutionary committees to take over police powers in every section (local district) or town. On 6 April 1793 the Convention established a Committee of Public Safety to provide direction to the government. And on 4 May 1793 it agreed to partial controls on grain prices.

The Girondin deputies had supported these emergency measures, but they did not want them to be under the control of the Parisian militants. To prevent this outcome, they arranged in April 1793 for the arrest of several leading journalists and section leaders. Most prominent among those arrested was Jean-Paul Marat, the editor of the vitriolic newspaper *The Friend of the People* and himself a deputy in the Convention. Marat had helped incite the prison massacres of September 1792, still continued to call for the execution of thousands more traitors, and advocated the establishment of a temporary dictatorship. When tried by the new Revolutionary Tribunal, he was acquitted and feted by the celebrating crowds. The Girondins then switched tactics; they established a Commission of Twelve to investigate insurrectionary activity in Paris and threatened to move the Convention to a more neutral site outside of Paris. The conflict between the Girondins and the Mountain finally ended when an armed crowd from the sections of Paris invaded the National Convention on 2 June 1793 and forced the deputies to order the house arrest of their twenty-nine Girondin colleagues.

The common people had intervened again, but this was no formless mass. Most were *sans-culottes*—that is, artisans or shopkeepers who avidly followed politics in popular clubs and their section committees. Women from the popular classes participated in many of their meetings and in the attack on the Convention, just as they had participated in the March to Versailles. One of the Girondins complained that members of the newly founded Society of Revolutionary Republican Women—"a troupe of furies, avid for carnage"—had armed themselves and egged the men on.

Setting the course for government and the war now fell to the Committee of Public Safety, composed of twelve deputies from the Convention. The chief spokesman of the committee was Maximilien Robespierre (see Fig. 3.1), a thirty-five-year-old lawyer who was known as "the incorruptible" for his stern honesty and fierce dedication. Because of his association with the Terror, which began officially in September 1793 when the deputies voted to "put Terror on the agenda," Robespierre remains one of the most disputed figures in world history. Germaine de Staël, the daughter of Louis XVI's finance minister, Necker, and herself a prominent writer, insisted that Robespierre was "neither more adept nor more eloquent than the others, but his political fanaticism had a character of calm and austerity that inspired fear in all his colleagues." Staël met Robespierre in 1789: "His features were coarse, his color pale, his veins of a greenish color, and he took up the most absurd theses with a cold-bloodedness that had the air of conviction." Robespierre believed that any sincere, reasonable person ought to support the Republic in its time of need and that only hypocrites and traitors would oppose it. Although he originally argued against both the death penalty and the war, he was convinced that the emergency situation of 1793 required severe measures, including death for those, such as the Girondins, who obstructed the Committee's policies.

Robespierre was a devoted disciple of Rousseau. "No one has given us a more just idea of the people than Rousseau," he insisted, "because no one has loved the people

Fig. 3.1   Robespierre by Claude-André Deseine (1791)

This bust of Robespierre, sculpted before the delegate made his way to the top, catches him in the full flower of his youthful idealism. Most later renditions show a more haggard look.

more." Since Robespierre tied his defense of the Terror—"the theory of revolutionary government"—to Rousseau's philosophy, he inadvertently helped foster the notion that Rousseau's thinking had totalitarian elements, that it encouraged the suppression of dissenting opinions. Robespierre loudly defended the people's right to democratic government, while in practice he supported many emergency measures that restricted their liberties. He personally favored a free-market economy, as did almost all middle-class deputies, but in this time of crisis he was willing to enact price controls and requisitioning. Like Rousseau, he believed the Republic would have to reform its citizens by establishing a new civic religion. In "On Political Morality," his speech to the Convention in February 1794, he concluded: "The first maxim of your policies must be to lead the people by reason and the people's enemies by terror. . . . If the mainspring of popular government in peacetime is virtue, amid revolution it is at the same time [both] virtue and terror: virtue, without which terror is fatal; terror, without which virtue is impotent." (CD-ROM p. 65) "Terror" was not an idle term; it seemed to imply that the goal of democracy justified totalitarian means.

Although he often spoke for the Committee of Public Safety, Robespierre never acted alone. He was no dictator. The members of the Committee were elected by the Convention and could be revoked. Robespierre's closest colleague on the Committee was the young and fiery Saint-Just, who like him was unmarried (a fact that would prompt the succeeding government to require deputies in the upper house to be married). A revolutionary purist, Saint-Just privately advocated the establishment of a new Spartan-style state in which children would be separated from their parents in order to mold them into true republicans. He threw himself tirelessly into the war effort, spending time at the front reorganizing the armies. "Those who would make revolutions in the world," he insisted, "must sleep only in the tomb." Many of his colleagues on the Committee worked eighteen-hour days. Joining Robespierre and Saint-Just were engineers known for their war expertise, an ex-priest who took charge of food distribution, and a small group that devoted its energies to the thankless task of managing the ups and downs of politics within the Convention. The Committee could only maintain its authority by winning the war, supplying food to Paris and the armies, defeating the mounting resistance to its policies, and establishing a political line that most of the deputies would willingly follow. In June 1793 the Convention had drafted a constitution for the Republic, which was approved by a popular referendum, but it shelved it for the duration of the war. As a result, the Committee of Public Safety exercised the executive function of government in 1793 and 1794.

Through a succession of determined measures, the Committee of Public Safety set the machinery of the Terror in motion. It sent deputies out "on mission" to purge unreliable officials, work with local leaders of the Jacobin Clubs and other popular societies to uncover dissidents, and organize the war effort. As an early version of the revolutionary commissars made notorious by the Russian Revolution of 1917, the deputies on mission had nearly absolute power over local affairs. In August 1793 the Convention voted the first universal draft of men in history: every unmarried man and childless widower between the ages of eighteen and twenty-five was declared eligible for conscription into the army. In areas of resistance to the Revolution, military commissions joined the Revolutionary Tribunals in dispensing quick justice. A Law of Suspects passed on 17 September 1793 defined treason in the broadest possible fashion: among those scheduled for arrest and trial were former nobles who had not shown their loyalty to the Revolution; anyone who emigrated, even if they returned; anyone dismissed from a government position; and anyone denied a certificate of patriotism by their local government (Document 2.5). To satisfy the economic demands of the sans-culottes, on 29 September 1793 the Convention set a maximum level on the prices of all staples (Document 2.6). The government confiscated the property of every convicted traitor.

A series of dramatic trials in Paris showed that the Convention meant to enforce its will. In October 1793 the Revolutionary Tribunal in Paris convicted Marie-Antoinette of treason and sent her to the guillotine. Even more than her husband Louis XVI, she had been vilified in pamphlets and newspapers. One especially vulgar and sensational newspaper, *Le Père Duchesne,* portrayed the queen as a lesbian sharing her counterrevolutionary hopes with one of her ladies-in-waiting. Calling her a monkey, a she-wolf, and the tigress of Austria, the editor Jacques Hébert suggested that she be chopped up like meat for pâté in revenge for all the blood she had caused to be shed in France. The Girondins went to the guillotine at the same time despite their vociferous protestations of innocence. One of them committed suicide at the announcement of the verdict in the courtroom. The queen was not the only prominent

Fig. 3.2 Noble Act of 500,000 Republicans

The revolutionary wars, which continued in one form or another until Napoleon's defeat in 1815, were different from other conflicts in early modern Europe. Both sides believed they were fighting for the triumph of good over evil. This image promoted the French as republicans fighting for a constitution. Note that the constitution is presented as two tablets, as in many renditions of the Ten Commandments. The opponents of the French are described as slaves.

woman to lose her life. Jeanne du Barry, the infamous mistress of Louis XV, was sentenced to death for counterrevolutionary activities. When Olympe de Gouges, author of the Declaration of the Rights of Women, and Manon Roland, wife of a former minister and herself a leading figure among the Girondins, climbed the scaffold to the guillotine in November 1793, a Parisian official denounced them for being "women-men," mixed beings who refused to stick to their ordained female roles.

The Terror won its greatest success on the battlefield, though victory was far from certain. As of April 1793, France was at war with every major European power except Russia. The allied powers had a chance to defeat France in 1793, when the French armies verged on chaos because of the emigration of noble army officers and the problems of integrating new draftees. At that very moment, however, Prussia, Austria, and Russia were preoccupied with clamping down on Poland, which they were about to partition for the second time before wiping it off the map altogether in 1795. For France this diversion meant a reprieve. Despite the enormity of the challenge facing them, the French had a new weapon at their disposal: nationalist pride. "The French have become the foremost people of the universe," proclaimed one deputy. The French were now free and had the obligation, they believed, to break the shackles of

tyranny weighing down their neighbors. French soldiers, drawn largely from the peasantry and the lower classes of the cities, fought for a revolution that they and their
brothers and sisters had helped make. Everyone had a role to play whether directly at
the front or back home making bandages, gathering saltpeter for gunpowder, or manufacturing guns in forges set up in the parks and gardens of Paris.

Because of the new national draft, the French had a huge and powerful fighting
force of 700,000 men by the end of 1793. (See Fig. 3.2 for a depiction of republican
soldiers.) But the army faced many problems in the field. As many as one-third of the
recent draftees deserted before or during battle. At the top, the tenure of generals
depended on their political reliability; defeat made them suspect, and they might face
the guillotine. Yet the patriotism created by democratic participation gave France an
undeniable advantage. Democracy even extended to the army: many officers had risen
through the ranks by skill and talent rather than by inheriting or purchasing their
positions. One young peasant boy wrote to his parents, "Either you will see me return
bathed in glory, or you will have a son who is a worthy citizen of France who knows
how to die for the defense of his country."

In the summer of 1794 the French armies invaded the Austrian Netherlands and
crossed the Rhine River. The army was ready to carry the gospel of revolution and
republicanism to the rest of Europe in a self-proclaimed war of liberation. But as the
French annexed more and more territory, "liberated" people in many places began to
view them as an army of occupation. Those in the territories on the northern and eastern frontiers reacted most positively to the French. In the Austrian Netherlands, Mainz,
Savoy, and Nice, French occupation meant the organization of Jacobin Clubs by French
officers and reliable middle-class locals. The clubs petitioned for annexation to France,
and French legislation was then introduced, including the abolition of seigneurial dues.
Despite resistance, especially in the Austrian Netherlands, these areas remained part of
France until 1815, and the legal changes were permanent. Like Louis XIV a century
before, most deputies in the National Convention considered the annexed territories to
be within France's "natural frontiers"—the Rhine, the Alps, and the Pyrenees.

The Republic of Virtue

The program of the Terror went beyond political and economic measures to include
efforts to "republicanize everything"—in other words, to effect a cultural revolution.
The government utilized every possible means to transform the old subjects of the
monarchy into virtuous republican citizens. While censoring writings deemed counterrevolutionary, the government encouraged republican art, set up civic festivals, and even
attacked the churches in a campaign known as de-Christianization. Because it could not
wait for the effects of a new program of elementary education, the Republic politicized
every aspect of daily life from the names of babies to the measures of space and time.

Refusing to tolerate opposition, the revolutionaries left no stone unturned in their
endeavor to get the republican message across. Songs—especially the new national

He [the Supreme Being] did not create kings to devour the human species. Neither did he create priests to harness us like brute beasts to the carriages of kings, and to give the world the example of baseness, pride, perfidy, avarice, debauchery, and falsehood. But he created the universe to celebrate his power; he created men to help and to love one another, and to attain happiness through the path of virtue.

—Robespierre, Speech at the Festival of the Supreme Being, 8 June 1794 (CD-ROM p. 118)

anthem, *La Marseillaise* (CD-ROM p. 181)—posters, pamphlets, newspapers, books, engravings, paintings, sculpture, even everyday crockery, embroidery, chamberpots, and playing cards conveyed republican slogans and symbols. Foremost among these symbols was the figure of Liberty known as Marianne (an early version of the Statue of Liberty now in New York harbor), which appeared on coins and bills, letterheads and seals, and as statues in festivals (see Fig. 3.3). Hundreds of new plays were produced, and old classics were revised. To encourage the production of patriotic and republican works, the government sponsored state competitions for artists. Works of art were supposed to "awaken the public spirit and make clear how atrocious and ridiculous were the enemies of liberty and of the Republic."

At the center of this elaborate cultural campaign were the revolutionary festivals modeled on Rousseau's plans for a civic religion. The festivals first emerged in 1789 when villagers and townspeople spontaneously planted liberty trees to celebrate the coming of the Revolution. Seeing an opportunity to encourage adherence to the new regime, the government organized a Festival of Federation on 14 July 1790 to mark the first anniversary of the fall of the Bastille. Simultaneous festivals took place all over the country, in which spectators watched while local officials and National Guardsmen took an oath to defend the new government. After the declaration of the Republic, Jacques-Louis David took over festival planning. David was one of the country's most famous painters. He had been elected as a deputy to the National Convention and became a close associate of Robespierre. David aimed to destroy the mystique of monarchy and transfer its sacred qualities to the Republic. His Festival of Unity on 10 August 1793, for example, celebrated the first anniversary of the overthrow of the monarchy. In front of the statue of Liberty built for the occasion, a bonfire consumed the crowns and scepters of royalty while a cloud of 3,000 white doves rose into the sky. This was all part of preaching the "moral order of the Republic . . . that will make us a people of brothers, a people of philosophers."

Some revolutionaries hoped that these civic festivals would replace the Catholic church altogether. They initiated a campaign of "de-Christianization" that included closing churches (Protestant as well as Catholic), selling many church buildings to the highest bidder, and trying to force even those clergy who had taken the oath of loyalty to abandon their clerical vocations and marry. The bishop of Paris was one of the first to renounce his functions. Under pressure, one rural priest wrote, "I am a priest, that is, a charlatan." Many priests were compelled to make such humiliating public statements. One in ten of the constitutional clergy married. As a result, some regions would have virtually no priests until well into the nineteenth century. "Revolutionary

Fig. 3.3 The Republic

Under the monarchy, the king was the country's symbolic center. Removing him and establishing a republic made necessary not only a new constitution but also a new set of symbols. Here the revolutionaries transformed "liberty" into "the republic." Without her pike and cap, she seems more matriarchal, framed by flourishing plants. Sometimes depicted in more aggressive posture, the Republic was always shown as a female figure, in part to avoid identification with any particular male politician or political group. The female Republic never appeared in contemporary dress; she was a symbol, above politics, not a French woman involved in revolutionary action.

armies," paramilitary bands that had been haphazardly organized by local revolutionary committees to carry out searches for hoarded grain, now jumped into action: they closed down the churches; seized church bells, crosses, and gold and silver sacramental objects; and destroyed any religious images and statues that could not be melted down, sold, or used for other purposes. Some of the greatest churches in Christendom became storehouses for arms or grain, or their stones were sold off to contractors. The medieval statues of kings on the façade of the cathedral of Notre Dame were beheaded.

In the ultimate step in de-Christianization, extremists tried to establish a cult of Reason to supplant Christianity. In Paris on 10 November 1793 a goddess of Liberty, played by an opera singer, presided over a Festival of Reason in Notre Dame cathedral. Deputies on mission to the provinces carried the de-Christianizing message. Joseph Fouché, for example, deconsecrated Catholic cemeteries, ordered secular funerals, and decreed that the gates of cemeteries should be inscribed with the slogan "Death is an eternal sleep." In a few places officials organized farces to mock the Catholic religion with a papier-mâché figure of the pope, or a donkey dressed as a bishop. Enlightenment philosophy seemed to have turned from anticlericalism to outright atheism.

The spread of de-Christianization alarmed many deputies in the Convention who were wary of turning devout, rural people against the Republic. Local people often resisted de-Christianization and demanded the return of their church bells and the reopening of the churches. Some villages forced priests who had resigned to say Mass again. Peasants attributed every natural disaster to the loss of their priests and their sacred objects. On 21 November 1793, just eleven days after the Festival of Reason in Notre Dame, Robespierre denounced the de-Christianizers in a speech at the Jacobin Club, insisting that they were the agents of foreign powers trying to discredit the Revolution. The de-Christianization campaign came to a halt, and a few months later, in June 1794, Robespierre tried to institute his own new religion, the cult of the Supreme Being. Robespierre objected to the atheism of the de-Christianization campaign; he favored a Rousseau-inspired deistic religion without the supposedly superstitious trappings of Catholicism, as the excerpt above from his speech at the festival demonstrates. Neither the cult of Reason nor the cult of the Supreme Being attracted many followers, but the attempts to establish them show the depth of the republican commitment to overturning the old order and all its traditional institutions.

In principle, the best way to ensure the future of the Republic was through the education of the young. The deputy Georges Danton, a lawyer who made his reputation in the Cordeliers Club of Paris, maintained "After bread, the first need of the people is education." The Convention voted to make primary schooling free and compulsory for both boys and girls. It took control of education away from the Catholic church and tried to set up a system of state schools at both the primary and secondary levels, but it lacked the trained teachers needed to replace those the Catholic religious orders had provided. As a result, opportunities for learning how to read and write actually may have diminished. In 1799 only one-fifth as many boys enrolled in the state secondary schools as had studied in church schools ten years earlier.

Although many of the ambitious republican programs failed, almost all aspects of daily life became politicized. Already in 1789 the colors one wore had political significance. The tricolor flag of red, white, and blue was devised in July 1789, and by 1793 everyone had to wear a cockade with the colors. And because using the formal forms of speech (in French the *vous* form for "you") or the title "Monsieur" or "Madame" might identify someone as an aristocrat, true patriots used the informal *tu* and called one another "Citizen" instead. Some people changed their names or gave their children new kinds of names; biblical and saints' names, such as Jean, Pierre, Joseph, or Marie, gave way to names recalling heroes of the ancient Roman Republic (Brutus or Gracchus), revolutionary heroes, or flowers and plants. Such changes symbolized adherence to the Republic and to Enlightenment ideals.

Even the measures of time and space were revolutionized. In October 1793 the Convention introduced a new rationalized calendar to replace the Christian one. Year one dated from the founding of the Republic on 22 September 1792. *Décades* of ten days each replaced the seven-day weeks; Sunday as the day of religion and rest gave way to *décadi*, simply the tenth day of the week. Each of the twelve months had exactly thirty days, with five public holidays tacked on to the end of the year. The names given the months reflected the seasons: thus the word *ventôse* spanning late

February and early March, came from the French word for "wind" (*le vent*). The calendar remained in force for twelve years despite continuing resistance to it. Needless to say, ordinary people did not much appreciate having their rest time reduced from four days in a month to three. Most people wanted to continue to celebrate Sunday rather than attending didactic festivals on *décadi*. More enduring in impact was the new metric system based on units of ten that was invented to replace the hundreds of local variations in weights and measures. Other countries in Europe and much of the rest of the world eventually adopted the metric system.

Revolutionary legislation also changed the rules of family life. The state took responsibility for all family matters away from the Catholic church and restricted the powers of fathers. Birth, death, and marriage registration now happened at the city hall, not the parish church. Marriage became a civil contract and as such could be broken. The new divorce law of September 1792 was the most far-reaching in the Western world: a couple could divorce by mutual consent or for such reasons as insanity, abandonment, battering, or criminal conviction. Thousands of men and women took advantage of the law to dissolve unhappy marriages, even though the pope had condemned the measure. In the past, men had simply walked away from marriages they disliked; now women could legally sever their connection from husbands who abandoned or abused them. In 1816 the government revoked the right to divorce, and not until the 1970s did French divorce laws return to the principles of the 1792 legislation. The government also limited fathers' rights over their children; they could not imprison them without cause or control their lives after the age of twenty-one. In one of its most influential actions, the revolutionary government passed a series of laws that created equal inheritance among all children in the family, including girls. The father's right to favor one child, especially the oldest male, was considered aristocratic and hence antirepublican. The National Convention even tried to legalize the rights of illegitimate children, but these laws were modified and then revoked by succeeding governments. In many ways, then, revolutionaries aimed to create equality of rights within the family just as they did within the state.

Resisting the Revolution

By intruding so often and so dramatically into religion, culture, and daily life, the Revolution inevitably provoked resistance. Every attempt to create new values and symbols produced a backlash among at least part of the population. When villagers and townspeople planted liberty trees to signal their support of the Revolution, the disgruntled could express their refusal to go along by tearing them out under cover of night. When revolutionaries sported the tricolor cockade, opponents wore other colors, outlandish versions, or none at all. The government's requirement of an oath of loyalty from the clergy made resisters out of those willing to shelter nonjuring priests

If the population of your beautiful countryside is almost entirely destroyed, if the voyager encounters in it only bones, ashes, and ruins, to whom can one impute these misfortunes, if not to the priests, who never separated their cause from that of religion and who overturned the universe in order to preserve their riches and their power?

—Charles Dupuis, speaking of the Vendée rebellion, *The Origin of All Religions* (1798)

(those who refused an oath of loyalty to the government) or attend masses officiated by nonjuring clergy. The de-Christianization campaign prompted some Catholic believers to organize defiant processions with statues of the Virgin Mary or to make pilgrimages to local shrines. Secret nighttime masses sometimes drew hundreds of worshipers. Resistance also took more violent forms, from riots over food shortages or religious policies to assassinations, uprisings, and, in the west of France, full-scale civil war.

Food and religion provided the most common sources of complaint, and in both areas women usually took the lead in criticizing the government. The constant need to supply the armies with food resulted in long bread lines in the cities that exhausted the patience of women already overwhelmed by the demands of housekeeping, child rearing, and working as shop assistants, fishwives, laundresses, and textile workers. Police spies reported their constant grumbling, which occasionally turned into spontaneous demonstrations or riots over high prices or food shortages (Document 2.9). The revolutionary government's conflicts with the Catholic church sparked women to action; women hid nonjuring priests, incited their menfolk to resist the confiscation of church bells, and led the way in demanding the reopening of churches. Sometimes these struggles mobilized whole communities. In one particularly striking example, 800 people were arrested in the village of La Ferté-Gaucher in December 1793 for assaulting officials who tried to carry away religious objects from the local church.

Some Catholics resented the granting of rights to Protestants and Jews. Although religion did not correlate in any precise way with political positions (Protestant deputies could be found both among the Girondins and the Mountain, for example), Protestants and Jews tended to support the Revolution, at least until the Terror. After Protestants gained full political rights in 1789, Catholics in southern France reacted by organizing their own unofficial companies of the National Guard to defend Catholic interests against local Protestants. Although plans to foment an insurrection against the new revolutionary government came to nothing, tensions boiled over in the town of Nîmes in June 1790. After Protestant National Guards defeated one of the unofficial Catholic companies in a pitched battle, the Protestants continued on a rampage against the Catholics. Some 200 to 300 Catholics died. A few southern Catholics continued to plot against the Revolution for years afterward. Jews fared less well in local conflicts than Protestants, because they were fewer in number and less well placed within local communities (many of the most important textile merchants in Nîmes, for example, were Protestants, whereas their workers were Catholics). In eastern France, where many Jews resided, anti-Semitic riots broke out in seventy villages in July 1789. Peasants resented the Jews who lent them money, and in the riots often destroyed the debt records. During the Terror, the de-Christianization movement attacked Protestant places of worship and Jewish synagogues as well as Catholic churches.

Political assassination was much less common than religiously motivated resistance but very dramatic in its impact. On the day of the king's execution in January 1793, a royalist killed one of the deputies who had voted for the death penalty. Fearful of a similar fate, his colleagues organized a public tribute to this "martyr of liberty." In July 1793, Charlotte Corday, a fervent supporter of the Girondin deputies who had been recently arrested, stabbed Jean-Paul Marat to death in his bath. She considered it her patriotic duty to kill the deputy who had constantly demanded more heads and more blood. Marat too was eulogized as a great martyr. Corday went to the guillotine vilified as a monster but confident in her own mind that she had "avenged many innocent victims." Assassination attempts on Robespierre and another member of the Committee of Public Safety heightened the atmosphere of insecurity and paranoia in the spring of 1794.

Charlotte Corday was not the only one upset by the arrest of the Girondin deputies. Two-thirds of the departments protested against the purge, and several attempted to organize their own armies to march on Paris. Most of these disbanded at the first sign of combat. More serious rebellions took place during the summer of 1793 in Bordeaux, Lyons, Marseilles, and Toulon. In Lyons, in clear contrast to Paris where the local sections constantly pushed for more radical measures, the neighborhood sections revolted against the Jacobin-dominated city government, took city hall by armed assault, and executed the pro-Terror head of the municipality. They also sent delegates off to Bordeaux and Marseilles to develop a common plan of action. The leaders of the revolt in Marseilles opened negotiations with the commander of the British fleet, while those in Toulon declared themselves for Louis XVII, the son of Louis XVI, and turned the city, along with France's Mediterranean fleet, over to the British.

The Convention promptly laid siege to these centers of "federalism," so-called because they favored less power for Paris and the National Convention and more for the rest of France. Although the insurgents gained considerable support in their home bases, they failed to establish workable links with one another, lost support when they seemed to endorse royalism, and proved ineffective at fighting against the regular army. Bordeaux and Marseilles fell in August 1793, but Lyons only surrendered in October after weeks of bombardment. Then a little-known artillery captain, Napoleon Bonaparte, gained a certain reputation when he played a leading role in the recapture of Toulon from the British. His skillful direction of French artillery devastated the other side.

The Convention did not let the rebels off lightly. After Toulon finally fell, the local Jacobins picked out 800 insurgents for execution. In Lyons, Collot d'Herbois, one of the members of the Committee of Public Safety, and Fouché, one of the architects of de-Christianization, took charge of the official punishment. They ordered 1,600 houses of the rich demolished. They set up a special commission to try rebels. It sentenced nearly 2,000 people to death; some were shot, the others were guillotined. They confiscated all the property of the condemned and changed the name of the city to Ville Affranchie (Liberated City). Although the Convention intended to destroy counterrevolutionary Lyons, the demolition proved incomplete; most of the houses of the rich lost only their façades, and the actions of the special commission created an enduring hostility to the revolutionary government.

Although these various forms of resistance created temporary problems for the Convention, they paled in comparison to the violence that erupted in the Vendée region of western France. Between March and December 1793, peasants, artisans, and weavers joined together under noble leadership to form a "Catholic and Royal Army." During his interrogation in the spring of 1794, one of the captured Vendée leaders, Maurice Gigost d'Elbée, was asked "What was the goal of the war that these rebels undertook?" He responded, "In principle the goal of the rebels in undertaking this war was only to escape the draft of republican troops destined to defend the frontiers. It became, soon afterward, a war to defend the throne and the clergy." The uprising took two different forms: in the Vendée region a counterrevolutionary army organized to fight the Republic; in nearby Brittany and Normandy, resistance took the form of guerrilla bands called *chouans* (Fig. 3.4), which united to murder republican officials and constitutional priests, stop grain shipments, or attack republican patrols, then quickly melted into the countryside. Great Britain provided money and underground contacts for these attacks, which were almost always aimed at towns. Town officials sold church lands, enforced measures against the clergy, and supervised conscription. In many ways this was a civil war between town and country, for the townspeople were the ones who supported the Revolution and bought church lands for themselves. The peasants had gained most of what they wanted in 1789 with the abolition of seigneurial dues, and they resented the government's demands for money and manpower and actions against their local clergy.

For several months in 1793 the Vendée rebels stormed the largest towns in the region. Both sides committed horrible atrocities. At the small town of Machecoul, for example, the rebels massacred 500 republicans, including National Guard members; many victims were tied together, shoved into freshly dug graves, and shot. Local officials wrote to Paris demanding help: "We cannot hide from you sirs, that a severe and swift example needs to be set" (Document 3.2). With the approval of the government, General L. M. Turreau sent draconian orders to his officers: "You will employ every means to discover the rebels, everyone will be bayoneted; the villages, farms, woods, wastelands, scrub and generally all which can be burned, will be put to the torch." Turreau complained that the rebel women had proved especially dangerous. "They stood out for their courage which was exceptional for women," he explained, "and especially for a ferocity that was shameful." Most terrifying in his view was the conduct of the

Fig. 3.4 Description of the Chouans and Other Counterrevolutionaries

The counterrevolution was a diverse movement that would, over time, engulf different parts of France from 1793 into the Napoleonic period. The most serious threat to the Republic came from the revolt in the west, which included both the Vendée insurrection (especially during 1793–94) and the more sporadic attacks of the chouans (strongest in 1795–96). The engraving mocks the "counterrevolution" by depicting its participants grotesquely and comically. It shows three effeminate-looking dandies identified as officers of the chouan army, setting forth "to assassinate, starve, and slit the throats of . . . patriots."

SIGNALEMENT DES CHOUANS ET AUTRES CONTREVOLUTIONAIRES.

Officiers généraux de l'armée thermidorienne sortant du Caffé de Chartres allant en expéditions armée de batons, sabres, et de tous les termes techniques reçu dans cette humaine confrairie, pour assassiner affamer et égorger le peuple et les patriotes par milliers.

1. *Vive la Convention.*   3. *Conspirations trouvé*
2. *A bas les Jacobins.*   *dans un mouchoir*

rebel women toward their victims: "after a victory they took part with barbarous joy in the long and bloody tortures inflicted on the unhappy [republican] prisoners." By the end of the fall, despite these obstacles, republican soldiers had turned back the rebels in the Vendée. Military courts ordered thousands executed, and republican soldiers slaughtered thousands of others. In the cities directly threatened by the rebels, revenge could take on horrifying proportions. In December 1793, Deputy-on-Mission Jean-Baptiste Carrier oversaw, or at least did nothing to stop, the drownings of some 2,000 prisoners in Nantes. Some had been convicted by the local military court, but others had simply been snatched from the prisons, including many priests. They were tied together on boats and then drowned in the river.

Even today, controversy still rages about the rebellion's death toll; estimates of rebel deaths alone range from about 20,000 to 250,000 and higher. Recent studies have concluded that about one-third of the inhabitants of the Vendée region died during the war, some in massacres and battles, others as a result of epidemics, famine, and general exhaustion. One-third of all farm animals also died. Many thousands of republican soldiers and civilians also lost their lives, though no exact count was ever made by the government. Even the low estimates reveal the carnage of this catastrophic confrontation between the Republic and its opponents. As the quotation opening this section demonstrates, many republicans blamed the violence on the narrow self-interest of Catholic priests who fomented rebellion among their parishioners and gathered a bitter harvest of "bones, ashes, and ruins." Republicans linked the priests to women's participation in the rebellion. Carrier underlined this connection in a letter he sent to the Committee of Public Safety on 11 December 1793: "You should know that it is the women along with the priests who have instigated and sustained the war in the Vendée, that it is the women who have had our poor prisoners gunned down, who cut the throats of many of them, who fight with the brigands and who ruthlessly kill our volunteers whenever they encounter any of them on patrol in the villages." From this moment on, republicans considered women particularly susceptible to priests, superstition, and fanaticism.

Although the republican armies gained the upper hand in the Vendée, the chouans continued to exact a toll; since they lacked a distinct military organization, they avoided pitched battles in favor of limited encounters. In many places in Brittany and Normandy the republican government exercised virtually no authority in 1793–94. The British continued to ship arms to the chouans and in June 1795 ferried 3,000 French émigrés to the Quiberon Peninsula in Brittany. They hoped to ignite a royalist insurrection when the aristocratic émigrés joined forces with the peasant chouans. This departure from the usual chouan tactics proved fatal to the rebels. A republican army quickly bottled up the invaders and their supporters; after their defeat, military commissions sentenced hundreds of émigrés to death. In December 1795 the national government assembled a large army to pursue the remaining guerrillas. It captured and executed the two main leaders of the chouans. The military threat ended for the time being, though the rebels revived their campaigns again in 1799 and in 1815.

The Fall of Robespierre and the End of the Terror, 1794–1799

In an atmosphere of paranoia that was fueled by overt resistance in places like the Vendée, Robespierre tried simultaneously to exert the Committee of Public Safety's control over popular political activities and weed out opposition among the deputies. In the fall of 1793 the Convention cracked down on popular clubs and societies. First to be suppressed were women's political clubs, in particular the Society of Revolutionary Republican Women. The deputies associated women's participation in the public sphere with political disorder and social upheaval. As Philippe Fabre d'Eglantine insisted,

women's clubs consisted of "adventuresses, female knights, eman-
cipated girls, and amazons." Amar continued, "Women are hardly
capable of lofty conceptions and serious cogitations" (Document
2.10). In subsequent years physicians and philosophers justified
women's inferior status by formulating "scientific" explanations
for women's "natural" differences from men.

> The courts, protectors of
> life and property, became
> butcheries, where
> confiscation and torture
> became just euphemisms
> for theft and murder.
> —Camille Desmoulins,
> *Le Vieux Cordelier*
> (Document 3.3)

The closing of women's clubs marked an important turning
point in the Revolution. From then on the sans-culottes and
their political organizations came increasingly under the thumb
of the Committee of Public Safety and the Jacobins in the Convention. Many young
militants were drafted into the army, while older ones joined the growing bureaucracy.
A Convention decree of 4 December 1793 subordinated all local governments and revolutionary committees to the central government. Local section assemblies could no
longer meet nonstop to gather denunciations of suspects or discuss politics; they were
limited to two meetings per *décade*. The city government in Paris, whose leaders
enjoyed close links to Robespierre and the Committee of Public Safety, increasingly
took control of local affairs away from the section assemblies. In short, popular militancy waned in the face of growing central authority.

Once its lines of command were firmly anchored, the Committee of Public Safety
then moved against those who still dared oppose its policies from within governing
circles. In March 1794 it arrested and executed a group labeled "ultrarevolutionaries,"
on the trumped-up grounds that they were plotting a military coup and new prison
massacres. Among the convicted "ultras," or extremists, were Hébert, editor of the *Le
Père Duchesne* newspaper and a leading militant in the Cordeliers Club; C. P. Ronsin,
the commander of the Parisian revolutionary army; and A. F. Momoro, an instigator
of de-Christianization. This surgical strike at the leaders of the popular movement in
Paris showed that local militants had been cowed.

Next came the other side, the "indulgents," so-called because they favored a moderation of the Terror. Included among them was the deputy Danton, himself once a
member of the Committee of Public Safety and a friend of Robespierre; Camille
Desmoulins, editor of *Le Vieux Cordelier,* who attacked the continuing Terror (Document 3.3); and Fabre d'Eglantine, one of the deputies who had led the charge
against women's clubs. All three had been active in the Cordeliers Club as well as the
Jacobins and were considered leading republicans. Under government pressure, in
April 1794 the Revolutionary Tribunal convicted them and their confederates of treason and sentenced them to death. As one of the Girondin victims of 1793 remarked,
"The Revolution was devouring its own children." Left or right, everyone was a
potential suspect.

Even after these supposed threats to the Committee's power had been eliminated, the
Terror continued and even worsened. A law passed on 10 June 1794 denied the accused
the right of legal counsel, reduced the number of jurors necessary for conviction, and

Fig. 3.5   Summoning to Execution

One of the most frightening parts of the Terror was its unpredictability. Thousands were denounced as suspects and faced unexpected, even nighttime, arrests. If convicted, they faced the terrors of death by guillotine. This English print captures the pathos of those final moments of fear and despair.

allowed only two judgments: acquittal or death (Document 3.4). The category of political crimes expanded to include those who "sought to inspire discouragement," "mislead opinion," or "disparage" the National Convention. Ordinary people risked the guillotine if they expressed any discontent, and the rate of executions in Paris rose from five a day in spring 1794 to twenty-six a day in the summer (Fig. 3.5). The political atmosphere darkened even though the military situation improved. On 26 June the French armies decisively defeated the main Austrian army at the battle of Fleurus and rapidly advanced through the Austrian Netherlands to Brussels and Antwerp. The emergency measures for fighting the war were clearly working.

Several factors combined to seal Robespierre's fate. Since the French armies had gone on the offensive, the emergency government of the Committee of Public Safety, and especially the new law broadening the definition of suspects, seemed less defensible (Document 3.5). Robespierre's central role at the Festival of the Supreme Being on 8 June 1794 angered many deputies who thought it signaled Robespierre's ambition for personal dictatorship. Finally, deputies who had either encouraged radical de-Christianization or supported Danton's moderation of the Terror still feared for their lives. On 26 July 1794 Robespierre appeared before the Convention promising to produce yet another list of deputies to be arrested. The next day (9 Thermidor year II on the revolutionary calendar) those who suspected they would be named ordered Robespierre arrested along with the president of the Revolutionary Tribunal in Paris, the commander of the Parisian National Guard, and Robespierre's colleague Saint-Just. Although the Paris city government tried to mount an armed uprising, it failed. Robespierre and his colleagues had destroyed the leadership of the sans-culottes, dispersed many of the rank-and-file militants, and may also have lost their confidence after the executions of the spring. Robespierre and Saint-Just, along with their supporters in city hall, went to the guillotine.

The men who led the attack on Robespierre did not intend to reverse all his policies, but that happened nonetheless. After a year of incredible tension, many longed for a respite from the Terror. The improvement of France's situation in the war seemed to justify a relaxation of the atmosphere of constraint. Newspapers attacked the Robespierrists as "tigers thirsting for human blood." The new government released hundreds of suspects. It purged Jacobins from local bodies and replaced them with their opponents. It arrested some of the most notorious "terrorists" in the National Convention, such as Carrier, and put them to death. Within the year the new leaders abolished the Revolutionary Tribunal and closed the Jacobin Club in Paris. Popular demonstrations met severe repression.

The last massive intervention of ordinary people occurred on 20 May 1795, when women's agitation over the shortage of bread culminated in an invasion of the Convention and the killing of one deputy (Fig. 3.6). The police reported, "The women, above all, seemed to be playing the principal role there; they were taunting the men, treating them as cowards. . . . A large number of them wanted to rush into insurrection" (Document 2.11). After the crowds dispersed, the government arrested and imprisoned hundreds of militants. As prorevolutionary militancy died out, counterrevolutionary aggression sprang into action. In the southeast of the country, in particular, a "White Terror" replaced the Jacobins' "Red Terror." Paramilitary bands that had tacit support from the new authorities harassed, assaulted, and often murdered former officials and local Jacobin leaders. In Lyons a mob several thousand strong murdered about 100 Jacobins; many of the Jacobins were hacked to death after fleeing the fires set to the prisons where they were jailed.

Across the country the official Terror had cost the lives of at least 40,000 French people, most of them living in the regions of major insurrections or near the borders with foreign enemies, where suspicion of collaboration ran high. The Terror hardly touched some parts of France, but overall the experience was undeniably traumatic. As many as 300,000 people went to prison as suspects between March 1793 and August 1794 (that is, one out of every fifty French). The toll for the aristocracy and the clergy was especially high. Many leading nobles perished under the guillotine, and thousands emigrated. Some 30,000 to 40,000 clergy who refused the oath emigrated, at least 2,000 (including many nuns) were executed, and thousands were imprisoned. The clergy were singled out in particular in the civil war zones: 135 priests were massacred at Lyons in November 1793, and 83 were shot in one day during the Vendée revolt. Yet many victims of the Terror were peasants or ordinary working people.

After the fall of Robespierre and the end of the official Terror (the so-called White Terror against former revolutionaries went on for some time), the deputies who remained in the National Convention prepared another constitution in 1795, which set up a two-house legislature and an executive body called the Directory, made up of

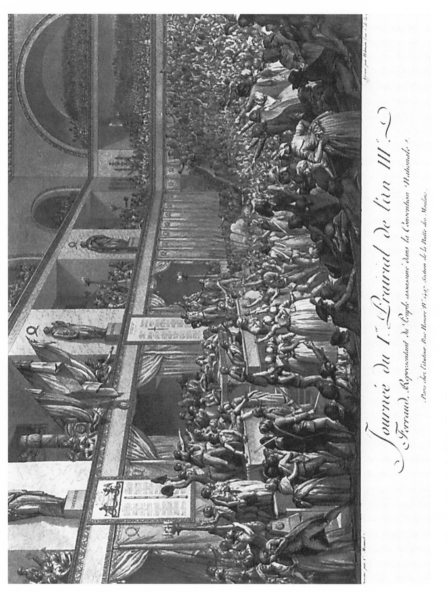

Journeé du 1.ᵉʳ Prairial de l'an III.

Ferraud, Représentant du Peuple assassiné dans la Convention Nationale.

Paris chez l'imprimeur Rue Honoré Nᵒ 1197, vis-à-vis de la Malte des Moulins.

Fig. 3.6 Day of 1 Prairial of the Year III

A mob of men and women threatens the deputies on 20 May 1795. They demanded "Bread and the Constitution of 1793." This uprising marked one of the last interventions of ordinary women into national politics.

five Directors. The Directory regime held tenuously on to power for four years, using force to annul elections that returned opponents from the right (the royalists) or the left (the Jacobins). The puritanical atmosphere of the Terror gave way to hedonism: low-cut dresses of transparent materials, the reappearance of prostitutes in the streets, fancy dinner parties, and "victims balls" where guests wore red ribbons around their necks as reminders of the guillotine. Bands of young men dressed in knee breeches and rich fabrics (the "gilded youth" or "jeunesse dorée") picked fights with known Jacobins and disrupted theater performances with loud antirevolutionary songs. All over France people banded together and petitioned to reopen churches closed during the Terror.

Although the Terror had ended, the Revolution had not. Between 1789 and 1799 France underwent monumental changes. Monarchy as a form of government gave way to a republic whose leaders were elected. Aristocracy based on rank and birth gave way to civil equality and the promotion of merit. Although successive governments learned how to control popular activism, elections continued to provide regular occasions for political education and mobilization in clubs and proto-parties. Even if turnout was often disappointing, the mere existence of national elections represented a fundamental change from before 1789. And thousands of men now held elective office and participated personally in revolutionary change. Women had not gained the right to vote, but they had formed their own clubs, marched in demonstrations, and published their political ideas. They gained the right to divorce and the right to equal inheritance. Between 1795 and 1799, the Republic and these gains in legal and political rights endured in France, but the Directory government directed a war effort abroad that would ultimately bring to power the man who would dismantle the Republic itself.

Documents

THE LOGIC OF THE TERROR

No part of the French Revolution has transfixed posterity as much as "the Terror." Contemporaries used that label to characterize the use of legalized violence during the period from the late summer of 1793 to the summer of 1794. How could a revolution that began with the promise of liberty, equality, and fraternity end up with hundreds of thousands of suspects in jail, summary trials, and tens of thousands of executions of political opponents? Was this transformation inevitable?

Scholarly debate on the causes of the Terror has been divided between two opposing camps: those who point to the urgent circumstances created by foreign war and internal counterrevolution versus those who focus on the impact of revolutionary ideology. The circumstances were dire. Even before France declared war on Austria in 1792, many leading nobles had emigrated and sought military support from foreign powers. Once war was declared, they openly joined counterrevolutionary armies. As the Vendée region erupted into revolt within France, the revolutionaries quickly concluded that potential enemies might be found everywhere, even among supposed friends. Wartime patriotism combined with fears of conspiracy to create a stark division between revolutionaries and counterrevolutionaries. Each side labeled the other absolutely evil and called for a fight to the death.

Although circumstances certainly go a long way toward explaining the revolutionary government's crackdown on presumed opponents and even political dissidents, war and counterrevolution cannot account for the continuation of the Terror once the revolutionary government began to win on both the foreign and domestic fronts in mid-summer 1794. As republicans themselves began to call for moderation of the Terror, the Committee of Public Safety, led by Robespierre, insisted on even broader definitions of suspects and even fewer rights for the accused, resulting in even more executions. Once set in motion, the Terror seemed to have an implacable logic. The room for dissent grew ever more constrained, until the whole system collapsed all at once.

Document 3.1: The Assembly Complains to the King About the Émigrés

Having received news of the support of Prussia and Austria for *émigré* French nobles, the Legislative Assembly considered itself threatened by invasion. Fearing that the king, despite his public acceptance of the constitution, had allied himself with this coalition, the assembly addressed Louis XVI and asked him to declare his opposition to the *émigrés* and if necessary to lead French forces against the Prussians and Austrians to preserve not only the constitution but also the more traditional concern of kings: the country's "glory."

Source: M. J. Mavidal and M. E. Laurent, eds., *Archives parlementaires de 1787 à 1860, première série (1787 à 1799),* 2nd ed., 82 vols. (Paris: Dupont, 1879–1913), 35:443. Translated by the *Exploring the French Revolution* project staff from original documents in French found in J. M. Roberts, *French Revolution Documents, 1792–1795,* vol. 1 (Oxford: Basil Blackwell, 1966), 446–47.

> *The National Assembly's Address to the King, 29 November 1791*
> Sire,
> The National Assembly had no sooner turned its gaze toward the state of the kingdom, than it noticed that the continuing troubles have their source in the criminal preparations of French *émigrés*.

Their audacity is supported by the German princes who flout the treaties signed between themselves and France.

They pretend to forget that they owe their Empire to the Treaty of Westphalia that guarantees their rights and security.

These preparations for hostilities and these threats of invasion require weapons that absorb immense sums that the nation would have gladly used to pay back its creditors.

Sire, it is your role to make them stop. It is your role to address these foreign powers with a language worthy of the King of the French People. Tell them that wherever people allow preparations to be made against France, France shall view them as nothing less than enemies. Tell them that we shall religiously abide by our oath to forswear all conquests, that we propose being good neighbors and offer them the inviolable friendship of a free and strong people. Tell them that we shall respect their laws and customs. Tell them that we shall respect their Constitutions, as long as they respect ours. Finally, tell them that if the princes of Germany continue to encourage preparations aimed against the French, that the French shall carry to them, not the sword and the torch, but liberty. It is up to them to foresee what can occur when nations are awoken.

For the last two years, as French patriots have been persecuted near the borders while the rebels there have found help, what Ambassador has spoken, as he should have, in your name? . . . None.

We ask you Sire: If the French, chased from their homeland by the revocation of the Edict of Nantes, were massed under arms at the frontier, if they were protected by the princes of Germany, what actions would Louis XIV have taken? Would he have put up with these gatherings? Would he have put up with the help being given by the princes who, in the name of allies, act as enemies? What he would have done for his authority, let your Majesty do for the salvation of the Empire and the safeguarding of our Constitution.

Sire everything, your interest, your dignity, the glory of the outraged nation, calls for some other language than that of diplomacy. The nation awaits from you energetic declarations aimed toward the ring of the Upper and Lower Rhine, the Princes of Trier, Mainz and other German princes.

Such as they are, let the hordes of *émigrés* be dissipated this instant. Stipulate a date in the near future beyond which no response, trying merely to gain time, shall be accepted. Let your declaration be underscored by the movement of the forces that have been entrusted to you, so that the nation is aware of who are enemies and who are friends. With these bold steps, we shall recognize the defender of the Constitution.

Thus you shall assure the serenity of the Empire, inseparable from your own. You shall also hasten the return of national prosperity, where peace shall bring back the order and reign of law, and where your happiness shall be mixed with that of all Frenchmen.

Document 3.2: Description of the Counterrevolution—the Vendée (25 August 1793)

The first groups of "brigands" formed in the west in mid-1792, in response most immediately to the call to all citizens to volunteer for the army. In this letter, a local government official, Choudieu, informs the National Convention that the detachment of soldiers it sent to the region has failed to dispel the brigands and asks for more forces, at just the moment when the Prussians have invaded from the north.

Source: Philippe-Joseph-Benjamin Buchez and Prosper-Charles Roux, *Histoire parlementaire de la Révolution Française,* vol. 17 (Paris: Paulin, 1834), 138–39. Translated by the *Exploring the French Revolution* project staff from original documents in French found in John Hardman, *French Revolution Documents 1792–1795,* vol. 2 (New York: Barnes & Noble Books, 1973), 7–8.

Niort, 25 August 1793, Year IV of Freedom [he dates 1789 as Year I]

The departmental adviser reported to you, in the last mail, the troubling events which occurred in the district of Châtillon. New information shows us that the crowd is continuing to gather, that the leaders of bandits, far from scattering them, every day battle with them anew and retreat anew. The council meanwhile has taken strong measures, and at this moment there are three thousand national guardsmen in the region to establish order. It is with the greatest of sorrow that we inform you that six patriots have already fallen victim to this rabble, but at least forty of their number were killed.

We had reason to hope that these gatherings would cease as soon as the public troops arrived. Our hopes were misguided, and this causes us the greatest of worries. Having already dispatched all of the armed force that was at our disposal, the departments of the Vendée, Loire-Inférieure, and Maine-et-Loire showed us unequivocal proof of their fraternity and neighborliness by coming to our aid during these circumstances. Without these departments, this unfortunate region would today have fallen to the rebels. . . .

We cannot hide from you sirs, that a severe and swift example needs to be set. Already several of these bandits have been arrested, and the departmental adviser requests that you issue a decree whereby the criminal court of Niort judges this case as the last resort. It is the only way to bring peace back to this unfortunate region. We hope that you will not refuse us this request.

Document 3.3: Revolution Devours Its Own—Le Vieux Cordelier

Despite the consolidation of power in the hands of the Committee of Public Safety and the creation of Revolutionary Tribunals across France to eliminate traitors to the Republic, the Convention continued to worry about conspiracies even among its political allies. By the end of 1793, the Committee of Public Safety feared the activities of those calling for an acceleration of the Revolution, notably followers of Jacques-Réné Hébert, as well as those who sought to moderate it, known as "Indulgents" and led by Georges Danton. This latter point of view was expressed by Danton's ally Camille Desmoulins in the newspaper *The Old Cordelier,* which made use of Roman history to warn that a republic could be undermined from within by "evil emperors"—by which Desmoulins implied the leadership of the Committee of Public Safety.

Source: Le Vieux Cordelier, 25 Frimaire Year II (15 December 1793), 1–8. Translated by the *Exploring the French Revolution* project staff from original documents in French found in John Hardman, *French Revolution Documents, 1792–1795,* vol. 2 (New York: Barnes & Noble Books, 1973), 186–93.

> Soon it would be a crime of lese majesty or counterrevolution for a town to raise a monument to its own who were killed at the siege of Modena, even though fighting for Augustus himself, but because Augustus fought with Brutus, and Nursia shared the fate of Pérouse, . . . a counterrevolutionary crime was committed by the journalist Cremutius Cordus for having called Brutus and Cassius the last Romans. A counterrevolutionary crime was committed by one of Cassius's descendants for having a portrait of his ancestors in his home. A crime of counterrevolution was committed by Mamercus Scaurus for having written a tragedy in which there were verses that could be interpreted in two different ways. A counterrevolutionary crime was committed by Torquatus Silanu, for having expenses. . . . A counterrevolutionary crime was committed for having taken off one's pants without emptying one's pockets, and for keeping a coin with a royal likeness on it in your coat, which showed a lack of respect for the sacred image of the tyrants. A counterrevolutionary crime was committed by complaining about the unfortunate times, since that was the government's job. A counterrevolutionary crime was committed by not calling upon the divine inspiration of Caligula. For failing to have done that, a large number of citizens were whipped to shreds, sent to the mines or to

the animals, and some were even cut in half. A counterrevolutionary crime was committed by the mother of the Consul Fusius Geminus for having cried at the fateful death of her son.

You should show joy at the death of one's friend or relative if you do not want to expose yourself to danger. Under Nero, several people close to some whom he had killed went to render homage to the gods, and they were cheerful. At least you should seem content, open and calm. You were afraid that seeming to be afraid would make you guilty.

Everyone gave homage to the tyrant. If a citizen was popular, he was a rival to the Prince, which could spark a civil war. Suspicious.

Did you therefore shun popularity? Did you stay home by the fire? This retired life made you noticeable and made you respected. Suspicious.

Were you rich? There was imminent peril that the People would be corrupted by your generosity. Suspicious.

Were you poor? Why? Invincible Emperor, you must watch that man more closely. There is no more enterprising person than he who has nothing. Suspicious.

Were you of a somber nature? Melancholy or unkempt? What was bothering you was that the general economy was doing well. Suspicious.

. . . Finally, had you made a name for yourself during the war? There is no one more dangerous than he who is talented, and there is something to be said for a General who is inept. If the latter is a traitor, he can deliver the army over to the enemy, but most of them will return. But if a victorious officer of Corbulon and Agricola are treasonous then not a single life would be saved. The best action would be to get rid of him. At least, your Highness, could you not spare yourself the trouble by quickly separating him from the Army? Suspicious.

We can believe that it used to be much worse if we were a grandson or ally of Augustus. One day we could have a claim to the throne. Suspicious.

The death of so many innocent and commendable citizens seems less a calamity than the insolence and outrageous fortune of their killers and denouncers. Every day, the untouchable informer made his triumphant entry into the house of the dead, reaping an impressive inheritance. All these denouncers adorned themselves with the best names, calling themselves Cotta, Scipion, Regulus, or Cassius Severus. Informing was the only way to succeed, and Regulus was named Consul three times for his denunciations. Also, everyone threw themselves into a career that had such great perquisites that were so easy to come by. And to distinguish oneself by an illustrious debut and to develop his group of informers, Marcus Serenus brought charges against his elderly father who was already in exile. After that, he was proud to be called Brutus.

As go accusers, so go judges. The courts, protectors of life and property, became butcheries, where confiscation and torture became just euphemisms for theft and murder. . . .

Document 3.4: The Law of 22 Prairial Year II (10 June 1794)

Although the most immediate threats to the security of the Republic—foreign invasion, the civil war in the Vendée, the Federalist uprisings, the grain shortage in Paris, and hyperinflation—had abated by June 1794, Robespierre and his allies on the Committee of Public Safety argued all the more strenuously that virtue needed to be enforced through terror. To this end, on 22 Prairial (10 June), they proposed a law that would free the Revolutionary Tribunals from control by the Convention and would greatly strengthen the position of prosecutors by limiting the ability of suspects to defend themselves. Furthermore, the law broadened the sorts of charges that could be brought, so that virtually any criticism of the government became criminal.

Source: John Hall Stewart, *A Documentary History of the French Revolution* (New York: Macmillan, 1951), 528–31.

The Revolutionary Tribunal shall divide itself into sections, composed of twelve members, to wit: three judges and nine jurors, which jurors may not pass judgment unless they are seven in number.

The Revolutionary Tribunal is instituted to punish the enemies of the people.

The enemies of the people are those who seek to destroy public liberty, either by force or by cunning.

The following are deemed enemies of the people: those who have instigated the reestablishment of monarchy, or have sought to disparage or dissolve the National Convention and the revolutionary and republican government of which it is the center;

Those who have betrayed the Republic in the command of places and armies, or in any other military function, carried on correspondence with the enemies of the Republic, labored to disrupt the provisioning or the service of the armies;

Those who have sought to impede the provisioning of Paris, or to create scarcity within the Republic;

Those who have supported the designs of the enemies of France, either by countenancing the sheltering and the impunity of conspirators and aristocracy, by persecuting and calumniating patriotism, by corrupting the mandataries of the people, or by abusing the principles of the Revolution or the laws or measures of the government by false and perfidious applications;

Those who have deceived the people or the representatives of the people, in order to lead them into undertakings contrary to the interests of liberty;

Those who have sought to inspire discouragement, in order to favor the enterprises of the tyrants leagued against the Republic;

Those who have disseminated false news in order to divide or disturb the people;

Those who have sought to mislead opinion and to prevent the instruction of the people, to deprave morals and to corrupt the public conscience, to impair the energy and the purity of revolutionary and republican principles, or to impede the progress thereof, either by counterrevolutionary or insidious writings, or by any other machination;

Contractors of bad faith who compromise the safety of the Republic, and squanderers of the public fortune, other than those included in the provisions of the law of 7 Frimaire;

Those who, charged with public office, take advantage of it in order to serve the enemies of the Revolution, to harass patriots, or to oppress the people;

Finally, all who are designated in previous laws relative to the punishment of conspirators and counterrevolutionaries, and who, by whatever means or by whatever appearances they assume, have made an attempt against the liberty, unity, and security of the Republic, or labored to prevent the strengthening thereof.

The penalty provided for all offenses under the jurisdiction of the Revolutionary Tribunal is death.

The proof necessary to convict enemies of the people comprises every kind of evidence, whether material or moral, oral or written, which can naturally secure the approval of every just and reasonable mind; the rule of judgments is the conscience of the jurors, enlightened by love of the Patrie; their aim, the triumph of the Republic and the ruin of its enemies; the procedure, the simple means which good sense dictates in order to arrive at a knowledge of the truth, in the forms determined by law.

It is confined to the following points.

Every citizen has the right to seize conspirators and counterrevolutionaries, and to arraign them before the magistrates. He is required to denounce them as soon as he knows of them.

The accused shall be examined publicly in the courtroom: the formality of the preceding secret examination is suppressed as superfluous; it shall take place only under special circumstances in which it is deemed useful for a knowledge of the truth.

If either material or moral proofs exist, apart from the attested proof, there shall be no further hearing of witnesses, unless such formality appears necessary, either to discover accomplices or for other important considerations of public interest.

All proceedings shall be conducted in public, and no written deposition shall be received, unless witnesses are so situated that they cannot come before the Tribunal; and in such case an express authorization of the Committees of Public Safety and General Security shall be necessary.

The law provides sworn patriots as council for calumniated patriots; it does not grant them to conspirators.

The pleadings completed, the jurors shall formulate their verdicts, and the judges shall pronounce the penalty in the manner determined by law.

The public prosecutor may not, on his own authority, discharge an accused person sent to the Tribunal, or one whom he himself has caused to be arraigned before it; in case there is no ground for accusation before the Tribunal, he shall make a written and motivated report thereon to the chamber of the council, which shall decide. But no accused person may be discharged from trial before the decision of the chamber has been communicated to the Committees of Public Safety and General Security, who shall examine it.

Document 3.5: Debate on the Law of 22 Prairial

Many in the Convention, including some on the Committee of Public Safety, opposed the proposed law, which they feared concentrated too much power in too few hands and would only further destabilize the Republic. This passage from the memoirs of Bertrand Barère, a member of the committee, reveals how opponents of the law had to confront the fear that opposition would expose adversaries to the Terror.

The passage of this law marked the beginning of the period known to historians as the "Great Terror," when violence, no longer necessary to protect the Republic, accelerated and became more focused, not only on former nobles and clergy but also, more broadly, on "the wealthy." From 22 Prairial until 10 Thermidor (10 June–28 July 1794), more than 1,300 people were executed in Paris and nearly 1,500 in the provinces, some 15 percent of the total number put to death in the entire fifteen-month reign of Terror.

Source: Bertrand Barère de Vieuzac, *Mémoires de B. Barère, membre de la Constituante, de la Convention, du Comité de Salut public, et de la Chambre des représentants,* vol. 2 (Paris: J. Labitte, 1842), 205–6. Translated by the *Exploring the French Revolution* project staff from original documents in French found in John Hardman, *French Revolution Documents, 1792–1795,* vol. 2 (New York: Barnes & Noble Books, 1973), 250.

In several evening sessions, the two Committees met to decide how to go about revoking the Law of 22 Prairial. After several debates that took place during the month of Messidor, they called in Robespierre and Saint-Just to force them to revoke the law themselves, which had been the result of a combination that all of the other members of the government had been unaware of. It was a very stormy session. Of the members of the National Security Committee, it was Vadier and Moïse Bayle who attacked the law and its authors with the most force and indignation. As for the Committee of Public Safety, they stated that they had played no role in the matter, and disowned the law completely. Everyone agreed that it would be revoked the next day. After this decision, Robespierre and Saint-Just stated that they would put the matter before the public. They stated that it was perfectly clear that a party had been created to ensure immunity for the enemies of the people and that in this way, Liberty's most ardent friends would be lost. But, they said, they would know how to protect the good citizens against the combined maneuvering of the two governmental committees. They departed, threatening members of the committee, including Carnot, among others, whom Saint-Just called an aristocrat and threatened to denounce to the Assembly. It was like a declaration of war between the two committees and the triumvirate.

4

The Revolution in the Colonies

IT IS NOT THAT WE THOUGHT THAT THE PATRIOTS OF THE COLONIES ARE YET UP TO THE LEVEL OF THE PRINCIPLES OF THE FRENCH REVOLUTION. EVERYBODY WANTS THEM TO HAVE LIBERTY, BUT THEY REFUSE THE RIGHT OF CITIZENSHIP TO COLORED PEOPLE, AND THEY WANT TO PERPETUATE SLAVERY AND THE SLAVE TRADE.
—*RÉVOLUTIONS DE PARIS,* 5 SEPTEMBER 1790

(DOCUMENT 4.3)

When revolution broke out in France in 1789, the French crown ruled over a variety of overseas colonies. Historians of the French Revolution have often overlooked the impact of the French Revolution in the colonies, but contemporaries certainly did not, as the quote from the newspaper *Révolutions de Paris* demonstrates. Political leaders in Paris vehemently disagreed among themselves about the fate of the colonies, and French policy frequently shifted during the revolutionary years. In the colonies themselves, conflict was no less intense: white planters wanted to maintain their privileges, free blacks aspired to new rights, and African slaves refused to sit quietly on the sidelines. Slavery was bound to become an intensely contested issue once the revolutionaries declared the universal "rights of man" in 1789. How could a country that had just recaptured its freedom continue to enslave others?

At first, the deputies of the National Assembly sought a way to reconcile revolution and continued slavery. In August 1791, however, a massive slave revolt erupted in Saint Domingue, the largest of the French Caribbean colonies. It would prove to be the first successful slave revolt in world history. In February 1794, in an attempt to keep control of Saint Domingue and their other colonies, the French abolished slavery and the slave trade. This bold stroke did not clarify the situation as much as might be expected, though, because warfare between France and its enemies Great Britain and Spain continued in the Caribbean, making the clear reestablishment of French authority difficult if not impossible. After Napoleon Bonaparte took power in France, he decreed the restoration of slavery in the colonies. However, Napoleon's soldiers failed to retake Saint Domingue, which won its independence as the republic of Haiti in 1804. But the French government restored slavery in the other French Caribbean colonies, and those colonies remain part of France today (slavery was finally abolished in 1848).

The Revolution of 1789 came at the end of a century of intense competition between France and Great Britain for colonial dominance in North America, the Caribbean, and India. By the terms of the peace treaty ending the Seven Years' War in 1763, France ceded Canada to the British, lost much of its territory in India, and gave up Louisiana to Spain. These losses constituted a diplomatic humiliation, but they translated into only minor economic disappointments because France's Caribbean colonies were much richer. France also retained control over two islands in the Indian Ocean, a small colony called Guiana on the northeast coast of South America, and a handful of bases in Africa for the slave trade that linked French port cities, the West African coastline, and the Caribbean islands. The French Caribbean colonies of Saint Domingue, Martinique, and Guadeloupe together made up twice the size in land area of the neighboring British Caribbean colonies. The French Caribbean colonies also produced nearly twice as much revenue in exports; the Caribbean colonies relied on slave labor to work large plantations that produced sugar, coffee, indigo (a vegetable dye), cacao, cotton, and tobacco. Saint Domingue, the western third of the island of Hispaniola (the remainder was Spanish), was the largest of the French Caribbean possessions, equaling in territory Martinique and Guadeloupe combined. Saint Domingue was the single most productive colony in the entire world in 1789, producing more wealth than the combined Spanish holdings in the New World.

The Colonies Under the Old Regime

The Caribbean colonies were located nearly 5,000 miles from France and were accessible only by a several weeks' voyage. As a result, they initially developed without much direction from the home country. The first white settlers of the mid-seventeenth century (who included some pirates) grew tobacco on relatively small plots of lands that over time grew to become large plantations cultivating indigo and sugar. Because sugar cultivation required intense labor, the slave system expanded. The district of Léogane typified the development of sugar plantations in Saint Domingue: in 1692 it had one sugar plantation, 54 indigo plantations, a few tobacco plantations, and a population of 973 whites and 625 slaves; by 1730, tobacco had disappeared, and the 59 sugar plantations now overshadowed the remaining 31 indigo plantations. The number of whites had fallen to 706, while the number of blacks had shot up to 7,646. In other words, as sugar displaced other crops, the population had increased fivefold, and the ratio of slaves to whites went from about 0.6 to 1, to nearly 11 to 1. By 1789, sugar production dominated in all the French Caribbean colonies. By that time, the ratio of slave to white was 8 to 1 in Martinique, 6.5 to 1 in Guadeloupe, and 15 to 1 in Saint Domingue.

> The interest of the French nation in supporting its commerce, preserving its colonies, and favoring their prosperity by every means compatible with the interests of the mainland has appeared to us, from every angle of vision, to be an incontestable truth.
> —Antoine-Pierre Barnave, Spokesman for the Colonial Committee of the National Assembly, 8 March 1790 (Document 4.2)

During the eighteenth century both slave trading and colonial commerce in the Caribbean expanded dramatically. In the "triangular system" established by Europeans to link their trade in African slaves to the establishment of plantations in the New World, Europeans exported manufactured goods (textiles, guns) to Africa, bought or captured slaves and transported them on their ships to the New World colonies, sold the slaves in the colonies and bought the staples produced on the plantations, and then shipped the raw goods back to Europe for refining and reshipment. Europeans also shipped and sold manufactured goods directly to the colonies. At the end of the seventeenth century, the French slave trade supplied the Caribbean colonies with only 1,000 or 2,000 slaves annually; by the 1780s, this had risen to an annual average of 37,000 slaves. By then, as many as one in eight French people depended in one way or another on colonial commerce for their livelihoods.

Between 1750 and 1789 the Caribbean colonies were virtually transformed by this rapid expansion of the slave trade; the slave population in the French Caribbean colonies doubled just in the twenty years before 1789. Ninety-nine slave ships arrived in Saint Domingue in 1789 alone. Between 1750 and 1789 the total population of Saint Domingue ballooned from 166,000 to 560,000. Martinique and Guadeloupe had smaller populations of about 100,000 each in 1789. The result of rapid growth, especially in Saint Domingue, was a society of extremes, in which recent arrivals from Africa made up a large proportion of the slave work force. There were 500,000 black slaves (89 percent of the total population) in Saint Domingue in 1789 and only 32,000 whites (6 percent), and 28,000 free people of color (5 percent of the population). The free people of color included both freed black slaves and mulattos, or people of mixed race. Free people of color could own plantations and slaves—they owned one-third of the plantations and one-fourth of the slaves in Saint Domingue—but they could not hold public office or practice most professions. It is worth noting that the Spanish portion of the island had a very different population mix: only 15,000 slaves, 40,000 whites, and as many as 80,000 free people of color. At the time, the entire United States had 700,000 slaves, the highest proportion of which—60 percent of the population—was in South Carolina.

As the number of slaves and the wealth of the colonies steadily increased, so too did the French presence. In 1685 Louis XIV published a "Black Code" to regulate slavery in the colonies. According to its provisions, non-Catholics could not own slaves, but in addition the law denied slaves any rights and privileges. They could not marry, sell produce, or gather in groups without their master's permission. They could not testify in court or carry weapons. A slave who struck a master or mistress was put to death. Those who ran away had their ears cut off and were branded on one shoul-

der; a second attempt was punished by cutting the hamstring muscle and branding the other shoulder; a third attempt was punished by death. (CD-ROM p. 129)

To maintain order the French government garrisoned some 4,000 to 5,000 troops in Saint Domingue with lesser forces in the other islands. After 1762 the government authorized companies of mulattos to hunt down runaway slaves. Whites, mulattos, and free blacks together formed local militia units to supplement the French army forces.

Because the number of slaves in Saint Domingue was so great and their conditions of life so harsh, an atmosphere of tension permeated the colony. Whites—and many mulattos—lived in dread of conspiracies among the slaves. The slaves developed a Creole language that combined French and various African tongues, and everyone born in Saint Domingue, whether black, white, or mulatto, could speak Creole. Many of the slaves practiced voodoo (vodun), a secret religious ritual. Médéric-Louis-Elie Moreau de Saint-Méry, a white lawyer born in Martinique who wrote at length on conditions in Saint Domingue, described the voodoo rituals: "One can see that fright has influenced them, to make them abandon the use of reason. In their transports of frenzy, they utter shouts, flee from other people's eyes, and excite pity. In a word, nothing is more dangerous, according to all the accounts, than this cult of

Voodoo." (CD-ROM p. 129) Despite fear of punishment, slaves frequently escaped (runaway slaves were called maroons) and formed outlaw bands and even permanent camps in the mountains. Those who stayed behind sometimes poisoned their masters, creating a paranoid fear among the planters. Faced with racial tension and a shortage of white women (there may have been five times as many white men as white women in Saint Domingue), white men turned to alcohol and prostitution. Two-thirds of the prostitutes in Saint Domingue were women of color. Saint Domingue attracted people who had a good reason to leave France; although it was a place where one might get rich quick, one might also die of a tropical disease, be poisoned by one's own slaves, or be done in by alcoholism, which reportedly was common. The average age at death for whites in the colony was thirty-eight.

Despite the manifest problems of life in a faraway tropical colony, white colonists worked hard to establish a society that resembled in every way—except slavery—life in mainland France. The biggest town in Saint Domingue, Cap Français, had 18,850 inhabitants in 1789, making it about the same size as Boston. It had a Catholic church, a convent, a prison, three poorhouses, a royal hospital, a theater that seated 1,500 people, a reading club, an official newspaper with 1,500 subscribers, two Masonic lodges, and a scientific society founded in 1784 that corresponded with its counterparts all over the world. The lodges and the scientific society showed that the Enlightenment had touched even the far-distant colonies. The Cercle des Philadelphes, the scientific society, investigated a wide range of scientific topics and aimed some of its efforts at increasing the profitability of slavery by improving the health of slaves.

From its very beginning, the slave trade had worried many Europeans. If according to Christianity all were equal in the eyes of God, how could some be enslaved by others? Agitation against the slave trade was slow to pick up steam, however, and became organized only after the 1770s. In Great Britain and the British North American colonies, the antislavery campaign had religious roots in evangelical Protestantism, especially among the Quakers. But in largely Catholic France, antislavery opinion drew most of its energies from the Enlightenment's very secular emphasis on the "rights of man," a concept that gained currency only in the 1760s.

The opening volley of the French antislavery campaign was Abbé Raynal's monumental history of European colonization, *Philosophical and Political History of the Settlements and Trade of the Europeans in the East and West Indies,* which was first published in 1770 but which more sharply attacked slavery in the 1780 edition and subsequent editions. Raynal and his collaborators (among them Diderot, editor of the *Encyclopedia*) denounced all the arguments based on custom or history that had been used to support slavery and even predicted a general slave revolt in the colonies. They detected signs of "the impending storm": "the Negroes want only a chief, sufficiently courageous, to lead them on to vengeance and slaughter." (CD-ROM p. 40) In 1785 Raynal published his *Essay on the Administration of Saint*

Domingue, in which he complained of the "pitiful degradation" of the slaves. But he saw no immediate prospects for improvement, much less abolition of either the slave trade or slavery.

Criticisms of the slave trade and of slavery as a labor system came from French writers living in France, not from the French living in the slave colonies. A leading disciple of the Enlightenment, the nobleman and philosopher Marie-Jean Caritat, Marquis de Condorcet, published a ringing condemnation of slavery in 1781, but he did so under a pseudonym, Mister Schwartz (*schwarz* is German for "black"). Condorcet denounced slavery as a crime because it deprived slaves of their rights. Because slavery qualified as a crime, the masters themselves enjoyed no rights over their slaves, he insisted. "It follows from our principles," he concluded, "that the inflexible justice to which kings and nations are subject like their citizens requires the destruction of slavery." Condorcet linked the fight against slavery to long-standing Enlightenment campaigns for abolition of legal torture, reform of the criminal law codes, and restoration of civil and political rights to the Calvinists. Colonists rejected these arguments. The permanent secretary of the Cercle des Philadelphes in Saint Domingue, Charles Arthaud, a physician born and educated in France, denounced the antislavery argument: "Some have even dared to discuss the emancipation of slaves in the colonies. If the specious reasoning brought in favor of this philosophical system could seduce our kings and rulers, the result would be that we would have to give up the colonies." The "license" and "insubordination" of freed slaves would cause social breakdown and overturn the natural order, which "destined" their masters to rule. Moreau de Saint-Méry described the African slaves in similarly negative terms as "indolent and idle, quarrelsome and talkative, and liars, and . . . addicted to stealing." Looking back a few years later, coffee planter P. J. Labourie insisted that the slave "would not labour" unless kept "in his natural state of thraldom." If proof was needed, revolutionary events in Saint Domingue provided them: "Here, let the philanthropic imprudent speculator [the abolitionist], view the present situation of things, correct his system, and profess contrition for the incalculable mischief he has done." (CD-ROM p. 130)

Despite the resistance of the colonists, abolitionist sentiment began to coalesce in the 1780s in Paris. Condorcet joined with other supporters of abolitionism to establish the Society of the Friends of Blacks in 1788, whose goal was to organize a public campaign against the slave trade and slavery itself. The Society was modeled on the London Committee for the Abolition of the Slave Trade, established the previous year, and its founders hoped that the French and the British might mount an international effort to eliminate the slave trade. The Friends of Blacks explicitly endorsed the idea of human rights; for its members the first of all truths was that "all men are born free and equal in rights." (CD-ROM p. 43) But in the constrained atmosphere of the monarchy the Society advanced its ideas only in the most tentative terms, knowing that the colonial and commercial interests invested in slavery still exercised great power. Few of the grievance lists composed in 1789 called for the abolition of slavery.

Revolution in the French Colonies

News of the fall of the Bastille on 14 July 1789 reached the Caribbean colonies in late September. But colonists had already been keeping track of developments in the home country. Planters in Saint Domingue had formed a committee in 1788 to petition for representation in the Estates General, and they sent delegates to Paris to make their case. The National Assembly granted them six deputies and eventually added deputies for Martinique and Guadeloupe. Because the white planters had excluded mulatto planters from their campaign, the mulattos of Saint Domingue promptly sent their own delegation to Paris.

> This Freedom, the greatest, the first of goods, is it made for all men?
> —Vincent Ogé, mulatto plantation-owner in Saint Domingue, in a pamphlet addressed to white planters sent as delegates to France, 1789
> (CD-ROM p. 43)

Vincent Ogé, a mulatto lawyer and slave-owner, presented the views of the mulatto delegates to the white planters who had come to Paris. He hoped to convince them that they shared many interests as property owners in the colonies. If they did not act in concert, if the whites did not grant equal rights to the free men of color, he warned, "we will see blood flowing, our lands invaded, the objects of our industry ravaged, our homes burnt, . . . the slave will raise the standard of the revolt, . . . commerce will be ruined, . . . we will lose everything." (CD-ROM p. 43) His appeal failed, for the white planters feared that any concession on the matter of color might set a dangerous precedent that would threaten the entire slave system.

Several prominent deputies in the National Assembly belonged to the Society of the Friends of Blacks, including the Marquis de Lafayette, whose experience with free black soldiers fighting for American independence made him suspicious of proslavery arguments. Faced with determined opposition to the abolition of either the slave trade or slavery, many deputies favorable to blacks turned instead to arguing that full civil and political rights be granted to free men of color in the colonies. This agitation created uncertainty in the colonies and raised expectations, especially among the free blacks and mulattos. In response, the white planters mounted their own counterattack and even began to contemplate demanding independence from France. In Cap Français, Moreau de Saint-Méry and Arthaud were expelled from the Cercle des Philadelphes—for being too favorable to the Revolution! Moreau de Saint-Méry had been in Paris at the time of the fall of the Bastille and taken a strong stand in support of the Revolution. The Cercle members wanted to punish Arthaud for seeming too favorable to the slaves; even while supporting the slave system, he had urged planters to treat their slaves with greater kindness. The other white planters now saw them both as traitors. The planters forced the leading royal officials to flee to France, and they put in motion plans to form an autonomous colonial assembly.

Less is known about the views of the slaves because hardly any of them could read and write, but the royal governor of Saint Domingue expressed his worries about the effects of the Revolution on them. In October 1789 he reported that the slaves considered the new revolutionary cockade of red, white, and blue a "signal of the manumission of the whites. . . . the blacks all share an idea that struck them spontaneously: that the white slaves killed their masters and now free they govern themselves and regain possession of the land"—in other words, the black slaves hoped to follow in the footsteps of their white predecessors, freeing themselves, killing their masters, and taking the land.

The governor of Guadeloupe was less specific but no less worried. In October 1789 he wrote back to Paris: "We must expect strange revolutions. Not only must we fear an insurrection by the whites but even one by our natural enemies [the slaves], whose behavior suggests hidden cabals." The slaves got their information about revolutionary events in France from former slaves who worked the many ships coming into the colonies and from slaves who worked at the docks unloading and loading the vessels.

As divisions hardened in the colonies, debate over slavery intensified in Paris. Letters, speeches, and petitions from the port cities on the Atlantic reminded the deputies in Paris that a major source of French wealth was endangered by such talk. In one such letter, a spokesman for the Chamber of Commerce of Nantes complained directly to Condorcet, who became president of the Society of the Friends of Blacks. "Consider the sixty million [francs] profit from their exports each year," he cautioned. And keep in mind that "our eternal rival [Britain]" would be eager to seize the opportunity to increase its "world-wide domination" (Document 4.1). The abolitionist side did not give in to these complaints. Jean-Louis Viefville des Essars echoed a growing chorus that proclaimed slavery to be "a violation of all the laws of society and of humanity." He offered a plan for gradual emancipation of the slaves (Document 4.5).

To quiet the unrest among the powerful white planters, especially in Saint Domingue, the colonial committee of the National Assembly proposed in March 1790 to exempt the colonies from the constitution and to prosecute anyone who attempted to prompt uprisings against the slave system. The spokesman for the committee, Antoine-Pierre Barnave, a lawyer from Grenoble (a city with no direct colonial interests), explained that France must preserve its colonies in order to maintain its commercial position: "Abandon the colonies, and these sources of prosperity will disappear or diminish" (Document 4.2). The majority of deputies shared his sentiments. Barnave would continue to support colonial interests, but by September 1791 he himself found the colonial regime problematic: "This regime [in the colonies] is oppressive, but it gives a livelihood to several million Frenchmen. This regime is barbarous but a still greater barbarity will result if you interfere with it without the necessary knowledge."

The decision of the National Assembly did not end the abolitionist campaign. Radical newspapers in Paris denounced the white planters and advocated the granting of political rights to men of color and the eventual abolition of the slave trade and slavery. In September 1790 the *Révolutions de Paris* predicted that Enlightenment-inspired principles would eventually triumph: "As for the slave trade and the slavery of Negroes, the European governments will find it useless to oppose the cries of philosophy and the principles of universal liberty that germinate and spread throughout nations" (Document 4.3). The next month the paper went back on the attack again: "It is not true that Negroes are narrow-minded. . . . As for what people say of their wickedness, it will never equal the cruelty of their masters" (Document 4.4). The Revolution in France and the responses it evoked in the colonies had brought the problem of racism out into the open.

The National Assembly may have satisfied the white planters, but it had done nothing about the political rights of free men of color, who continued to press their demands both in Paris and in Saint Domingue. When whites began lynching mulattos who publicly demanded rights, the mulattos prepared an insurrection. Ogé returned home in October 1790 to lead 350 mulattos in an attack on Cap Français. French army troops cooperated with local planter militias to defeat and arrest them. In February 1791 Ogé and other mulatto leaders were publicly executed. But the event did not go unremarked in Paris. Ogé had joined the Society of the Friends of Blacks and had become friendly with the leaders of the abolitionist movement in London. His martyrdom to freedom was commemorated in a play performed to packed houses in Paris, and supporters of rights for free men of color now demanded the floor in the National Assembly. Robespierre boldly proclaimed, "Perish the colonies if the price is to be your happiness, your glory, your liberty." On 15 May 1791, under renewed pressure from the Society of the Friends of Blacks, the National Assembly granted political rights to all free blacks and mulattos who were born of free mothers and fathers. Although this proviso limited rights to a few hundred men, the deputies rescinded the decree a few months later on 24 September 1791, having decided to leave such decisions up to local colonial authorities—for the moment.

In the midst of this political struggle, the entire situation changed dramatically when on 22 August 1791 the slaves of Saint Domingue rose in revolt. The signal was reportedly given by Boukman Dutty, a coach driver and high priest of voodoo, during a nocturnal voodoo ceremony. Within a few days, half the sugarcane plantations near Cap Français had been burned to the ground. On 12 October 1791 the *Pennsylvania Gazette* in Philadelphia published a letter written on 28 August that detailed the devastation: "No longer than Monday last, this great space [the plain extending thirty miles from Cap Français] was filled with beautiful villas, elegant seats, and nearly the whole covered with sugarcane; the greatest part of which are laid and now laying in ashes. Almost the whole is destroyed!" (CD-ROM p. 136) All the horrors predicted by Raynal were now realized as the slaves wreaked their vengeance on their masters with pillage, rape, torture, mutilation, and death. In retaliation, whites massacred black prisoners as they were being escorted by soldiers back to town. Within weeks as many as 100,000 slaves joined the revolt, burning down 180 sugar plantations and hundreds of coffee and indigo plantations.

The slave revolt made the position of mulattos even more critical, because they were plantation and slave owners too. The governor of Guadeloupe reinforced the plantation patrols, worried that "the free [men of color] might form a party with the slaves and that this colony too will become in its turn the theater of a massacre." In Martinique the white planters granted mulattos the vote. They could afford this gesture of generosity because whites in Martinique outnumbered mulattos two to one, and in Guadeloupe more than four to one. In Saint Domingue, however, where whites and mulattos were about equal in number, the whites refused to extend rights to mulattos, a move that prompted the mulattos once again to take up arms against the whites. As the revolt spread, the French colonists appealed to the British governor of Jamaica for help. The planters blamed the abolitionists for the revolt. The abolitionists traced it instead to the refusal to grant rights to mulattos.

In the hope of gaining the support of mulattos for French authority, the newly elected Legislative Assembly finally granted civil and political rights to the free men of color at the end of March 1792. By now the deputies had recognized that they faced an unprecedented and dangerous situation. In the debate in the Legislative Assembly, Armand-Guy Kersaint, a former noble and slave-owner, explained why he now favored rights for free men of color: "The moment has arrived," he insisted, "to change the social system of the colonies, to reintegrate into it humankind" (Document 4.6). The Assembly had to grant rights to free men of color, he argued, if France was to check the spreading slave revolt and stop the white colonists from seeking foreign aid to gain their independence from France. Slave owners in the United States shared the alarm about the situation. On 16 May 1792 the *Pennsylvania Gazette* published a letter from Cap Français written on 15 April: "We are willing to hope that the ocean which surrounds Hispaniola will check the extension of the spirit of revolt; for,

 if it should become general through the islands, it will require almost half Europe to subdue it." (CD-ROM p. 136)

Even though the Legislative Assembly left slavery untouched and showed its determination to put down the slave revolt by dispatching 6,000 men from France, the white planters would not compromise and accept free men of color as fellow citizens. After France declared war on Great Britain in January 1793, the white planters in both Saint Domingue and Martinique made agreements with British agents to declare British sovereignty over the islands. To complicate matters further, Spain, which controlled the rest of the island of Hispaniola and had joined Great Britain in the war against France, offered freedom to individual slave rebels who joined them as long as they agreed to maintain the slave regime for the other blacks. The British invaded Martinique in June 1793, the Spanish invaded Saint Domingue from across

Fig. 4.1 Toussaint L'Ouverture

A slave inspired by the French Revolution's egalitarianism, Toussaint rose rapidly to prominence and agreed to fight for the French if they abolished slavery. Nonetheless, he had no intention of letting whites rule, for he wanted blacks to control their own destinies. By 1801 he had conquered Saint Domingue for France and for his fellow slaves.

their common border, and the British joined the effort in Saint Domingue soon after. By March 1794 the British had gained control of both Martinique and Guadeloupe. The British expected that their conquests would soon pay for themselves.

With the rebel slaves of Saint Domingue joining the Spanish armies in droves, the French troops were clearly outnumbered. In any case, only 3,500 French soldiers remained, and many of them were ill or ready to desert. To prevent complete military disaster, the French commissioner in Saint Domingue freed all the slaves in his jurisdiction in August 1793, acting without permission from the government at home. In February 1794, overcoming fears that abolition was a British plot, the National Convention formally abolished slavery and granted full rights to all black men in the colonies. Although these actions risked alienating the United States as well as all the

European colonial powers, they had the desired effect in Saint Domingue. One of the ablest black generals allied with the Spanish, the ex-slave François-Dominique Toussaint L'Ouverture (Fig. 4.1), changed sides and committed his troops to the French. The National Convention ordered an expeditionary force to sail for the Caribbean and free the slaves on the other islands by force. The tide had turned.

In the summer of 1794 the French gradually retook Martinique and Guadeloupe. Victor Hugues, sent by the Convention with the expeditionary force, first defeated the royalists in Guadeloupe and then freed the slaves and enrolled them in army units to fight the British. He brought with him a guillotine, which he used to execute royalists, and a printing press, which he set to work making copies in Spanish, Portuguese, Dutch, and English of revolutionary decrees and the Declaration of the Rights of Man and Citizen. French agents set off to try to provoke slave uprisings in British, Spanish, Portuguese, and Dutch colonies. Hugues dispatched 500 French soldiers to the British island of Saint Vincent to help a coalition of mulattos, slaves, and black Caribs (born of shipwrecked slaves and natives) fight the British. In 1795 the Spanish ceded the eastern part of Hispaniola to the French. Faced with the prospect of turning tables, the British sent 100 ships and 30,000 men to the Caribbean and managed to retake Saint Vincent. But their efforts to capture Saint Domingue failed. The French had few troops of their own, but they had the increasingly disciplined forces of Toussaint. In 1798 the British negotiated their withdrawal directly with Toussaint. By then they had suffered 60,000 casualties.

The French had appointed Toussaint governor of Saint Domingue as a reward for his efforts, but he had effectively established his control without them. Toussaint fascinated everyone who met him and remains one of the most compelling of historical figures. Born a slave but freed by his owner, he had learned to read and write and reportedly read the writings of Raynal (a bust of Raynal adorned the governor's palace). Through marriage, he acquired a plantation that was worked by a dozen or more slaves. He gradually made a name for himself during the fighting after the outbreak of the revolt. He took the slogans of the French Revolution for his own: "I want liberty and equality to reign in Saint Domingue." His secretaries (usually whites) prepared his decrees, letters, and proclamations. His staff of advisers included whites and mulattos, but to firmly establish his authority he eventually forced many of the leading mulattos to leave the island. He feared, with reason, that mulattos—many of whom were slave and plantation owners—wanted at least to maintain their superiority over the slaves, if not maintain the slave system itself. The mulattos went to France. Most of the officers in Toussaint's army were former slaves, though a handful were white or mulatto.

The country Toussaint governed in 1800 hardly resembled what it had been a mere decade before. The vicious fighting and the flight of whites left the economy in ruins: in 1800 only 10,000 whites remained, as many as one-third of the former slaves had died in the fighting, and the plantations produced only one-fifth of what they had in

1789. Toussaint relied on his generals to exercise control over the freed slaves. Army officers or officials took over the plantations and kept all those working in agriculture under military discipline. General Jean-Jacques Dessalines, for example, personally expropriated thirty-three sugar plantations. He and other generals soon amassed great fortunes. The former slaves were bound to their plantations like serfs and forced to work in exchange for an autonomous family life and the right to maintain personal garden plots. Hugues set up a similar agricultural regime in Guadeloupe.

Toussaint remained in charge until 1802, when France's new ruler, Napoleon Bonaparte, sent 16,000 French soldiers to regain control of the island. Among the generals sent by the French were two of the mulattos Toussaint had forced out of Saint Domingue. Bonaparte's wife, Josephine, owned plantations in Saint Domingue and Martinique. Moreau de Saint-Méry, who had spent years in exile in Philadelphia, had returned to France and was now a member of Bonaparte's Council of State. The French arrested Toussaint and transported him to France, where he died in prison in 1803.

Toussaint instantly became a hero to abolitionists everywhere. The first historian of Haiti, Marcus Rainsford, hailed Toussaint's character: "If during this early period of his life, the black general had shone conspicuously, through every disadvantage, with the brightest talents and the milder virtues, he now rose superior to all around him, with the qualities and rank of an exalted chief. Every part of his conduct was marked by judgment and benevolence." (CD-ROM p. 135) One French general called him "the Negro, the Spartacus foretold by Raynal, whose destiny it was to avenge the wrongs committed on his race."

Bonaparte intended to restore slavery and the slave trade in the Caribbean. He succeeded quickly in Martinique, because there the slave plantations remained intact. Armed force was required in Guadeloupe. Although Victor Hugues had been replaced as governor in 1798, former slaves had taken over many plantations, and they now fought the French soldiers alongside the black general Louis Delgrès. After Delgrès was killed in battle, the French left the black soldiers free but promptly returned all those working the plantations to their former status. Saint Domingue proved to be a different story. Fighting continued there after the capture of Toussaint, and the French suffered heavy casualties. The French soldiers who survived the fighting began to succumb to yellow fever. In November 1802 the commander of the French forces died of the disease.

In a last, desperate effort to enforce his will on Saint Domingue, Bonaparte sent yet another 15,000 troops, who in frustration began to massacre everyone in their path (Fig. 4.2). The remaining black generals joined together under the leadership of Dessalines and now openly fought for an independent republic. In November 1804 the remaining French had to beg the British navy to evacuate them as prisoners of war. They and their white colonist collaborators sailed to Jamaica. The whites left behind were slaughtered by the black soldiers. In all, Bonaparte had sent 35,000 soldiers to

The Mode of exterminating the Black Army, as practised by the French

Fig. 4.2   The Mode of Exterminating the Black Army

When Napoleon sent his troops to reconquer Saint Domingue in 1802, a bloody war ensued. This print shows the French throwing their prisoners overboard. Although the French captured Toussaint, they ultimately lost the colony, which proclaimed its independence as Haiti in 1804.

Saint Domingue: 20,000 died of disease and 8,000 died in battle. No less than nineteen white generals died in the futile effort to recapture Saint Domingue.

The victorious generals formally declared the independence of the new republic of Haiti on 31 December 1804. Dessalines, an ex-slave, had already had himself crowned emperor, using a crown given to him by merchants in Philadelphia. He faced even more severe problems than those confronted by Toussaint. After setting up an imperial court that siphoned off most of the available tax revenues, he was assassinated in 1806, inaugurating a long period of political instability and economic uncertainty. Thirteen years of brutal military struggle had made armed force the primary determinant of power, leading to a continuing history of military conspiracies and coups. The economic structure of the country changed dramatically because the ex-slaves preferred to farm individual plots, a shift that made production of such cash crops as sugar nearly impossible. Yet with peace the population recovered and began to grow rapidly in numbers.

The French Revolution brought the message of freedom to the colonies. Paradoxically, the message took root most firmly in the colony with the largest number of slaves, Saint Domingue. The prized jewel of the Caribbean, the richest colony of them all, proved to be the hardest to retain. The huge number of recently arrived African slaves, the relatively small number of whites, and the competition between whites and free people of color combined together to make Saint Domingue the one place where the chains of slavery were broken. The French broadcast the message of liberty and equality but it was the black Haitians who defended that message against the French themselves. The formerly enslaved of Saint Domingue would not give up their hard-won freedom, even when the French turned their backs on the concepts they had done so much to promote.

Documents

SLAVERY AND THE REVOLUTION

The liberty and legal equality promised by the Declaration of Rights of Man and Citizen seemed to undermine the validity of slavery, yet French legislators initially rejected any idea of emancipation. Under pressure from colonists and merchants in France, the deputies decided to treat the colonies separately—that is, to maintain the slave trade and slave labor. They defended their decision as economically and politically necessary: France's economy depended on the slave trade and plantation production in colonies, and change would only benefit Great Britain, France's chief colonial rival. As the slave revolt in Saint Domingue spread, abolitionist arguments in Paris gained more force until they finally prevailed in 1794.

Document 4.1: Letter from Monseron de l'Aunay to the Marquis de Condorcet, President of the Society of the Friends of Blacks (24 December 1789)

This letter appears in the *Journal de Paris* as part of a debate over a performance of a play by noted feminist Olympe de Gouges, that concerns the abolition of the slave trade. The letter is written by a deputy of the Chamber of Commerce of the port city of Nantes, which had close ties to the Caribbean economy. He would like to protect French interests against potential British incursion.

Source: Supplement to the *Journal de Paris,* vol. 362 (28 December 1789).

> You send me alarming news from our sugar islands, principally from Saint Domingue. The inhabitants of that island may all be currently being held at knife point by the Negroes in revolt.
>
> Perverse men abuse the purity of your intentions, criminally interpreting the decrees of the National Assembly and making their treacherous plans undo what humanity and liberty have done for the happiness of its citizens in another hemisphere. In the name of this humanity, of which

you are a worthy apostle, and in the name of the homeland that counts you among its best citizens, I beg you sir, add your voice to the cries of pain of all the residents of our islands, of the colonial land-owners living in France, and of the uncountable mass of Frenchmen who live off the commerce of the colonies. Consider that these colonies are France's destiny. Consider the sixty million [*francs*] profit from their exports each year, and the enormous importance of the income already lost. Consider that their capital of three billion [*francs*] is the sacred property of their owners, and that this capital is the security against the four-hundred million [*francs*] that they owe continental France. Consider that six million men live there along with eighty-thousand Frenchmen, and that half of France would be plunged into sadness and misery [if the islands were lost].

Our eternal rival [Britain], whose ambitious policies may be having them underhandedly sharpen their swords, smile at our misfortunes and, beneath this horrible rubble, foresee the scepter of their world-wide domination that no human force would be able to take from them.

We must not wait Sir, for verified reports to confirm our misfortunes. By the time the first spark will have reached us, the fire will have consumed everything. Five hundred leagues away, doubt is more awful than certainty. There are no words to gauge the horrified imagination and public terror that lead the best minds astray. The suspension of all work and a long delay in the contribution of a fortune so uncertain, are but a faint sketch of the ills that are easier felt than expressed.

Let us meet then Sir, to beg the National Assembly to protect the life and property of the French, and by a solemn decree arm the executive power with the fullness of the force [and] enjoin them to make sure that the Colonies are not damaged in the least.

SIGNED, MONSERON DE L'AUNAY.

Document 4.2: Barnave, Speech for the Colonial Committee of the National Assembly (8 March 1790)

Here Antoine-Pierre Barnave, a well-connected and influential lawyer from Grenoble, spoke for the Colonial Committee, which advocated separate treatment for the colonies. The committee took the side of the colonists, insisting that France's prosperity depended on maintaining the current slave system of plantation production. Barnave's proposals were adopted almost without debate.

Source: The materials listed below appeared originally in *The French Revolution and Human Rights: A Brief Documentary History,* translated, edited, and with an introduction by Lynn Hunt (Boston/New York: Bedford/St. Martin's, 1996), 109–11.

The interest of the French nation in supporting its commerce, preserving its colonies, and favoring their prosperity by every means compatible with the interests of the mainland has appeared to us, from every angle of vision, to be an incontestable truth. . . .

Abandon the colonies, and these sources of prosperity will disappear or diminish.

Abandon the colonies, and you will import, at great price, from foreigners what they buy today from you.

Abandon the colonies at the moment when your establishments there are based on possessing them, and listlessness will replace activity, misery abundance: the mass of workers, of useful and hardworking citizens, will pass quickly from a state of ease into the most deplorable situation; finally, agriculture and our finances will soon be struck by the same disaster experienced in commerce and manufactures. . . .

You should only, you can only speak here one language, that of truth, which consists in disavowing the false extension that has been given [to some of your decrees]. You have not been able to change anything in all of what concerns the colonies, for the laws that you have decreed did not have them in mind; you have not been able to change anything because public security and humanity itself would offer insurmountable obstacles to what your hearts might have inspired in you [the abolition of the slave trade or slavery itself]. Let us say it then at this moment, since doubts have been raised: you have broken no new ground. This declaration will suffice; it can leave no alarm remaining. It is only just to accompany it with an arrangement suitable for reassuring the colonies against those who, with criminal plots, would seek to bring trouble there, to excite uprisings there. These men whom some have affected to confuse with peaceful citizens occupied with seeking through reflection means for softening the destiny of the most unfortunate portion of the human race [the slaves], these men, I say, only have perverse motives and can only be considered as enemies of France and of humanity. . . .

Here then, Sirs, is the project for a decree that your committee has unanimously voted to propose to you:

The National Assembly, deliberating on the addresses and petitions from the cities of commerce and manufacturing, on the items recently arrived from Saint Domingue and Martinique, addressed to it by the Minister of the Marine, and on the representations made by the deputies from the colonies,

Declares that, considering the colonies as a part of the French empire, and desiring to enable them to enjoy the fruits of the happy regeneration that has been accomplished in the empire, it never intended to include them in the constitution that it has decreed for the kingdom or to subject them to laws which might be incompatible with their particular, local proprieties. . . .

Moreover, the National Assembly declares that it never intended to introduce innovations into any of the branches of indirect or direct commerce between France and its colonies [thus it leaves the slave trade untouched] and hereby puts the colonists and their properties under the special protection of the nation and declares criminal, toward the nation, whoever works to excite uprisings against them. Judging favorably the motives that have inspired the citizens of the said colonies, it declares that there is no reason to pursue them for any charge [there had been widespread agitation among the planters to establish greater independence from Paris]; it expects from their patriotism the maintenance of public peace and an inviolable fidelity to the nation, the law, and the king.

Document 4.3: A Left-Wing Newspaper Links the Revolution to the Abolition of Slavery (September 1790)

During the explosion of newspaper publishing after 1789, the *Révolutions de Paris* consistently supported radical positions, including the abolition of slavery in articles like this one entitled "No Color Bar."

Source: Les Révolutions de Paris, no. 63 (5 September 1790), 523–24.

However, it is not that we thought that the patriots of the colonies are yet up to the level of the principles of the French Revolution. Everybody wants them to have liberty, but they refuse the right of citizenship to colored people, and they want to perpetuate slavery and the slave trade. It is true that the aristocrats have included colored people in their party; but they do so only in order to oppress the friends of the constitution, firmly resolved to leave them in contempt, and to add to their chains when they think they can do without them.

As for the slave trade and the slavery of Negroes, the European governments will find it useless to oppose the cries of philosophy and the principles of universal liberty that germinate and spread throughout the nations. Let them learn that it is never in vain for people to be shown the truth, and that once the impetus is given, they must totally give way to the flood that will wash away the old abuses. The new order of things will rise up despite all the precautions that have been taken to prevent it. Yes! We dare to predict with confidence that the time will come, and that day is not far off, when you will see a frizzy-haired African, with no other recommendation than his good sense and his virtues, come and participate in the legislative process at the heart of our national assemblies.

Document 4.4: A Left-Wing Newspaper Continues the Attack on Slavery (October 1790)

In this article the influential newspaper *Révolutions de Paris* asks whether Africans and their descendants are "born to slavery" as part of a general consideration of the situation in the French colonies.

Source: *Les Révolutions de Paris,* no. 66 (9–16 October 1790), 13–17.

> But it is said that Negroes are a type of men born to slavery . . . they are narrow-minded, deceitful, and wicked. Even they admit to the superiority of Whites, and almost to the legality of their state.
>
> It is not true that Negroes are narrow-minded. Experience has proven that they have succeeded in the sciences, and if the mindlessness in which they are plunged makes them believe that Whites are a superior race, liberty will soon bring them up to the same level. As for what people say of their wickedness, it will never equal the cruelty of their masters.

Document 4.5: Viefville des Essars, On the Emancipation of the Negroes (1790)

This bold project to free the slaves in the French colonies was presented to the National Assembly. The vast majority of deputies opposed abolition of slavery or the slave trade until 1794, when France faced the loss of its colonies.

Source: Jean-Louis Viefville des Essars, *Discours et projet de loi pour l'affranchissement des negrès ou l'adoucissement de leur régime, et réponse aux objections des colons* (Paris, n.d.).

> Freedom is the first right that man receives from nature. It is a sacred and inalienable right, and nothing should take it from him. Slavery is therefore nothing more than an abuse of power.
>
> France has had the good fortune of seeing [slavery] disappear from its continent. But unjustly, it had the cruelty to establish it in its colonies. It is a violation of all the laws of society and of humanity. If ever there is an opportunity to banish this barbarous abuse from French soil, if ever an opportunity presents itself to break the chains of slavery, it is no doubt now at a moment when man is more imbued than ever with the truth that all men are equal in the eyes of their Creator and before the eternal law that an invisible hand has inscribed in their hearts. It is at this moment

that all their efforts to abolish and erase to the last trace of their former enslavement come together.

Gentlemen, it seems to me that the time has come to present to you possibly the largest, the most noble, and most dignified of projects for posterity which alone could immortalize this august body—the abolition of slavery.

Raise up the nature of man degraded and demeaned, return man to his dignity, restore to him his basic rights . . . this is an action worthy of French generosity. Atone for so many centuries of this affront to humanity, and, if possible, erase all crimes of cupidity. It is an act worthy of our sense of justice.

Already a rival nation, which has so many claims to our esteem, has taken care of this matter. Let us take heed of its generous scope. The task of setting this important example is up to France, it is up to you Sirs, and it will earn you the homage and veneration of the whole world. I admit it . . . the heart is seduced and drawn to such a beautiful and noble enterprise. It is so very pleasant to exercise charity by placing alms into the hands of the poor and spread happiness there. It is impossible not to feel, I would not say pity and compassion, but rather tenderness, and a powerful interest in those poor unfortunate people, those unhappy victims of our excesses and of our insatiable and cruel avarice.

There is no kind of cruelty or barbarity to which they [the slaves] have not been exposed, nor is there any hideous crime which we have not committed towards them. The most horrendous of means are used to make the slave trade profitable. We incite war and carnage in their country, and by the lure of a few trivial items, we purchase the awful right to enchain them and treat them like a vile herd of cattle. . . .

[He then traces the horrors of slave ships and chattel auctions. Then Essars begins enumerating the reasons for abolishing the slave trade and concludes with a draft of the law abolishing the trade:]

Article I. Slavery shall be and shall remain abolished in every country under French rule in the manner described in the following articles. Men, arriving there, shall be free and shall there enjoy all of their rights.

II. The slave trade is and shall remain abolished upon publication of this decree. All Blacks who arrive or who are brought to French colonies or to any other part of the realm, by any means or by any person, shall be free six months after said publication.

III. All of the slaves currently residing in the French colonies shall be successively freed and placed at liberty over a sixteen year period, one-sixteenth each year, the first being freed upon publication of this decree.

IV. Slaves above the age of seventy shall be the first to be freed. However they shall remain the charges of their masters who shall be required to feed and care for them, or to provide an annual stipend for their feeding and care in a charity home that shall be built for that purpose.

V. Married slaves who have the most children shall be the next to be freed, and freedom shall be granted to all members of the family at the same time. As freed fathers and mothers, their children cannot be slaves.

VI. Children on a property below the age of fifteen having neither father nor mother shall continue to be raised and fed until the time established for the complete end of slavery. Then, steps shall be taken to provide for their subsistence and any payments that may be due to the masters that have fed them, without their making a profit from it.

VII. All Blacks who have worked for twenty years on the same property or who are forty years of age and not able to earn a living and who prefer to remain shall be fed. This shall also apply to the disabled and ill on a property. If they do not like their masters, their subsistence shall be paid for in the charity home to be built.

VIII. The slaves who shall be freed shall enjoy, from that moment on, all of the benefits of the law to contract, sell, purchase and make commerce as well as all of the other rights of a citizen.

IX. From this day, the Black Code is and shall remain abolished and repealed as inhuman and barbarous. It is forbidden for property foremen, masters, and slave drivers to punish [Blacks] or have them punished, or to arbitrarily strike them or have them struck by reason of their authority for any motive or pretext. And it is forbidden for any person to claim the right to inflict any sort of punishment on [the Blacks], and from this moment on they are placed under the protection of the law.

X. A legal system shall be established in each quarter that shall be made up of eight notables who, without remuneration, will deal exclusively with the problems concerning the Blacks in conformance with the law which shall be passed. The notables must be a majority of five in order to pass judgment.

XI. The master who has reason to complain about his slave may not dispense his own justice as stated in Article IX at the risk of punishment in accordance with the requirements of the case. He shall be required to refer to the system of justice previously mentioned.

XII. Blacks shall be allowed to marry amongst themselves regardless of their master's opposition. That is to say those who profess the Catholic religion in accordance with the conventions prescribed by the Church and the laws of the realm, the others following the conventions established for non-Catholics. The master to whom the man belongs shall be obliged to purchase the woman should she belong to another master, or, if he prefers, may sell the other master his Black at a set price, in order that [the couple] may live together. They shall be given a separate cabana.

XIII. It is expressly forbidden to require the wife to work during the last six weeks of her pregnancy and during the first six weeks after delivery.

XIV. The master who best treats those living on his property shall receive a reward that shall be decided by factoring in how many children were born there and the number and gender of his slaves.

XV. Property belonging to all persons of color who die without children and without having disposed of their property shall be given to the black family having the most children who have neither property nor means of subsistence. If the property is large, it shall be divided in as many portions as deemed necessary for each family. The poorest, and those with the most children, shall receive preference.

XVI. If there are infertile or abandoned grounds that are applicable, they shall be divided and distributed as those identified in the previous Article and it shall be passed to new colonists if deemed necessary for the first year of ground clearing.

XVII. The commissioners chosen and appointed to oversee the execution of this decree, shall see to the means of ensuring the subsistence of the newly-freed slaves, in order to attach them to the soil through ownership, and to [seal] the principles of humanity and justice, with all that those ideas can bring to the safety and prosperity of the colonies.

Document 4.6: Kersaint, "Discussion of Troubles in the Colonies" (28 March 1792)

This speech by a former noble who had served as a naval officer reveals the deep ambivalence of the deputies about moving too quickly to emancipate the slaves. Caught between the planters, who threatened to rebel if emancipation was passed, and the dangerous slave revolt that had already broken out, Kersaint hoped for a gradual process of emancipation that would help France hold on to its most valuable colony. He was later executed during the Terror.

Source: The materials listed below appeared originally in *The French Revolution and Human Rights: A Brief Documentary History,* translated, edited, and with an introduction by Lynn Hunt (Boston/New York: Bedford/St. Martin's, 1996), 112–15.

Your fears are of three kinds: the first, the revolt of the slaves; the second, that [white planters in Saint Domingue] not call upon foreigners and not wish to make [the colony] independent; the third, that it not protest against national power [the power of the assembly] in order to only recognize royal authority. In effect, the reasons for these different fears are well-founded, but how will you succeed in dissipating them? One sole means should suffice.

There exists in Saint Domingue a numerous class of men who love France, who cherish the new laws, who are in general honest, enlightened, hardworking men who live in a state of few means from the fruits of their daily labor and who owe no debts [poor whites]. This class is reinforced by that of the free black property owning men; this is the party of the National Assembly in this island; this is the class that must be supported by all means combined. [He then goes on to attack the 24 September 1791 decree rescinding the political rights of free blacks.] . . .

It cannot be denied that when the French nation proclaimed these sacred words, "Men are born and remain free and equal in rights," it did not break the chains of humankind. The action of this truth, which ought to level the world, had to first fall on us. The fears of our colonists are therefore well-founded in that they have everything to fear from the influence of our Revolution on their slaves. The rights of man overturn the system on which rests their fortunes. No one should be surprised therefore that [the colonists] have become the most ardent enemies of the rights of man; they are right to read in them their condemnation. . . .

I do not belong to the Society of the Friends of Blacks. But, as a friend of all men, I am not indifferent to the goal of the work of this society. The improvement of the lot of the Africans, transported to the European colonies, always appeared to me to be the most worthy subject for exciting the zeal of any being born sensitive to the sufferings of his fellow man. . . .

I lived for a long time in the colonies. I have owned black slaves; a part of my fortune is still in that country; and I cannot therefore wish for the destruction of it. Planters who read me, tell yourselves: He has the same interests as us and his opinions are different; let us see, let us examine; at issue here are the most cherished interests of life, and partiality and prejudice are capable of losing everything irrevocably. . . .

The moment has arrived to change the social system of the colonies, to reintegrate into it humankind, and in this greater view will be found the salvation of all the interested parties, justice and utility, interest and glory.

The free men of color demand justice: the rights of citizens in all their extension will be accorded to them. The colonists will no longer refuse them; they will remember that misfortune makes men sensitive, that those men whom they push away are their sons, their brothers, their nephews. They will honor finally the breast that nourished them, no matter what the color, and this first act of justice will guide them toward another, virtues following from each other as do vices.

Among the slaves you will call to freedom pure and simple all the artisans whose names will be furnished by their former masters, on the sole condition of a tax by head, which you will convert into an indemnity for those whom they made rich in the past.

The Negroes born in the colonies will then be called without distinction to the enjoyment of conditional liberty. It will have as its base the obligation to be reunited on the land of their former masters and to work there for them for a fixed time, after which they will enjoy liberty on the same conditions as the artisan Negroes. I think that this term can be fixed at ten years for those who are 30 years old or older, and at fifteen years for those who are less than 30 years old. But only the Negro fathers of families should be called to enjoy this advantage; the others should be held to 20 years of work. . . .

Every Negro who has come from Africa, is married for at least 10 years, has a garden in good order and six children, will enjoy first freedom for three days work a week along with his wife. After 20 years of marriage and with four children still living, they will be considered freed . . . ; their children will enjoy the same advantages at 25 years of age, and their grandchildren will be free without conditions. . . .

But some will ask if I am keeping or destroying the slave trade? My pen refuses to trace those words: "You will buy men," but this trade can change character, and the effect of the law that I propose for the colonies would modify the most odious part. It would no longer be slaves that you would export from Africa but farmers, inhabitants that you would abduct from their tyrants to educate them one day by work and instruction to the dignity of free men.

5

The Rise and Fall of Napoleon Bonaparte, 1799–1815

THE NATION MUST HAVE A HEAD, A HEAD RENDERED
ILLUSTRIOUS BY GLORY AND NOT BY THEORIES OF
GOVERNMENT, FINE PHRASES, OR THE TALK OF IDEALISTS,
OF WHICH THE FRENCH UNDERSTAND NOT A WHIT.
— NAPOLEON BONAPARTE'S CONVERSATION DURING
THE ITALIAN CAMPAIGN (1 JUNE 1796) AS REPORTED BY
ANDRÉ-FRANÇOIS MIOT DE MELITO, SPECIAL MINISTER
FROM THE DIRECTORY TO PIEDMONT

(CD-ROM p. 141)

Napoleon Bonaparte was one of those rare individuals in history who towered over an era. He fundamentally reshaped the political landscape of the nineteenth century. He came to prominence as a general in the 1790s, became supreme leader of the French Republic in 1799, then made himself emperor of the French in 1804. He ended the democratic revolution and installed the first modern police state, yet he maintained many of the administrative and legal changes inaugurated by the revolutionaries. Bonaparte's military conquests—and failures—had far-reaching effects. By 1810 he ruled most of western Europe and had much of eastern Europe at his feet, but he lost France's most important colony in the Caribbean, sold the Louisiana Territory to the United States, and failed to dislodge the British from India. Wherever he triumphed he redrew political boundaries, abolished feudalism, and instituted legal equality, even for religious minorities. Like most military conquerors, however, Napoleon did not stop while he was ahead. His armies of occupation, demands for tribute, and reckless disregard for local customs eventually provoked resistance and opened the way to his defeat. Although his sixteen-year rule was relatively short, in combination with the innovations of the 1790s it transformed European politics and diplomacy forever.

Napoleon's Rise to Power

Napoleon Bonaparte was an unlikely candidate for conqueror of Europe and emperor of the French. Short and physically unimpressive, he spoke French with an accent because he was a Corsican by birth. France took over the island of Corsica from Genoa only in 1768, the year before Napoleon's birth. The son of a minor noble, Bonaparte had attended military school in France and served as an artillery officer in the revolutionary army. Unlike many noble French officers, he did not emigrate and rapidly rose through the ranks. Only twenty years old when the Revolution began in 1789, he played a key role in the recapture of Toulon in 1793 and then helped put down an insurrection in Paris in October 1795 during the last days of the National Convention. The Parisian insurgents demanded the revocation of the Convention's "Two-Thirds Decree," which required that two-thirds of the incoming deputies be chosen from among the current ones. The Convention wanted to ensure continuation of a moderate republican regime. Early in his career Bonaparte had supported the Jacobins, but now he inclined toward order and backed the government. He was rewarded soon after with command of the Army of Italy.

Bonaparte's appointment hardly constituted a guarantee of success; he was only twenty-seven, had no experience commanding an army, and his opponents, the Austrians, outnumbered him two to one. To make matters worse, his soldiers had no uniforms, had not been paid, and had little in the way of food and supplies. The Directory government elected to replace the Convention at the end of 1795 had not yet decided what its foreign policy would be: should it just defend the new frontiers established during the Terror, or should it launch a more aggressive policy? When Prussia declared neutrality in 1795, French armies invaded the Dutch Republic and created a Batavian Republic. It was supposed to be a "sister republic" but in fact was a French satellite. The Directors decided that these gains would best be preserved if Austria, long France's chief foe on the continent, were defeated. They sent major armies across the Rhine to engage the Austrians and planned to use Bonaparte as a diversion in Italy. But within a month of taking command, before the armies to the north had even swung into action, Bonaparte had gone on the offensive: he marched into Milan, invaded Tuscany and the papal states, captured major Austrian fortresses, and forced every territory he conquered to offer tribute in cash so that he could pay his soldiers himself. He confiscated art treasures and rare manuscripts, set up a Cisalpine Republic based on Milan, and handed Venice, an independent republic, over to the Austrians in exchange for a peace agreement, which he negotiated himself. The French public enthusiastically followed the young general's bulletins from the field, which were published in the newspapers. The bulletins invariably cast Bonaparte in a heroic role.

> His powdered hair, which was cut in a peculiar, square fashion below the ears, fell down to his shoulders. He had on a straight coat, closely buttoned up, decorated with a very narrow gold embroidery, and wore a tri-colored plume in his hat. At first glance the face did not seem to me a fine one, but the striking features, a quick and searching eye, and abrupt, animated gestures, proclaimed an ardent soul, while the broad, serious forehead showed a deep thinker. . . . His speech was quick and at this time very incorrect.
> —Miot de Melito, describing Napoleon during the Italian campaign, 1796 (CD-ROM p. 141)

The Directory government gave in to the temptation of using victories abroad to overcome divisions at home. It found itself caught between royalists, who wanted a restoration of the monarchy, and former Jacobins, who still believed that the Republic needed a controlled economy and firm measures against counterrevolutionaries. The government's situation had deteriorated as prices rose in 1795 and 1796 after the abolition of the maximum. Conditions in the cities were desperate. People died of hunger in the streets of Paris as government rations fell precipitously down to two ounces and then just one ounce of bread per person per day. In May 1796 the police arrested Gracchus Babeuf for plotting a revolutionary coup to install the Constitution of 1793 and eventually establish some kind of proto-communist utopia. The intentions of Babeuf's "Conspiracy of Equals" are not easy to pin down, but he apparently advocated either the elimination of private property altogether or its more equal division to help the poor. At his trial, Babeuf denounced the Directorial Republic: "The aim of the Revolution also is the well-being of the greatest number; therefore, if this goal has not been achieved, if the people have not found the better life that they were seeking, then the Revolution is not over. This is true despite what those who want only to substitute their own rule for somebody else's say, or hope it to be" (Document 1.5). A special court acquitted most of his confederates but sent Babeuf and a collaborator to the guillotine in May 1797.

The tide had already turned in the opposite direction, for in the elections of March 1797 the royalists won a stunning victory. Royalists had established solid bases in many big cities and decided to participate in the electoral process. In response, on 4 September 1797, with the assistance of soldiers sent to Paris by Bonaparte, the three committed republicans among the five Directors arrested their other two colleagues as suspected royalists, annulled the election results in forty-nine departments, ordered the incarceration of thirty-two journalists, and banned forty-two newspapers. Fifty-three deputies were deported. As the government rooted out presumed royalists, the Jacobins made a comeback in the elections of 1798. They set up "constitutional circles" (revived Jacobin Clubs), organized processions on *décadi,* planted liberty trees, and offered "civic soups" to potential voters. Faced with this swing too far in the other direction, the government closed the circles, suppressed left-wing newspapers, and refused to let 127 newly elected deputies take their seats. Since 1792 voting in elections had been in decline; it now reached as low as 10 percent in some places as voters lost confidence in the electoral process itself.

The Directors were able to act so unilaterally because of the structure of the new constitutional government. Once elected by the deputies, the five Directors were not subject to the control of the two-house legislature. The Directors exercised considerable executive authority, having jurisdiction over diplomacy, the military, the execution of the laws, and the appointment process. Given the cumbersome nature of the legislative process, in which Directors could not initiate or veto legislation, the temptation to intervene by military force proved irresistible.

Dependent on force, the Directors now relied more and more on their generals and gave them greater freedom of action in the field. French armies invaded the Swiss cantons in 1798, annexed Geneva to France, and set up a Helvetic Republic. They also conquered the Papal States in 1798 and installed a Roman Republic; the pope fled to Siena. The same year, Napoleon took a great army, originally raised to attack England, across the Mediterranean Sea to Egypt. The Directory hoped that an occupation of Egypt would strike a blow at British trade by cutting the route to India and thus compensate France for its losses there years before. Once the army disembarked, however, British Admiral Horatio Nelson destroyed the French fleet while it was anchored in Aboukir Bay.

The French soldiers arrived in Egypt dreaming of glory, but they soon awoke to the reality of determined resistance. As Napoleon's young secretary reported, "Egypt was no longer the empire of the Ptolemies, covered with populous and wealthy cities; it now presented one unvaried scene of devastation and misery. Instead of being aided by the inhabitants, whom we had ruined, for the sake of delivering them from the yoke of the beys [Ottoman rulers], we found all against us." (CD-ROM p. 147) After an outbreak of the bubonic plague, Bonaparte's armies retreated from a further expedition in Syria. But the French occupation of Egypt lasted long enough for that largely Muslim country to experience the same kinds of Enlighten-

Fig. 5.1 The Saving of France

Although the plotters had included Napoleon only for his ability to bring military support, in one short month he completely upstaged them. In the new government, which was dominated by three consuls, Napoleon became the First Consul. In this metaphorical representation, Napoleon receives the mantle of leadership. This piece, clearly produced for its propaganda value, reminds us of Napoleon's consistent use of the media to promote his own image.

Le Soutien de la France

ment-inspired legal transformations that had been introduced in Europe: Bonaparte abolished torture, introduced equality before the law, eliminated religious taxes, and proclaimed religious toleration.

Even the disasters of the Egyptian campaign did not diminish Bonaparte's luster. He had taken scores of France's leading scientists with him on the expedition, which had given him a reputation as a man of culture. And his own propaganda kept the French public largely ignorant of the failures of the campaign. With his troops pinned down, he slipped out of Egypt in October 1799 and made his way secretly across the Mediterranean to southern France and then to Paris. His timing could not have been better. The war in Europe was going badly; the Belgian departments had revolted against new conscription laws; deserters swelled the ranks of the chouans in western France; a royalist army had tried to take the city of Toulouse in the southwest; and many government leaders wanted to revise the Constitution of 1795. Leading the plotters was Abbé Sieyès (the author of *What Is the Third Estate?* of 1789), who had been elected a Director in May 1799. He enlisted Bonaparte's support in overturning the Constitution of 1795.

On 9 November 1799 (18 Brumaire, Year VIII, by the revolutionary calendar), the conspirators persuaded the deputies to move out of Paris to avoid an imagined Jacobin plot. Never one to wait patiently for the unfolding of events, Bonaparte nearly botched the planned coup the next day by bursting into the new meeting place in a Paris suburb and demanding immediate changes in the constitution. He was greeted by cries of "Down with the dictator." His quick-thinking brother, Lucien, president of the Council of Five Hundred (the lower house), saved him by summoning soldiers guarding the hall and claiming that the deputies had tried to assassinate the popular general. The troops ejected the deputies, and a hastily assembled rump voted to abolish the Directory and establish a new three-man executive called the Consulate.

Bonaparte became First Consul, a title revived from ancient Rome (see Fig. 5.1). The other two consuls were Sieyès and a nonentity, Roger Ducos. In short order a new constitution was submitted to the voters; millions abstained, and the government falsified the results to give an appearance of even greater support to the new regime. Although Bonaparte was only the first of three consuls, he quickly established his superiority. In Italy and Egypt he had already proved himself a master of propaganda. Now, he struck just the right note as the man above party factionalism: "All parties came to me, confided to me their designs, disclosed their secrets, and requested my support; I refused to be the man of a party" (Document 5.1).

From Consulate to Empire

Your first task is to destroy irrevocably, in your department, the influence of those events which for too long have dominated our minds. Do your utmost to bring hatred and passion to an end, to extinguish rancor, to blot out the painful memories of the past.

—Lucien Bonaparte,
Minister of the Interior,
to his prefects, 1800
(Document 5.2)

When Napoleon Bonaparte came to power in 1799, his coup d'état at first appeared to be just the latest in a long line of upheavals in revolutionary France. Within the year, however, he had effectively ended the French Revolution and set France on a new course. Step by step he created an authoritarian state: military officers, engineers, and scientists took most of the honors; the police maintained order through censorship, harassment, and house arrest; and a paternalistic legal code buttressed the authority of fathers over children, husbands over wives, and employers over workers. As emperor after 1804, Napoleon dreamed of European integration in the tradition of Alexander the Great, Julius Caesar, and Charlemagne, but he also mastered the details of practical administration. To achieve his goals, he compromised with the Catholic church and with exiled aristocrats willing to return to France and relentlessly worked to enhance his own reputation as ruler, military man, intellectual, and even arbiter of taste.

Napoleon made the most of every opportunity. The new constitution made him the First Consul with the right to name the Council of State, which drew up all laws. He and his advisers also handpicked the members of the new legislature from a small pool of "notables." Three bodies made up the legislature: a Tribunate of 100 members to discuss proposed legislation; a Legislative Body of 300 to vote on bills but not discuss them; and a Senate of 60 to decide on the constitutionality of any proposed laws. While thus hobbling the legislature, Napoleon aimed to centralize and strengthen executive power even more than under the absolutist monarchy or the Terror. Almost immediately (February 1800) he instituted the office of Prefect to supervise government operations in each department. His brother Lucien, appointed Minister of the Interior with direct responsibility for the prefects, explained that the prefect was to "be always the first magistrate of your department, never the man of the revolution" (Document 5.2). Owing their loyalty to the Bonapartes, the prefects sent regular reports about their progress in ensuring "the most complete security" (Document 5.3). Elections and participation in clubs and societies now gave way to the top-down exercise of power. Sieyès himself had declared that the maxim of government ought to be "confidence from below, authority from above." The prefects named mayors in towns of less than 5,000 people; elected officials now had largely advisory roles.

The new regime severely limited political expression. Napoleon never relied on mass executions to achieve control, but he refused to allow those who opposed him to meet in clubs, influence elections, or publish newspapers. In 1800 a decree reduced the number of newspapers in Paris from seventy-three to thirteen (and then finally to four in 1811), and the newspapers that remained became government organs. Censors had to approve all operas and plays, and they banned "offensive" artistic works just as they had under the monarchy. Former terrorist Joseph Fouché, now Minister of Police, could impose house arrest, arbitrary imprisonment, and surveillance of political dissidents. Political contest and debate shriveled to almost nothing. When a bomb attack on Napoleon's carriage failed in 1800, Fouché suppressed the evidence of a royalist plot and instead arrested hundreds of former Jacobins.

Napoleon's most pressing concern was to reconcile to his regime the millions of Catholics who had been alienated by revolutionary policies. Klemens von Metternich, the Austrian foreign minister and then chancellor, admired Napoleon's ability to push through this reconciliation: "Personally indifferent to religious practices, he respected them too much to permit the slightest ridicule of those who followed them." Napoleon understood the value of religion in maintaining social order. According to Metternich, Napoleon saw Catholicism as "the form of worship most favorable to the maintenance of order and the true tranquility of the moral world." (CD-ROM p. 142) In 1801 a Concordat with Pope Pius VII ended a decade of church-state conflict (Document 5.4). The pope validated all sales of church lands, and the government agreed to pay the salaries of bishops and priests who would swear loyalty to the state. The state also paid Protestant pastors' salaries. Catholicism was officially recognized as "the religion of the great majority of French citizens." The pope thus brought the huge French Catholic population back into the fold, and Napoleon gained the pope's support for his regime.

Once Napoleon had gained the allegiance of Catholics, he turned his attention toward enhancing his own personal power. Although he had supported the Republic in his youth, he showed little hesitation about moving away from democratic elections and representative government. In 1802 he had himself named First Consul for life, and in 1804, with the pope's blessing, he crowned himself emperor. In explaining his decision to have himself named hereditary emperor, he claimed that "a state as vast as France" had to be ruled by a "hereditary power." He overcame his own reluctance, he insisted, in order to thwart "the hopes of our enemies" and respond to the "pressure of public opinion." "There was no alternative left," he claimed, because "he realized that his death might ruin his whole work." (CD-ROM p. 144) Referendums ratified these moves, but because voting did not take place by secret ballot, opposition was squelched. A noticeable decline in enthusiasm can be charted, however: in the southwestern district comprising the city of Toulouse, for example, 12,452 voters approved the life consulate in 1802, but only 8,888 voted for hereditary empire in 1804. (CD-ROM p. 145) The virtual absence of opposition—Toulouse recorded only two "no" votes in 1802, and one in 1804—could not conceal growing political apathy.

To accompany the development of hereditary empire, Napoleon created a new social elite, eventually reviving noble titles. Again he moved step by step. He first took control of naming senators, selecting the nation's most illustrious generals, ministers, prefects, scientists, rich men, and former nobles. In 1802 he took the next step by founding a Legion of Honor. Members of the Legion received lifetime pensions along with their titles. By 1814 the Legion had 32,000 members, only 5 percent of them civilians. The new elite had been created with the intention of mediating between the old nobility of birth and the Republic's strict emphasis on equality; Napoleon revived noble status but granted it for service, thus recognizing the importance of merit. In 1808 he introduced a complete hierarchy of noble titles, ranging from princes down to barons and chevaliers. Titles could be inherited but had to be supported by wealth—a man could not be a duke without a fortune of 200,000 francs, or a chevalier without 3,000 francs. Napoleon gave his favorite generals huge fortunes, often in the form of estates in the conquered territories, as well as titles. Napoleonic nobles had all served the state, came from varied social backgrounds, and would lose their status if they lost their wealth. Economic power was thus tied explicitly to political power.

Even while installing this new social elite, Napoleon worked hard to win over nobles from the Old Regime, many of whom eventually joined his regime. The wife of the Count of La Tour du Pin wrote that many of her friends had rallied to the government because of the Concordat with the papacy. Later she enjoyed dinner with the emperor and select members of his court: "This dinner was one of the events of my life of which I have preserved the most agreeable recollection" (Document 5.5). Yet none of the trappings of Old Regime nobility such as legal privileges or venality of office were restored, and old nobles had to be incorporated into the new imperial nobility if they wanted to have titles. Napoleon created more than 3,000 nobles after 1808; 60 percent were military officers, and 22 percent came from the Old Regime nobility.

Although Napoleon ran roughshod over his political critics, he rooted his authority in a newly rationalized legal system. The revolutionary governments had tried to unify and standardize France's multiple legal codes, but only Napoleon successfully established a new one, partly because he personally presided over the commission that drafted the new Civil Code. Called the Napoleonic Code as a way of further embellishing his image, it defined and ensured property rights, guaranteed religious liberty, and established a uniform system of law that ensured equal treatment for all adult males and affirmed the right of men to choose their professions.

With its curtailment of women's rights and its insistence on the authority of fathers and employers, the Code also laid the foundations for a more paternalistic society. Discussions of women's rights were forthright. One leading jurist remarked, for example, "There have been many discussions on the equality and superiority of the sexes. Nothing is more useless than such disputes. . . . Women need protection because they are weaker; men are free because they are stronger." The framers of the Civil Code used women's supposed innate weakness as justification for limiting the participation of women in public life and for legally protecting their separate, domestic roles to help reaffirm their wifely and motherly virtues. The law obligated husbands to support their wives, but the husband alone controlled any property held in common; a wife could not sue in court, sell or mortgage her own property, or contract a debt without her husband's consent. Not until 1965 did French wives gain legal status equal to that of their husbands.

The Civil Code took the male revolutionary ambivalence about women's political participation a step further, modifying even those few revolutionary laws that had been favorable to women, and in some instances denying rights women had under the monarchy. Divorce was still possible but severely restricted, especially for women (Document 5.6). Adultery was acceptable grounds for divorce, but the law considered a wife's infidelity more contemptible than a husband's. A wife could petition for divorce only if her husband brought his mistress to live in the family home! In contrast, a wife convicted of adultery could be imprisoned for up to two years. The Code's framers saw these discrepancies as a way to reinforce the family and make women responsible for private virtue, while leaving public decisions to men. Similar views of women's roles were shared by most leaders in Europe and the newly founded United States.

The Civil Code reasserted a father's control of his children. It restored most paternal powers, which revolutionary legislation had limited. For example, fathers could send their children under sixteen to prison for up to a month with no hearing of any sort. At the same time, the code insisted on fathers' responsibilities to provide for their children's welfare. Napoleon himself encouraged the establishment of private charities to help indigent mothers, and one of his decrees made it easier for women to give up their children anonymously to a government foundling hospital. Napoleon hoped such measures would discourage abortion and infanticide, especially among the poorest classes in the fast-growing urban areas.

Under the new code, the status of employees resembled that of children. The state required all workers to carry a work card attesting to their good conduct, and it prohibited all workers' organizations. The police considered workers without cards vagrants or criminals and could send them to workhouses or prison. Arbitration boards settled labor disputes after 1806, but they took employers at their word while treating workers as minors, demanding that foremen and shop superintendents represent them. Strikes occasionally occurred, led by secret, illegal journeymen's associations, or *compagnonnages,* but wage workers generally lived under the thumb of their employers, many of whom laid off employees when times were hard, deducted fines from their wages, and dismissed them without appeal for being absent or making errors. These limitations on workers' rights won Napoleon the support of French business.

The economy, education, and even morals came under government supervision. Napoleon created a Bank of France to facilitate government borrowing and relied on gold and silver coinage rather than paper money. In periods of economic crisis his regime set up soup kitchens, but in time-honored fashion it also arrested beggars and sent them to newly established workhouses. Believing that education was crucial to military success and national wealth, Napoleon inaugurated the *lycées,* state-run secondary schools for boys from better-off families. Students in these schools wore military uniforms, and drum rolls signaled the beginning and end of classes. (Without the military trappings, the *lycées* are now coeducational, socially diverse, and still the heart of the French educational system.) As might be expected, Napoleon took little interest in girls' education, believing that they should spend most of their time at home learning religion, manners, and such "female occupations" as sewing and music. "Public girls"—prostitutes—were more closely regulated than ever before. The police arrested prostitutes who worked on their own, but they tolerated and even supervised brothels, requiring the women to have monthly medical examinations for venereal disease.

Every aspect of this authoritarian state was stamped with Napoleon's personality. His visage and name adorned coins, engravings, histories, paintings, and public monuments. His favorite painters helped create his legend by depicting him as a warrior-hero of mythic proportions. In his imperial court, Napoleon staged his entrances carefully to maximize his personal presence: his wife and courtiers would all be dressed in regal finery, and he would be announced with great pomp—but he would arrive dressed in a simple military uniform with no medals. He encouraged the spread of stories that he worked prodigiously, sleeping only a few hours a night. In fact, he made a very big impression, even on his harshest critics. Germaine de Staël, whose books were banned in France and who was eventually forced to live in exile, recounted her personal reaction to Napoleon: "Far from recovering my confidence by seeing Bonaparte more frequently, he constantly intimidated me more and more. I had a confused feeling that no emotion of the heart could act upon him. He regards a human being as an action or a thing, not as a fellow creature. He does not hate more than he loves; for him nothing exists but himself; all other creatures are ciphers."

To further this sense of intimidation, Napoleon embarked on ostentatious building projects. Government-commissioned architects built the Arc de Triomphe, the Stock Exchange, fountains, and even slaughterhouses. Most of his new construction reflected his neoclassical taste for monumental buildings set in vast empty spaces. Old, winding streets with their cramped houses were demolished to make way for these improvements. At the same time, Napoleon did everything possible to promote French scientific inquiry, especially that which could serve practical ends. He closely monitored the research institutes established during the Revolution, sometimes intervening personally to insist on political conformity. An impressive outpouring of new theoretical and practical scientific work rewarded the state's efforts. Experiments with balloons led to the discovery of laws about the expansion of gases, and research on fossil shells prepared the way for new theories of revolutionary change later in the nineteenth century. The surgeon Dominique-Jean Larrey developed new techniques of battlefield amputation and medical care during Napoleon's wars, winning an appointment as an officer in the Legion of Honor and a baron's title along with a pension.

Throughout all these remarkable changes, Napoleon stuck by his Corsican family. He named his older brother, Joseph, king of Naples (1806) and then king of Spain (1808). He made his younger brother, Louis, king of Holland in 1806. At age twenty-three his stepson Eugène de Beauharnais was proclaimed viceroy of Italy, and his sister Caroline and brother-in-law General Murat became king and queen of Naples in 1808. Napoleon wanted to establish an imperial succession, but he lacked an heir. In thirteen years of marriage his wife, Josephine, had borne no children, so in 1809 he divorced her and in 1810 married the eighteen-year-old Princess Marie-Louise of Austria. The next year she gave birth to a son to whom Napoleon immediately gave the title King of Rome.

Although ruling for his own benefit and perhaps that of his family, Napoleon left a legacy in France that should not be seen as entirely antithetical to the Revolution. Because he left intact the property changes forced through by the revolutionaries, he in effect strengthened the position of the rich commoners and weakened the nobles of the monarchy. The class divide of the Old Regime between nobles and commoners gave way to a new mixed elite of "notables," which resembled in many ways the society desired by the revolutionaries of 1789. Napoleon's restructuring of the state reinforced many trends in rationalization and modernization first initiated by the revolutionary authorities in 1790–91. In conquered lands, he abolished traditional customs and replaced local officials with a new elite chosen for its talents not its birth. His support for scientific research and his emphasis on education also bespeak his interest in enlightened modernization. Despite his move toward a hereditary empire aligned with a new noble caste, Napoleon continued many policies that revolutionaries had made the cornerstone of their own efforts in overturning the Old Regime.

The Road to Waterloo and Final Defeat

Because immediate usurpation was easy, he believed it could be durable, and once he became a usurper, he did all that usurpation condemns a usurper to do in our century. . . . a usurper's sole resource is uninterrupted war.

—Benjamin Constant,
The Spirit of Conquest and Usurpation (1814)
(Document 5.7)

Although Napoleon left an indelible stamp on French institutions and political life, his fame and much of his power rested on his military conquests (Fig. 5.2). Building on innovations introduced by the republican governments before him, Napoleon revolutionized the art of war with tactics and strategy based on a highly mobile army. By 1810 he ruled an empire more extensive than any in the West since the time of ancient Rome. Yet within two years that empire had begun to crumble, and with it went Napoleon's power at home. Napoleon's empire failed because it was based on a contradiction: Napoleon tried to reduce virtually all the European states to the status of colonial dependents when they had long been independent. The result, inevitably, was a great upsurge in nationalist feeling that has dominated European politics right up to the present. Even before his final fall, critics such as Benjamin Constant complained that "Bonaparte was compelled to distract public attention by bellicose enterprises" (Document 5.7). Those bellicose enterprises proved to be his undoing, but not before he had dazzled the world with a string of astounding military victories.

Napoleon attributed his military success "three-quarters to morale" and the rest to leadership and having more soldiers at the point of attack. Conscription provided the large numbers: 1.3 million men age twenty to twenty-four were drafted between 1800 and 1812, another million in 1813–14. So many agreed to go because the Republic had taught them to identify the army with the nation. Military service was both a patriotic duty and a means of social ascent. The new men who rose through the ranks to become officers were young, ambitious, and accustomed to the new ways of war. Consequently, the French army had higher morale than the armies of other powers, most of which rejected conscription as too democratic and continued to restrict their officer corps to the nobility. Only in 1813–14 did French morale plummet, as defeat cast in a darker light Napoleon's insatiable demands for more men.

When Napoleon came to power in 1799, France had been at war for almost seven years, and its military position was precarious. Desertion was rampant, and the various

Fig. 5.2 Bonaparte, First Consul of the French Republic, 18 Brumaire, Year VIII

From the beginning it was clear that Napoleon's political support was closely tied to his fortunes in war. This engraving celebrates the victory over the Austrians at the Battle of Marengo in Italy, June 1800. In fact, he almost lost this battle, but government propaganda rarely mentioned such problems. Both in this image and in the war bulletin, it is described as a major victory.

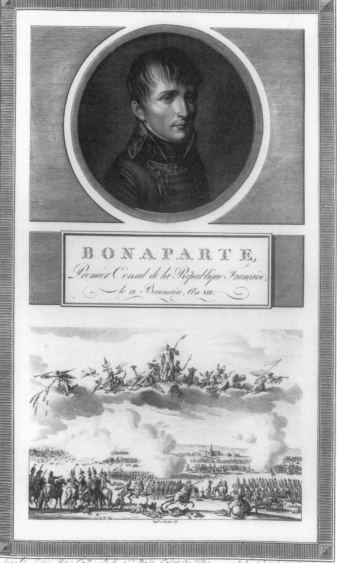

BONAPARTE,
Premier Consul de la République Française,
le 18 Brumaire, An VIII.

Bataille de Marengo, commandée par le premier Consul, le 25 Prairial, An VIII

republican armies vied for predominance. Napoleon ended this squabbling by uniting all the armies into one Grand Army under his command. By 1812 he personally commanded 700,000 troops; while 250,000 soldiers fought in Spain, others remained garrisoned in France. Between 70,000 and 180,000 men, not all of them French, fought for France in any given battle. Life on campaign was no picnic—ordinary soldiers slept in the rain, mud, and snow, and often had to forage for food—but Napoleon nonetheless inspired almost fanatical loyalty. He fought alongside his soldiers in some sixty battles and had nineteen horses shot from under him. One opponent said that Napoleon's presence alone was worth 50,000 men.

Napoleon's military command, like his domestic role, was personal and highly centralized. He essentially served as his own operations officer: "I alone know what I have to do," he insisted. Employing a pragmatic and direct approach to strategy, Napoleon went for the main body of the opposing army and tried to crush it in a lightning campaign. He gathered the largest possible army for one great and decisive battle, then followed with a relentless pursuit to break enemy morale altogether. His armies' victories at Marengo and Hohenlinden in 1800 forced the Austrian emperor to sue for peace. Britain agreed to the Treaty of Amiens soon afterward (1802), but peace lasted only until 1803. Napoleon used the breathing space to send an expeditionary force to Saint Domingue and capture Toussaint L'Ouverture, the leader of the slave revolt. Continuing resistance among the black population, and an epidemic of yellow fever, forced Napoleon to withdraw his troops from Saint Domingue and abandon his plans to extend his empire to the western hemisphere. As part of his retreat, he sold the Louisiana Territory to the United States in 1803.

Napoleon considered the peace with Great Britain merely a truce and used the time to consolidate his position before again taking up arms. When hostilities resumed, the British navy once more proved its superiority by blocking an attempted French invasion and by defeating the French and their Spanish allies in a huge naval battle at Trafalgar in 1805. France lost many ships; the British lost no vessels, but their renowned admiral, Lord Nelson, perished. On land, however, Napoleon remained invincible, which he proved immediately in 1805, when Austria took up arms again after France demanded that it declare neutrality in the conflict with Britain. Napoleon promptly captured 25,000 Austrian soldiers at Ulm in Bavaria in 1805. After marching on to Vienna, he again trounced the Austrians, who had been joined by their new Russian ally. The Battle of Austerlitz, often considered Napoleon's greatest victory, was fought on 2 December 1805, the first anniversary of his coronation.

When Prussia ended its decade of neutrality in 1806, the French promptly destroyed the Prussian army at Jena and Auerstadt. In 1807, Napoleon defeated the Russians at Friedland. As a result of personal negotiations between Napoleon and the young Tsar Alexander I, Prussian lands west of the Elbe River became the kingdom of Westphalia under Napoleon's brother Jerome, and Prussia's Polish provinces became the duchy of Warsaw. Alexander recognized Napoleon's conquests in central and western Europe and promised to help him against the British in exchange for Napoleon's support against the Turks. Neither party kept the bargain.

Wherever his Grand Army conquered, Napoleon's influence soon followed. By annexing some territories and setting up others as satellite kingdoms with much reduced autonomy, Napoleon attempted to colonize large parts of Europe. He brought the disparate German and Italian states together in order to rule them more effectively and to exploit their resources for his own ends. In 1803, Napoleon consolidated the tiny German states by abolishing some of them and attaching them to larger units. In July 1806 he established the Confederation of the Rhine, which soon included almost all the German states except Austria and Prussia. The Holy Roman Emperor gave up his title and became simply the emperor of Austria, ending the Holy Roman Empire that had lasted a thousand years, since the coronation of Charlemagne in 800. Napoleon established three units in Italy: the territories directly annexed to France, the kingdom of Italy, and the kingdom of Naples. Italy had not been so unified since the Roman Empire.

Napoleon forced French-style reforms on both the annexed territories and the satellite kingdoms. Annexed territories became departments with administrations identical to those in France. There and in the satellite kingdoms, French reforms included abolishing serfdom, eliminating seigneurial dues, introducing the Napoleonic Code, suppressing monasteries, and subordinating church to state, as well as extending civil rights to Jews and other religious minorities. The experience in the kingdom of Westphalia was typical of a French satellite. When Jerome Bonaparte and his wife Catherine arrived as king and queen in 1807, they relied on French experts who worked with a hand-picked committee of Germans to write a constitution and install legal reforms. The Westphalian army had the first Jewish officers in the German states, and the army, administration, and judiciary all opened to the middle classes. As time passed, however, the German subjects began to chafe under French rule. German officials enforced French decrees only halfheartedly, and the French army had to forbid its soldiers to frequent local taverns and shops because their presence often started fights.

As the example of Westphalia shows, reactions to Napoleonic innovations were always mixed. Napoleon's chosen rulers often made real improvements in roads, public works, law codes, and education, yet almost everyone had some cause for complaint. Republicans regretted Napoleon's conversion of the sister republics into kingdoms after his coronation. Tax increases and ever-rising conscription quotas fomented discontent in all the satellites. The annexed territories and satellite kingdoms paid half the French war expenses. The removal of internal tariffs, on the other hand, often fostered the growth of factories.

Almost everywhere conflicts arose between Napoleon's desire for standardized, central government and local insistence on maintaining customs and traditions. Sometimes his own relatives sided with their new countries. Louis would not allow conscription in Holland, for instance, because the Dutch had never had compulsory military service. He established a National Council for Public Health, enforced vaccination for smallpox, and tried to encourage breast-feeding of babies. When Napoleon tried to introduce an economic policy banning trade with Great Britain, Louis's lax enforcement prompted the frustrated emperor to complain, "Holland is an English province." In 1810 Napoleon annexed the satellite kingdom because his brother had become too sympathetic to Dutch interests.

Napoleon's victories forced defeated rulers to rethink their political and cultural assumptions. In response to the crushing defeat of 1806, Prussia's Frederick William III abolished serfdom and allowed nonnobles to buy and enclose land. The king's advisers also overhauled the army to make the high command more efficient and to open the way to the appointment of middle-class officers. Prussia instituted these reforms to try to compete with the French, not to promote democracy. As one reformer wrote to Frederick William, "We must do from above what the French have done from below." Even Tsar Alexander I set up reform commissions: he created Western-style ministries, lifted restrictions on importing foreign books, founded six new universities, and encouraged nobles to voluntarily free their serfs.

One power proved completely immune to the threat of Napoleonic domination: Great Britain. As Constant acerbically remarked, "While a single country remained free, Bonaparte was never safe." In an effort to bankrupt this "nation of shopkeepers" by choking its trade, Napoleon inaugurated a Continental System in 1806 that prohibited all commerce between Great Britain and France, as well as France's dependent states and allies. At first the system worked: British exports dropped 20 percent in 1807–8, and industrial production declined 10 percent, creating unemployment and igniting a strike of 60,000 workers in northern England. In the midst of continuing wars, however, the system proved impossible to enforce, and widespread smuggling brought British goods into the European market. French and other continental industries nonetheless benefited from this temporary protection from British exports.

Resistance to Napoleonic rule usually began as local opposition to French demands for money or draftees and then turned into nationalist revival. In southern Italy gangs of bandits harassed the French army and local officials; 33,000 Italian bandits were arrested in 1809 alone. But resistance continued via a network of secret societies called the *carbonari*, which in the mid-nineteenth century would play an important role in Italian unification. Spain and Portugal turned local protest into a major drain on Napoleon's armies. In 1807, Napoleon sent 100,000 troops through Spain to invade Portugal, Great Britain's ally. The Portuguese royal family fled to Brazil, but fighting continued, aided by a British army. Napoleon managed to get his brother Joseph named king of Spain in place of the senile Charles IV and his heir, Prince Ferdinand. In response, the Spanish clergy and nobles raised bands of peasants called *guerrillas* (the origin of the term "guerrilla warfare") who fought pitched battles and then melted away into the countryside like the chouans in western France. Even Napoleon's taking personal command of the French forces failed to quell the Spanish, who for six years fought a war of national independence that pinned down thousands of French soldiers far from the eastern front. Madame de Staël commented that Napoleon "never understood that a war might be a crusade. . . . He never reckoned with the one power that no arms could overcome—the enthusiasm of a whole people."

The war in Spain had aspects of a religious crusade. Like their Vendée counterparts, Spanish peasants hated French requisitioning of their food supplies and sought to

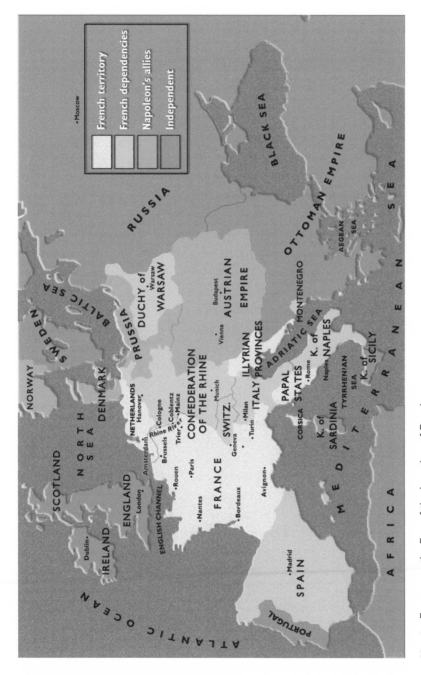

Map 3 Europe on the Eve of the Invasion of Russia

By 1812 Napoleon controlled, either directly or indirectly, most of Europe. Only Adolf Hitler, between 1940 and 1944, would exercise comparable dominance over European affairs, and Hitler would lose his grip for almost exactly the same reasons that Napoleon lost his: fighting a war on two distant fronts at once (in Napoleon's case, Spain and Russia) and failing to subdue Great Britain and Russia. When Napoleon's armies disintegrated under the impact of the Russian winter, British money and military aid fanned the smoldering resistance to Napoleonic rule into the fires of all-out war.

defend their priests against French anticlericalism. The Spanish church spread anti-French propaganda that equated Napoleon with heresy. A catechism issued for the occasion included the following: "Question: Who is the enemy of our happiness? Response: The Emperor of the French. Question: Who is he? Response: A new and infinitely evil ruler, a greedy chief of all evil men and the exterminator of the good, the

 essence and receptacle of every vice. Question: How many natural forms does he assume? Response: Two. One a devil and the other human." (CD-ROM p. 151)

In this tense atmosphere, and assisted by the British, the Spanish guerrillas countered every French massacre with atrocities of their own. They tortured their French prisoners (they boiled one general alive) and lynched collaborators.

Despite opposition, Napoleon had assembled an extensive empire by 1812. Only two major European states remained fully independent—Great Britain and Russia—but joined together they would prove to be his undoing. In order to take on the French, Tsar Alexander I made peace with the Ottomans and allied himself with Great Britain and Sweden. Napoleon invaded Russia in 1812 with a host of at least 250,000 horses and 600,000 men, including contingents of Italians, Poles, Swiss, Dutch, and Germans. He followed his usual strategy of trying to strike quickly, but the Russian generals avoided confrontation and retreated eastward, destroying anything that might be useful to the invader. In September, on the road to Moscow, Napoleon finally engaged the main Russian force in the gigantic battle of Borodino. French casualties were 30,000 men, including 47 generals; the Russians lost 45,000, either killed or wounded.

Once again the Russians retreated, leaving Moscow undefended. Napoleon entered the deserted city, but the victory turned hollow because the wooden city was soon on fire, probably set by the departing Russians. Within a week, three-fourths of it had burned to the ground. Philippe Ségur, one of Napoleon's chief aides, described Napoleon's personal reaction: "This mighty conquest, for which he had sacrificed everything, appeared now like a phantom which had been long pursued by him, which

 he had vainly thought he had at length grasped, but which, after all, he now saw vanishing in air, in a whirlwind of smoke and flames." (CD-ROM p. 152)

Alexander still refused to negotiate, and French morale plunged with worsening problems of supply. Weeks of constant marching in the dirt and heat had worn down the foot soldiers, who were dying of disease or deserting in large numbers.

In October, Napoleon began his retreat; in November came the cold. Napoleon himself reported that on 14 November the temperature fell to –4 degrees Fahrenheit. Even the official bulletin from the army sounded a note of desperation: "The cold began on the 7th [of November]; from this moment on, we lost each night several hundred horses who died in bivouac. We had already lost many cavalry and artillery horses by the time we reached Smolensk. More than 30,000 horses died in a few days.

 We had to destroy a good part of our guns, our munitions, and our food supplies." (CD-ROM p. 152) A German soldier in the Grand Army described trying to cook fistfuls of raw bran with snow in order to make something like bread. For him the retreat was "the indescribable horror of all possible plagues." Ségur was heartbroken as he described his men in retreat: "Their wet clothes froze upon them, this covering of ice pierced their bodies, and stiffened all their limbs. A cutting and violent wind stopped their breath, or seized upon it at the moment it was exhaled and converted it into icicles, which hung upon their beard round their mouths. The unhappy men crawled on, with trembling limbs, and chattering teeth, until the snow collecting round their feet in masses, like stones, some scattered fragment, a branch of a tree, or the body of one of their companions made them stagger and fall." (CD-ROM p. 152) Russian forces harassed the disintegrating French army, now more pathetic than grand. By December only 100,000 troops remained, one-sixth the original number, and the retreat had turned into a rout: the Russians had captured 200,000 soldiers, including 48 generals and 3,000 other officers.

Napoleon had made a classic military mistake, one that would be famously repeated by Adolf Hitler in World War II: fighting a war on two distant fronts simultaneously. The Spanish war tied up 250,000 troops and forced Napoleon to bully Prussia and Austria into supplying soldiers of dubious loyalty. But even without the war with Spain and Portugal, the logistical and communications problems of marching to Moscow were simply too overwhelming given early nineteenth-century conditions.

Spain and Russia were the beginning of the end, but Napoleon was not yet finished. By the spring of 1813 the French emperor had replenished his army with

Fig. 5.3   Napoleon Is Unable to Digest Leipzig

After the defeat in Russia, with renewed allied forces arrayed against him, Napoleon prepared once again to go to war. In 1813 at Leipzig, the Emperor was soundly defeated in the Battle of the Nations. This allowed the allies to press a successful campaign, leading to French surrender in 1814. Napoleon would return the next year, only to be defeated at Waterloo and exiled far from Europe.

another 250,000 men. In response the other European powers formed a coalition against him. With British financial support, Russian, Austrian, Prussian, and Swedish armies met the French outside Leipzig in October 1813 and defeated Napoleon in the Battle of the Nations (Fig. 5.3). One by one Napoleon's German allies deserted him to join the German nationalist "War of Liberation." Napoleon's French Empire crumbled. The Confederation of the Rhine dissolved, and the Dutch revolted and restored the prince of Orange. Joseph Bonaparte fled Spain, and a combined Spanish-Portuguese army under British command invaded France. In only a few months the allied powers crossed the Rhine and marched toward Paris. The French Senate deposed Napoleon, who abdicated when his remaining generals refused to fight. Napoleon went into exile on the island of Elba off the Italian coast.

Napoleon still had one last chance. The allies restored the Bourbon monarchy to postrevolutionary France: Louis XVI's brother, the count of Provence, became King Louis XVIII (Louis XVI's son was known as Louis XVII even though he died in prison in 1795 without ever ruling). The new king tried to steer a middle course by "giving" France a charter that established a British-style monarchy with a two-house legislature and guaranteed civil rights. Discontent was nonetheless widespread. The rank and file of the army were happy to come home, but many professional officers lost their jobs. Sensing an opportunity, Napoleon escaped from Elba in early 1815 and landed in southern France, then made swift and unimpeded progress to Paris. His popularity surged as he promised to liberalize his regime. Louis XVIII fled across the border, and the period known as the Hundred Days began.

Napoleon quickly moved his armies into present-day Belgium. At first it seemed that he might succeed in separately fighting the two armies arrayed against him: a Prussian army and a joint force of Belgian, Dutch, German, and British troops led by Sir Arthur Wellesley, Duke of Wellington. But the Prussians evaded him and joined with Wellington at Waterloo. Completely routed, Napoleon had no choice but to abdicate again. This time the victorious allies banished him permanently to the remote island of St. Helena, far off the coast of West Africa, where he died in 1821 at the age of fifty-two. "Thus terminates in exile, and in prison," wrote the *London Times* on 5 July 1821, "the most extraordinary life yet known to political history." (CD-ROM p. 155)

The cost of Napoleon's rule was high: 750,000 French and 400,000 soldiers from annexed and satellite states died between 1800 and 1815. Yet no other military figure since Alexander the Great had made such an impact on world history. His plans for a united Europe, his insistence on spreading the legal reforms of the French Revolution, his extension of police powers, and even his inadvertent awakening of national sentiment set the agenda for European history in the modern era.

The death of Napoleon Bonaparte in 1821 brought forth a cascade of commentary on his remarkable rise and fall. Even his greatest enemies had to admit his grandeur as a figure. The *London Times* wrote, for example, "The varieties of fortune which

Buonaparte experienced . . . embrace both extremes of the condition of man in society, and therefore address themselves to all ranks of human beings." (CD-ROM p. 155) The most influential French poet of the nineteenth century, Victor Hugo, captured the nostalgia that many French people felt in the decades after Napoleon's meteoric appearance. In his poem "To the Column" (1830) Hugo mourned, "Thy rugged St. Helena keep, / Where, of thy fortune's proudest steep, / The dazed eye sees the sad reverse; . . . There, free from outrage, dost thou sleep, / And, oft aroused, thou near dost feel / Those who from rage and sorrow weep / The red-clad soldiers o'er thee kneel." (CD-ROM p. 156) As Hugo indicated with that last line about the "red-clad soldiers," Napoleon's military men felt the greatest sense of loss because they had so personally participated in Napoleon's rise and fall. Napoleon brought countless young men up through the ranks with him to positions of wealth, status, and political power.

Napoleon's story captured everyone's imagination because he was Europe's first truly self-made ruler. His career traced out the new prospects for social mobility: he became consul and then emperor not because he was born to high position but because he was a great military leader who made himself into the symbolic incarnation of French glory and achievement. His memory lived on in a thousand different ways. Alphonse de Lamartine, a leading poet and republican politician of the 1840s, described how peddlers sold colored prints of Napoleon's victorious battles: "The peasant would come out of his cottage and, with eyes shining in wonder, would see a display of heroic portraits, listen to tales of combat, and for one sou he would buy the history of these feats of arms. He nailed them to the walls of his house, or had his wife sew them to the serge curtain around his bed; for him and for his family, this was the whole history of France in great deeds." (CD-ROM p. 156) Napoleon, the little Corsican artillery captain, represented not a fleeting moment of glory but a continuing dream of France's greatness.

Documents

NAPOLEON: BUILDING POWER

In a period characterized by much uncertainty, Napoleon's first contribution was consolidation. His manner of coming to power at first made his role as a stabilizer seem unlikely. He achieved political position through a coup d'état that once again used force, unsettling the political process. Once in power, however, Napoleon immediately acted to stabilize the new regime. He centralized administrative and political power in the new office of Prefect, he made peace with the Catholic church, and he won over many Old Regime nobles to his rule, in part by guaranteeing order through the new Civil Code, which reaffirmed the authority of fathers, husbands, and employers. Napoleon's unflagging enthusiasm for foreign wars always threatened to undermine his achievements. Again and again, he called up new recruits, borrowed more money, and demanded additional contributions of men and money from those he conquered. "Liberated" peoples increasingly resisted French control, and criticism eventually grew within France, even though Napoleon kept the French press on a short leash. In the end, Napoleon's regime could not survive his defeat in battle.

Document 5.1: Napoleon's Own Account of His Coup d'État (10 November 1799)

Napoleon glosses over the conspiracy to overthrow the Constitution of 1795 and the duly elected legislature. This conspiracy was organized in part by his younger brother Lucien. He does, however, admit that some of the deputies opposed his endeavor and tried to arrest him. At this moment, Napoleon portrays himself as a simple "soldier of liberty, a citizen devoted to the Republic."

Source: John Hall Stewart, ed., *A Documentary Survey of the French Revolution* (New York: Macmillan, 1951), 763–65.

> On my return to Paris [from Egypt] I found division among all authorities, and agreement upon only one point, namely, that the Constitution was half destroyed and was unable to save liberty.
>
> All parties came to me, confided to me their designs, disclosed their secrets, and requested my support; I refused to be the man of a party.
>
> The Council of Elders summoned me; I answered its appeal. A plan of general restoration had been devised by men whom the nation has been accustomed to regard as the defenders of liberty, equality, and property; this plan required an examination, calm, free, exempt from all influence and all fear. Accordingly, the Council of Elders resolved upon the removal of the Legislative Body to Saint-Cloud; it gave me the responsibility of disposing the force necessary for its independence. I believed it my duty to my fellow citizens, to the soldiers perishing in our armies, to the national glory acquired at the cost of their blood, to accept the command.
>
> The Councils assembled at Saint-Cloud; republican troops guaranteed their security from without, but assassins created terror within. Several deputies of the Council of Five Hundred, armed with stilettos and firearms, circulated threats of death around them.
>
> The plans which ought to have been developed were withheld, the majority disorganized, the boldest orators disconcerted, and the futility of every wise proposition was evident.
>
> I took my indignation and grief to the Council of Elders; I besought it to assure the execution of its generous designs; I directed its attention to

the evils of the *Patrie* [Fatherland] . . . ; it concurred with me by new evidence of its steadfast will.

I presented myself at the Council of Five Hundred, alone, unarmed, my head uncovered, just as the Elders had received and applauded me; I came to remind the majority of its wishes, and to assure it of its power.

The stilettos which menaced the deputies were instantly raised against their liberator; twenty assassins threw themselves upon me and aimed at my breast. The grenadiers of the Legislative Body whom I had left at the door of the hall ran forward, placed themselves between the assassins and myself. One of these brave grenadiers had his clothes pierced by a stiletto. They bore me out.

At the same moment cries of "Outlaw" were raised against the defender of the law. It was the fierce cry of assassins against the power destined to repress them.

They crowded around the president, uttering threats, arms in their hands they commanded him to outlaw me; I was informed of this: I ordered him to be rescued from their fury, and six grenadiers of the Legislative Body secured him. Immediately afterwards some grenadiers of the legislative body charged into the hall and cleared it.

The factions, intimidated, dispersed and fled. The majority, freed from their attacks, returned freely and peaceably into the meeting hall, listened to the proposals on behalf of public safety, deliberated, and prepared the salutary resolution which is to become the new and provisional law of the Republic.

Frenchmen, you will doubtless recognize in this conduct the zeal of a soldier of liberty, a citizen devoted to the Republic. Conservative, tutelary, and liberal ideas have been restored to their rights through the dispersal of the rebels who oppressed the Councils.

Document 5.2: Establishing a New Administrative Order (1800–1801)

Naming his brother Lucien to the key post of Minister of the Interior, Bonaparte quickly moved to establish his political control over the country. He set up "prefects" for every administrative region known as a department; these appointees had final say in such important matters as finances, politics, and the conscription of troops.

Source: Martyn Lyons, *Napoleon Bonaparte and the Legacy of the French Revolution* (London: Macmillan, 1994), 70.

Lucien Bonaparte, Minister of the Interior, Explains the Mission of the Prefects, 1800

This post demands a wide range of duties, but it offers you great rewards in the future: you have been summoned to assist the government in its noble design to restore France to her ancient splendor, to revive in her all that is great and generous, and to establish this magnificent edifice on the unshakable foundations of liberty and equality. . . .

You will not be called upon to carry out the whims or passing desires of a fickle government, unstable in its operation, and anxious about its future. Your first task is to destroy irrevocably, in your department, the influence of those events which for too long have dominated our minds. Do your utmost to bring hatred and passion to an end, to extinguish rancor, to blot out the painful memories of the past. . . . In your public decisions, and even in your private lives, be always the first magistrate of your department, never the man of the revolution. Do not tolerate any public reference to the labels which still cling to the diverse political parties of the revolution; merely consign them to that most deplorable chapter in the history of human folly. . . . You will receive from the War Minister all the instructions necessary for the administrative responsibilities within his jurisdiction. I will simply limit myself to a reminder to apply yourself immediately to the conscription draft. . . . I give special priority to the collection of taxes: their prompt payment is now a sacred duty. Agriculture, trade, the industries and professions must resume their honored status. Respect and honor our farmers. . . . Protect our trade, whose freedom can never have any limit except the public interest. . . . Visit our manufactures; bestow your highest compliments on those distinguished citizens engaged in them. . . . Encourage the new generations; fix your attention on public education, and the formation of Men, Citizens, and Frenchmen.

Document 5.3: A Prefect in Action (1800–1801)

The prefect of the Haute-Garonne department headquartered in Toulouse reported on his efforts to establish control in a region known for its rebelliousness.

Source: Martyn Lyons, *Napoleon Bonaparte and the Legacy of the French Revolution* (London: Macmillan, 1994), 75–76.

Prefect of the Haute-Garonne to the Minister of the Interior, Toulouse, 3 Germinal Year IX (24 March 1801)

A year has now passed, Citizen Minister, since I was given the honor of administering the department of the Haute-Garonne. It is not without a certain satisfaction that I consider the situation in this region when I arrived, and compare it to its present condition. In Germinal Year VIII

[1799], the department of the Haute-Garonne was beset by troubles and disorder. Toulouse was in open revolt . . . a seditious crowd had forced the sale of grain at a low price; authority was flouted, property was violated with the consent of local government, trade was destroyed, and the troops had been disarmed by the multitude . . . there were garrisons everywhere, and two half-brigades of infantry and a regiment of cavalry did not suffice to contain the rebels and troublemakers. . . .

A great number of factious subjects dominated the countryside and tyrannized citizens. They defied every law with impunity; they attacked and beat in broad daylight those whose clothing or manners did not meet with their approval. . . .

Today the department enjoys the greatest tranquility, despite the fact that it is completely without troops and supplies, especially bread, are excessively expensive. Anxiety and troubles have given way to the most complete security. Each citizen is calmly enjoying his property and his industry, blessing the government which protects him, and provides him with the benefits of order. . . . Administrative matters are dispatched with speed and impartiality. Crime is rare and the guilty are promptly apprehended and punished. The spirit of faction is nowhere in evidence, and the brawls which used to occur daily are not repeated. In a word, I dare to suggest, there is not a calmer department in the Republic.

Document 5.4: Making Peace with the Catholic Church (1801–1802)

One of Napoleon's first priorities was to reestablish good relations with the papacy, which had fought the revolutionary church settlement tooth and nail. Napoleon gained everything he desired in the Concordat: he appointed the bishops and archbishops of the French church, and all bishops had to swear an oath of fidelity to the French Republic.

Source: Frank M. Anderson, ed., *The Constitutions and Other Illustrative Documents of the History of France,* 2nd ed., rev. (New York: Russell and Russell, 1908), 296–97.

The government of the French Republic recognizes that the Roman, catholic and apostolic religion is the religion of the great majority of French citizens.

His Holiness likewise recognizes that this same religion has derived and in this moment again expects the greatest benefit and grandeur from the establishment of Catholic worship in France and from the personal profession of it which the Consuls of the Republic make.

In consequence, after this mutual recognition, as well for the benefit of religion as for the maintenance of internal tranquility, they have agreed as follows:

1. The Catholic, apostolic and Roman religion shall be freely exercised in France: its worship shall be public, and in conformity with the police regulations which the government shall deem necessary for the public tranquility. . . .

4. The First Consul of the Republic shall make appointments, within the three months which shall follow the publication of the bull of His Holiness to the archbishoprics and bishoprics of the new circumscription. His Holiness shall confer the canonical institution, following the forms established in relation to France before the change of government. . . .

6. Before entering upon their functions, the bishops shall take directly, at the hands of the First Consul, the oath of fidelity which was in use before the change of government, expressed in the following terms:

"I swear and promise to God, upon the holy scriptures, to remain in obedience and fidelity to the government established by the constitution of the French Republic. I also promise not to have any intercourse, nor to assist by any council, nor to support any league, either within or without, which is inimical to the public tranquility; and if, within my diocese or elsewhere, I learn that anything to the prejudice of the state is being contrived, I will make it known to the government."

Document 5.5: Winning Over the Nobles

To make his new hybrid state work, Napoleon curried the favor of the Old Regime nobles. He needed their approval to make his empire convincing. Although he set up his own form of nobility, granted largely for exceptional military service, he wanted to amalgamate these new nobles with the old nobility of the monarchy. The memoirs of Henriette-Lucie Dillon, wife of Frédéric-Séraphin, Comte de La Tour du Pin, show his success.

Source: Walter Geer, ed. and trans., *Recollections of the Revolution and the Empire by la Marquise de La Tour du Pin* (New York: Brentano's, 1920), 320–21, 358–60.

My aunt and Monsieur de Lally wrote us from Paris that all the persons whom we had formerly known had rallied to the government. The Concordat had just been published and the reestablishment of religion had a prodigious effect in the provinces. Until this moment, divine services were only held in private rooms, if not entirely in secret, and the priests were almost always returned *émigrés*. There was therefore universal joy when Monsieur d'Aviau de Sanzai, a man highly esteemed, was appointed Archbishop at Bordeaux. We had the honor of entertaining him at Le Bouilh during the first two days which followed his taking possession of the diocese. We brought together to receive him all the good curés of our former estate which comprised nineteen parishes. The greater part, recently appointed, had returned from foreign countries. Others had been concealed with their parishioners or in private houses. Our Archbishop was adored by all and his entry into Bordeaux was a triumph. The gratitude which all felt went out to the great man who held the reins of government. When he proclaimed himself Consul for Life, this gratitude was shown by the almost unanimous approbation of those who were called upon to vote upon this proposition.

A little later there appeared in the communes the lists upon which it was necessary for the voters to inscribe their names and respond by "yes" or "no" to the question as to whether the Consul for Life should be proclaimed Emperor.

Monsieur de La Tour du Pin was in a state of great indecision before he decided to write "yes" upon the list at Saint-André-de-Cubzac. I saw him walk up and down alone in the garden, but I did not try to penetrate his thoughts. Finally one evening he entered and I learned with pleasure that he had just written "yes" as a result of his reflections. . . .

The following day [1810, almost a decade after the preceding passage] there was to be a grand ball at the Hôtel de Ville. I was therefore somewhat put out when I was invited to dinner at Laeken, as I did not well see how I could find a moment to change my toilette, or at least my gown, between the dinner and the ball. However, the pleasure of seeing and listening to the Emperor during a period of two hours was so great that I could not but appreciate the value of such an invitation. The Duc d'Ursel accompanied me, and as we were to go afterwards to the Hôtel de Ville to receive the Emperor, I ordered my femme de chambre to be there with another toilette all ready.

This dinner was one of the events of my life of which I have preserved the most agreeable recollection. Here is the way in which the guests, to the number of eight, were placed at the table: The Emperor; at his right, the Queen of Westphalia; then Maréchal Berthier; the King of Westphalia; the Empress; the Duc d'Ursel; Mme. de Bouillé; finally myself, at the left of the Emperor. He talked to me nearly all the time, regarding the manufactures, the laces, the daily wages, the life of the lace-makers; then of the monuments, the antiquities, the establishments of charity, the manners of the people, the *béguines*. Fortunately I was well posted regarding all of these subjects. The Emperor demanded of the Duc d'Ursel: "What are the wages of the lace-maker?" The poor man was embarrassed in the endeavor to express the sum in centimes. The Emperor saw his hesitation, and turning to me asked: "What is the name of the money of the country?" I replied: "An *escalin,* or sixty-three centimes." "Ah! c'est bien," said he. . . .

The Emperor and his wife left the following morning. A yacht highly decorated took them to the end of the Canal of Brussels where they found the carriages which conveyed them to Antwerp. On boarding the yacht, my husband noticed the Marquis de Trazegnies, the Commander of the Guard of Honor. Fearing that the Emperor would not invite him to take a place on the yacht, where there was only room for a few persons, he named him, at the same time adding: "His ancestor was Constable under Saint Louis." These words produced a magic effect on the Emperor, who immediately summoned the Marquis de Trazegnies and had a long talk with him. A short time later, his wife was named Dame du Palais. She pretended to be displeased over this nomination, although secretly she was delighted.

Document 5.6: The French Civil Code (1804)

Napoleon brought to completion a project dear to the hearts of the revolutionaries: the drafting of new law codes. The Civil Code was the most important because it institutionalized equality under the law (at least for adult men), guaranteed the abolition of feudalism, and, not least, gave the nation one single code of law replacing the hundreds in effect in 1789. As the following excerpts show, however, it also codified the subservience of women in marriage. Divorce was still allowed (it had been established in 1792), but under conditions that were quite unfavorable to wives.

Source: Bryant Barrett, trans., *The Code Napoleon, Verbally Translated from the French,* 2 vols. (London: W. Reed, 1811), 1:47, 49, 57.

> Of the Rights and Respective Duties of Husband and Wife:
> Husband and wife mutually owe to each other fidelity, succor, and assistance.
> The husband owes protection to his wife, the wife obedience to her husband.
> The wife is obliged to live with her husband, and to follow him wherever he may think proper to dwell: the husband is bound to receive her, and to furnish her with everything necessary for the purposes of life, according to his means and condition.
> The wife can do no act in law without the authority of the husband, even where she shall be a public trader, or not in community, or separate in property.
> Of Causes of Divorce:
> The husband may demand divorce for cause of adultery on the part of his wife.
> The wife may demand divorce for cause of adultery on the part of her husband, where he shall have kept his concubine in their common house.

Of the Provisional Measures to Which the Demand of Divorce for Cause Defined May Give Cause:

The provisional administration of the children shall remain with the husband plaintiff or defendant in divorce, unless it shall be otherwise ordered by the tribunal, at the request either of the mother, or of the family, or of the imperial proctor, for the greater benefit of the children.

Document 5.7: Benjamin Constant, Leader of French Liberal Opposition to Napoleon

Benjamin Constant (1767–1830) spent the early years of the French Revolution in a post at a minor German court. He moved to Paris in 1795 and became active in French politics (and became the lover of Staël). He published pamphlets attacking Napoleon but later reconciled to him during the Hundred Days. He then joined the opposition to the restored Bourbon monarchy. The following comes from the fourth edition of *The Spirit of Conquest and Usurpation* (1814, thus before Constant's reconciliation with Napoleon).

Source: Benjamin Constant, *Political Writings,* ed. and trans., Biancamaria Fontana (Cambridge: Cambridge University Press, 1988), 161–63. Reprinted with the permission of Cambridge University Press.

Surely, Bonaparte is a thousand times more guilty than those barbarous conquerors who, ruling over barbarians, were by no means at odds with their age. Unlike them, he has chosen barbarism; he has preferred it. In the midst of enlightenment, he has sought to bring back the night. He has chosen to transform into greedy and bloodthirsty nomads a mild and polite people: his crime lies in this premeditated intention, in his obstinate effort to rob us of the heritage of all the enlightened generations who have preceded us on this earth. But why have we given him the right to conceive such project?

When he first arrived here, alone, out of poverty and obscurity, and until he was twenty-four, his greedy gaze wandering over the country around him, why did we show him a country in which any religious idea was the object of irony? When he listened to what was professed in our circles, why did serious thinkers tell him that man had no other motivation than his own interest? If he discovered easily enough that all the subtle interpretations through which, once the principle had been stated, we sought to elude its implications, were illusory, it was because his instinct was sound and his judgment quick. As I never attributed to him virtues which he did not possess, I am not obliged to deny him the faculties which he did. If in the heart of man there is nothing but interest, tyranny has only to frighten or to seduce him in order to dominate him. If in the heart of man there is nothing but self-interest, it is not true that morality—that is, elevation, nobility, resistance to injustice—is in accord with real self-interest. Properly understood, self-interest, in this case, given the certainty of death, is nothing but enjoyment, combined, since life can be more or less long, with that prudence which grants to enjoyment a certain duration. Finally, when in a France torn apart, tired of suffering and lamenting, and demanding only a ruler, he offered to become that ruler, why did the multitude hasten to solicit from him enslavement? When the crowd is pleased to show its love for servitude, it would be too much for it to expect its master to insist on giving it liberty instead.

I know, the nation slandered herself, or let herself be slandered by unfaithful interpreters. Despite the wretched affectation which mimicked incredulity, not all religious sentiment had been destroyed. Despite the fatuity which proclaimed itself selfish, egoism did not reign alone; and whatever acclamations may sound in the air, the national desire was not for servitude. But Bonaparte must have deceived himself over this, he whose reason was not enlightened by sentiment, whose soul was incapable of being exalted by a generous whim. He judged France by her own words, and the world by France as he imagined her to be. Because immediate usurpation was easy, he believed it could be durable, and once he became a usurper, he did all that usurpation condemns a usurper to do in our century.

It was necessary to stifle inside the country all intellectual life: he banished discussion and proscribed the freedom of the press.

The nation might have been stunned by that silence: he provided, extorted, or paid for acclamation which sounded like the national voice.

Had France remained at peace, her peaceful citizens, her idle warriors would have observed the despot, would have judged him, and would have communicated their judgments to him. Truth would have passed through the ranks of the people. Usurpation would not have long withstood the influence of truth. Thus Bonaparte was compelled to distract public attention by bellicose enterprises. War flung onto distant shores that part of the French nation that still had some real energy. It prompted the police harassment of the timid, whom it could not force abroad. It struck terror into men's hearts, and left there a certain hope that chance would take responsibility for their deliverance: a hope agreeable to fear and convenient to inertia. How many times have I heard men who were pressed to resist tyranny postponing this, during wartime till the coming of peace, and in peacetime until war commences!

I am right therefore in claiming that a usurper's sole resource is uninterrupted war. Some object: what if Bonaparte had been pacific? Had he been pacific, he would never have lasted twelve years. Peace would have re-established communication among the different countries of Europe. These communications would have restored to thought its means of expression. Works published abroad would have been smuggled into the country. The French would have seen that they did not enjoy the approval of the majority of Europe: their prestige could not have been sustained. Bonaparte perceived this truth so well that he broke with England in order to escape the British newspapers. Yet even this was not enough. While a single country remained free, Bonaparte was never safe. Commerce, active, adroit, invisible, indefatigable, capable of overcoming any distance and of insinuating itself through a thousand roundabout means, would sooner or later have reintroduced into the empire those enemies whom it was so important to exile from it. Hence the Continental blockade and the war with Russia.

LIBERTY, EQUALITY, FRATERNITY

6

Legacies and Interpretations

WE HAVE NOW TO CONSIDER THE FRENCH REVOLUTION
IN ITS ORGANIC CONNECTION WITH THE HISTORY OF
THE WORLD; FOR IN ITS SUBSTANTIAL IMPORT THAT
EVENT IS WORLD-HISTORICAL.

—GERMAN PHILOSOPHER GEORG WILHELM FRIEDRICH
HEGEL, ON THE MEANING OF THE FRENCH REVOLUTION
FOR THE PHILOSOPHY OF HISTORY (1830–31)

(CD-ROM p. 164)

Until Napoleon fell from power, Europeans could not be sure that the French Revolution was over. For some, Napoleon represented a natural continuation of the French Revolution because he brought its principles of legal equality and religious toleration to other peoples. For others, Napoleon, turning a fledgling democracy into an authoritarian state dependent on military conquest, represented a perversion or distortion of those principles. Still others condemned the French Revolution and Napoleon alike. Whatever their response to the events, most contemporaries agreed with Hegel (see quotation above) that the French Revolution had fundamentally changed the course of world history. In sorting through the legacies and interpretations of the period, it is helpful to keep in mind that the definition of the French Revolution constantly shifted as the French passed through constitutional monarchy, two forms of democratic republic (the Terror and the Directory), a consulate, and an empire. Similarly, memories, lessons, and histories drawn from the French Revolution changed as different moments in the experience came into view. Few events in world history have provoked as many clashing views, whether about its causes, its effects, or its ultimate significance.

Political Legacies

The liberty of the whole earth was depending on the issue of the contest, and was ever such a prize won with so little innocent blood? My own affections have been deeply wounded by some of the martyrs to this cause, but rather than it should have failed, I would have seen half the earth desolated.

—Thomas Jefferson,
letter to William Short,
3 January 1793
(Document 6.3)

The French Revolution provoked controversy from its beginning in July 1789, and possible positions on it were almost infinitely various. Most reactions eventually fed into four main political streams: conservative, liberal, radical democratic, and revolutionary. These fundamentally different political philosophies, often called *ideologies,* first took shape in response to the French Revolution and have continued to exercise influence right down to the present day. Much of modern political conflict can be traced back to the political legacies left by the French Revolution.

Conservatives defended the traditional order that was challenged during the revolutionary era. The first influential spokesman for the conservative position was Edmund Burke, whose *Reflections on the Revolution in France* (1790) argued that political change would work only if it was carefully rooted in "the practice of their ancestors" and "the fundamental laws of their country" and then tested by "long experience." Burke opposed rapid or radical change based on reason ("political metaphysics") rather than tradition. Government founded solely on natural rights was inevitably faulty, he insisted, because it encouraged selfishness, unrestrained ambition, and excessive individualism. The "abstract perfection" of natural rights was "their practical defect"; people actually had to give up their natural rights if they were to live in civil society (Document 6.1).

Although Burke published his reflections in 1790, long before the Terror or Napoleon, his outline of conservative principles had a European-wide impact. Unlike many supporters of royal absolutism, Burke did not simply resist the idea of change: he did not argue that everything must remain the same over time. Instead, he advocated gradual, incremental changes that did not overthrow the basic principles of a government. He came from a country, after all, that had experienced revolutionary upheaval in the 1640s (including the killing of the king) and a second revolution in 1688. Burke himself supported the cause of the American revolutionaries.

Many European royalists, in contrast, held more reactionary conservative views: they completely rejected any notion of natural rights, constitutional guarantees, representative government, legal equality, and certainly democracy. Like Burke they argued that political authority could not be derived from the people; it could only come directly from God or indirectly from history and tradition. Following Burke, they also attacked the idea that reason alone could construct a new, just society; in place of natural rights they advocated reliance on traditional institutions and established churches.

Conservatives constantly invoked the specter of revolutionary violence, arguing that it proved the bankruptcy and even criminality of revolutionary principles. French nobleman François-René Chateaubriand denounced the Jacobins (the favorite target of all conservatives) as the true authors of revolutionary evil: "Thus was the unhappy nation bandied about by the hands of powerful faction [the Jacobins], suddenly transported into another world, stunned by the cries of victims, and the acclamations of victory resounding from all the frontiers, when God, casting a look towards France, caused these monsters to sink into nothingness." (CD-ROM p. 164) Joseph de Maistre, another aristocrat, made the connection of conservatism to established religion even clearer when he railed against the immorality of the event: "Now what distinguishes the French Revolution and makes it an event unique in history is that it is radically bad. No element of good disturbs the eye of the observer; it is the highest degree of corruption ever known; it is pure impurity." Like many conservatives, Maistre traced the evil nature of the Revolution to the Enlightenment, and especially to Voltaire. The solution he proposed was a return to absolutism in politics and religion.

It is not surprising that most of the monarchs of Europe embraced the conservative creed. One of Metternich's aides, Friedrich von Gentz, declared in 1819: "As a preventive measure against the abuses of the press, absolutely nothing should be printed for years. . . . With this maxim as a rule, we should in a short time get back to God and the Truth." Many conservatives of the early 1800s followed Maistre in arguing that authority is derived from God and is therefore not an invention of man or dependent on a social contract. They rejected the principles of the Enlightenment along with those of the French Revolution.

During the nineteenth century, conservatism lost its automatic connection with monarchy, but conservatives continued to reject the French Revolution because they viewed it as the fount of democratic politics, or what they called "mob" politics. Hippolyte Taine, for example, published a series of books in the 1870s and 1880s under the general title *The Origins of Modern France,* in which he denounced the mob principle at the heart of the Revolution of 1789. This "formidable, destructive, and shapeless beast" still threatened French politics in the form of democracy. In Taine's view, the Jacobins were "fanatical, brutal or perverse enough to have lost respect for others"; "insurrections, usurpations, pillaging, murders, assaults on individuals, on magistrates, on assemblies, violations of law, attacks on the State, on communities— there is no outrage not committed by [them]." (CD-ROM p. 168)

The attack on democracy took increasingly explicit form as the French along with many other European governments adopted the principle of universal manhood suffrage. Some conservatives veered off into authoritarian nationalism, anti-Semitism, and racist forms of nationalism. The most noteworthy proponent of this direction was Charles Maurras, a founder of the right-wing political group "Action française." Maurras denounced every revolutionary principle, including equality: "The second of the revolutionary ideas, the principle of equality, essence of the democratic system, handed over power to the most numerous, that is to say the most inferior elements of the nation, to the least vigorous producers, to the most voracious consumers, who do the least work and the most damage." (CD-ROM p. 169)

Just as conservatism by its very name emphasized conservation of the old, so too liberalism as a term reflected its proponents' insistence on "liberty." Liberals accepted the principles of the Enlightenment and the innovations of the constitutional monarchy, including especially the Declaration of the Rights of Man and Citizen, but rejected the violence of the Terror. Liberals shared with Burke a distrust for abstract ideals in politics, and with conservatives a belief that rapid change would threaten the social order itself. But unlike most conservatives, they advocated political and economic reforms, in particular the implementation of constitutions that guaranteed individual rights and laws favoring free trade. Liberals held that such measures were necessary to avoid the threat of revolution.

Many leaders of the American War of Independence from Great Britain took the liberal position. Alexander Hamilton, for example, insisted that "as long therefore as the Revolution of France bore the marks of being the cause of liberty it united all hearts and centered all opinions." But, he continued, this enthusiasm had rightly diminished as a result of "the excesses which have constantly multiplied." Hamilton deplored the "partiality" of his fellow citizens for the French Revolution, even when it was "the most cruel, sanguinary, and violent that ever stained the annals of mankind" (Document 6.4). Hamilton's views resembled those of the French nobleman Marquis de Lafayette. Lafayette had fought alongside the Americans in the War of Independence, and he took a leading role in the first years of the French Revolution, only to desert the cause when the revolutionaries turned against King Louis XVI. After 1815, Lafayette would return to France and commit himself again to moderate constitutional change. Other

European liberals, such as Anne-Louise-Germaine de Staël, a noted writer and daughter of Louis XVI's Swiss finance minister, Jacques Necker, likewise deplored the violence of the French Revolution but insisted that it resulted from an inevitable popular revulsion against a domineering nobility, an overweening Catholic church, and a monarchical government that failed to reform in time.

Because they accepted the Enlightenment and many of the reforms of the French Revolution even while rejecting the Revolution's more violent aspects, liberals had to maintain a delicate balancing act. Conservatives accused them of encouraging popular disorder with their demands for change; the radical democrats and revolutionaries attacked them for pursuing improvements in the current system rather than challenging it more fundamentally. The most influential liberal of the nineteenth century, British reformer Jeremy Bentham, rejected the notion of natural rights and called the Declaration of the Rights of Man and Citizen "a hodge-podge of confusion and absurdity." Yet he argued that democracy was inevitable because government by the majority ensured his "principle of utility": the greatest good of the greatest number. Bentham's "utilitarianism" drew directly from the principles of the Enlightenment but advocated practical reforms of trade, parliament, prisons, the criminal law, and education rather than revolution. Like most liberals, he wanted more political and economic liberty, but not at the cost of violence. Bentham's most influential follower, John Stuart Mill, publicly defended the actions of the revolutionaries of 1789–91 against their conservative critics and described his thrill in the 1820s at learning that the idea of democracy had its roots in the French Revolution: "I learnt with astonishment, that the principles of democracy, then apparently in so insignificant and hopeless a minority everywhere in Europe, had borne all before them in France thirty years earlier, and had been the creed of the nation." (CD-ROM p. 167)

Radical democrats, as their name suggests, fastened on the democratic promise of the French Revolution. They believed that the French revolutionaries had been correct when they tried to implement Enlightenment principles and had endorsed violent measures only in reaction to the treachery of the aristocracy and the monarchy. The most influential statement of the radical democratic position in the 1790s came not from France but from Great Britain and the pen of Thomas Paine. Paine wrote his most famous work, *The Rights of Man* (1791), to refute Burke. He insisted that natural rights must be the foundation of all legitimate government and that they could be protected only under written constitutions, like those recently drawn up in the United States and France (Great Britain did not have a written constitution). He derided the notion that the British Parliament could establish precedents that had to be followed ever after: "Every age and generation," he insisted, "must be as free to act for itself in all cases as the age and generations which preceded it. The vanity and presumption of governing beyond the grave is the most ridiculous and insolent of all tyrannies" (Document 6.2). Reason, not tradition, should be the judge of what is right and just in government. Paine's views influenced generations of British radical democrats.

Thomas Jefferson endorsed the radical democratic position too. In his letter to William Short of January 1793, he bemoaned the violence of the French Revolution, but also to some extent condoned it as inevitable: "It was necessary to use the arm of the people, a machine not quite so blind as balls and bombs, but blind to a certain degree. . . . Were there but an Adam and an Eve left in every country, and left free, it would be better than as it now is" (Document 6.3). In these famous—or infamous—lines, Jefferson suggested his support for radical renewal much along the lines of Paine: true liberty would result only if the tyranny of the past were to be broken. Jefferson held out in favor of the French Revolution much longer than most American political figures, and he suspected that those who, like Hamilton, preached against revolutionary excesses, secretly desired to return to a monarchical form of government.

In the nineteenth century, radical democrats agitated for universal manhood suffrage (only a few embraced the logic of women's rights), republicanism, and nationalism. They often identified themselves with the Jacobins of the French Revolution. But nationalists, in particular, wanted to take the French Revolution a step further. Italian nationalist Giuseppe Mazzini (1805–72), for example, argued that the French Revolution offered not only an important example but also a warning, especially in regard to nationalism: "Wherever, in fact, individual rights are exercised without the influence of some great thought that is common to all [nationalism]; where every individual interest is not harmonized by some organization that is directed by a positive ruling principle, and by the consciousness of a common aim, there must be a tendency for some to usurp others' rights." (CD-ROM p. 167) Only nationalism could really ensure rights, he insisted, because common interests must take priority over individual interests. Radical democrats might on occasion participate in revolutions, as Mazzini and many others did in 1848, but in the second half of the nineteenth century they preferred to work through pamphlets, newspapers, political parties, parliaments, voluntary societies, and, when necessary, massive popular demonstrations.

As the radical democrats' enthusiasm for revolutionary action waned, revolution became increasingly associated with socialism, and especially communism. This version of the revolutionary legacy was articulated most influentially in the writings of Karl Marx and Friedrich Engels, founders of the international communist movement, but it could be traced back to Gracchus Babeuf and those inspired by his "Conspiracy of Equals" of 1796. Although Babeuf had few followers in 1796, his dream of a revolutionary seizure of political power by a secretly organized conspiratorial group lived on through the efforts of Italian revolutionary Filippo Buonarroti. Buonarroti (1761–1837), a member of Babeuf's circle in 1796, wrote a history of the Conspiracy of Equals in 1828. It brought the message of revolutionary seizure of power to secret societies throughout Europe. One of Buonarroti's followers, French revolutionary socialist Auguste Blanqui (1805–81), combined Buonarroti's appeal for a secret revolutionary brotherhood with the idea of a "dictatorship of the proletariat," a term coined by Blanqui to define the political goal for socialism.

Marx and Engels incorporated these notions into their doctrine of communism: communists would seize political power through revolution and install a dictatorship of the proletariat in order to abolish private property, destroy the dominance of the bourgeoisie over the workers, and replace the capitalist mode of production with a socialist or communist one. Babeuf and his followers, who talked vaguely of sharing all wealth, had not tied their conspiratorial projects to an analysis of the emerging industrial society. In fact, Babeuf went to his death before industrialization took off in France. Marx pushed far beyond the ideas of the Jacobins and even Babeuf to imagine a fundamental simultaneous restructuring of politics, society, and the economy.

Marx and Engels made constant reference to the French Revolution in their writings. (CD-ROM p. 170) It was the great revolution against which all its nineteenth-century imitators had to be compared, but it had only begun the task of transforming the world. In 1880, Engels summarized their view of the French Revolution: "We saw how the French philosophers of the eighteenth century, the forerunners of the Revolution, appealed to reason as the sole judge of all that is. A rational government, rational society, were to be founded; everything that ran counter to eternal reason was to be remorselessly done away with. . . . The French Revolution had realized this rational society and government. But the new order of things, rational enough as compared with earlier conditions, turned out to be by no means absolutely rational." (CD-ROM p. 170) The French Revolution had brought the bourgeoisie to power and enabled capitalism to triumph over feudalism; now the proletariat had to seize power and overthrow the bourgeoisie. The means to accomplish this upheaval had been revealed by the French Revolution, but revolution in the communist movement was increasingly interpreted to mean not mass uprising, as in 1789, but a workers' party secretly organized to achieve its end through political dictatorship, based on the political model suggested first by Babeuf.

Through Marx and Engels the revolutionary political legacy took root in the worldwide communist revolutionary movement. Communist revolutionaries even in the twentieth century continued to think long and hard about the lessons of the French Revolution of 1789. Leon Trotsky, for example, one of the architects of the Russian Revolution of 1917, along with Lenin, constantly kept the French Revolution in his sights. "History does not repeat itself," he insisted. "However much one may compare the Russian Revolution with the Great French Revolution, the former can never be transformed into a repetition of the latter. The nineteenth century has not passed in vain." (CD-ROM p. 171) Yet to prove how far the Russian Revolution had advanced beyond the French Revolution, he had to return again and again to comparisons with the French Revolution, to defend the Jacobins against their liberal critics, and then to argue how communism had surpassed Jacobinism. The French Revolution, in other words, became a necessary stage in the communist view of world history: because it brought the bourgeoisie to power and thereby facilitated the development of capitalist industry, it directly prepared the way for the next stage in history, in which the proletarian revolution would overthrow the bourgeoisie and replace capitalism with the socialist organization of production. The incorporation of the French Revolution into this notion of the stages of history ensured that the French Revolution would continue to be a focus of controversy right down to the present.

Communists, radical democrats, liberals, and conservatives drew contradictory lessons from the French Revolution because they held contradictory opinions about revolution as a mode of political action. Communists viewed revolution as the best instrument for fashioning a fundamentally new world; radical democrats considered revolution an occasional necessity to be entered upon only in times of extremity; liberals accepted revolutions only when they were made for constitutional guarantees; and conservatives considered revolution a sign of human pride, a fundamentally mistaken activity that could only bring in its train political disaster and attacks on religion and morals. Because revolution still generates controversy in the present day, the French Revolution, as the first modern revolution and as the model for communist revolution, has lost none of its ability to provoke discussion and debate.

Scholarly Interpretations

Independent of every thing that is accounted for in the French Revolution, there is something unaccounted for in its spirit and its acts. I sense where the unknown object is, but try as I may, I cannot raise the veil that covers it.

—Alexis de
Tocqueville (1858)
(CD-ROM p. 167)

Because the French Revolution gave rise to so many competing political legacies, it is hardly surprising that it has generated disputes among scholars as well. In the century after its occurrence, until the outbreak of the Russian Revolution in 1917, the French Revolution provoked more scholarly controversy than any other moment in Western history. The first histories of the French Revolution were written by authors who wanted to directly shape the public's memory of its legacy. Memoirs by participants, and "reflections" and "considerations" by those not far removed from the action, appeared as soon as Napoleon Bonaparte left the scene. The most influential of these was Germaine de Staël's *Considerations on the French Revolution,* published in 1818 just after her death. Staël swam against the currents set in motion by the restored monarchy in France; she justified the Revolution as an attempt to regain sovereignty for the nation from an absolute monarchy that had deprived the French of their rights. Although she denounced the "regime of blood" and "political fanaticism" of Robespierre, she blamed the nobility and the clergy for bringing down the monarchy. Their insistence on maintaining their privileged position had made constitutional monarchy impossible. At a time when royal officials suppressed any reminder of the events between 1789 and 1815 as contrary to order and good morals, Staël's *Considerations* announced a program for the opposition: they would tell the history of the Revolution as a way of criticizing the restored monarchy.

The pattern set by Staël continued right up to the 1870s: criticism of the regime in France often took the form of histories of the French Revolution. The first full-length histories of the Revolution appeared in the 1820s, written by François-Auguste Mignet and Adolphe Thiers, journalists and editors in the political opposition. Like Staël, they took the liberal position, opposing the violence of the Terror but defending the notion of a constitutional monarchy. When a constitutional monarchy came to power under King Louis-Philippe after the Revolution of 1830, historians briefly turned their attention to gathering and publishing documents about the revolutionary era. Then, in the late 1840s, growing opposition to the reign of Louis-Philippe from a revived republican movement again took the form of new histories of the French Revolution. Two of the republican historians, Alphonse Lamartine and Louis Blanc, took leadership roles in the revolution of 1848 that overthrew Louis-Philippe. A third republican historian, Jules Michelet (1798–1874), wrote the most popular history of the Revolution in the nineteenth century.

Michelet fulminated against the powers of the Catholic clergy and exulted in the uprising of the people. In lyric prose reminiscent of his contemporaries among romantic poets, Michelet interpreted the Revolution of 1789 as a joyous expression of national feeling. The Revolution had not destroyed the nobility, he claimed; rather, it made of the French 34 million nobles. The "true" France was the France of the Revolution of 1789, the France that carried on the generous ideals of a nation identified with Joan of Arc. Robespierre had perverted this revolutionary spirit of peace, justice, and fraternity, but the people, Michelet insisted, would eventually reclaim their democratic heritage. The regimes of Louis-Philippe and his successor Napoleon III made every effort to muzzle Michelet, who was forced to retire in 1853 from his university position just as he finished writing his history of the Revolution.

It was a critic of democracy, however, who wrote the most enduringly influential account of the French Revolution. Alexis de Tocqueville (1805–59), a contemporary of Michelet and an aristocrat, landowner, and brilliant social commentator, also opposed the regime of Napoleon III, but from a perspective at odds with that of Michelet. Tocqueville had made an international reputation for himself in 1835 when he published *Democracy in America,* based on his travels to the United States. In this early work he expressed some optimism about democracy, at least in its American setting. By 1856, however, when he published *The Old Regime and the French Revolution,* he had become much more pessimistic. Democracy and despotism seemed to go hand in hand in France: the Revolution of 1789 led to Napoleon Bonaparte; the Revolution of 1848, which brought Tocqueville briefly to a ministerial position, ended in the elevation of Napoleon Bonaparte's nephew, Napoleon III.

Tocqueville took it as his task to explain how revolutions made in the name of liberty could end up in a common subservience to one-man rule, how "the head of Liberty" had been grafted "onto a servile body." He did not write a new narrative of the French Revolution; instead, he offered an analysis of French political culture, an

analysis that still resonates today. He traced France's problem in establishing enduring liberty to the legacy of the absolute monarchy. By suppressing all the powers of
the nobility, the monarchs of France had eliminated opportunities for learning to participate in political life, removed the only restraints on royal power, and inadvertently
created resentment against the nobles, who no longer had political functions to justify their social privileges. The centralization of royal authority thus created a kind of
equality of political passivity. Into the vacuum created by the royal destruction of
noble powers stepped the writers of the Enlightenment. Lacking any forum for practical political discussion, Enlightenment writers advanced wildly utopian and abstract
ideas (here Tocqueville showed Burke's influence). Adopting the Enlightenment position, the revolutionaries "nursed the foolish hope that a sudden, radical transformation of a very ancient, highly intricate social system could be effected almost
painlessly, under the auspices of reason and by its efficacy alone." The revolutionaries
carried the centralization of power even further, and as a consequence their emphasis
on equality and democracy only paved the way to dictatorship, a form even worse
than monarchy, in Tocqueville's view.

Tocqueville's account exercised more influence in the second half of the twentieth
century than it did in the century following its publication. In the heat of continuing
French conflicts over the form of government, which recurred with alarming fre-
quency right up to 1958 (the date of the establishment of the present fifth republic),
Tocqueville was often dismissed as an aristocrat nostalgic for the Old Regime, or simply neglected because he did not write a narrative history of the Revolution. In the
past fifty years, however, all sides have finally claimed him as their own, and his analysis has become standard reading everywhere because it so astutely deciphers many of
the enduring patterns in French politics.

As history became an academic profession in the last decades of the nineteenth
century, professors gradually displaced the writers and politicians who had shaped the
image of the French Revolution in the past. They still waged their political wars
through narrative histories, but now wrote in an increasingly analytical fashion,
reflecting the changes in history as a discipline. On one side of the political struggle
was the left, the supporters of the Republic (France became a republic again in 1870
and has remained one, with variations, since then), and eventually socialists and communists. On the other side was the right, Bonapartists and monarchist opponents of
the Republic and—once the Republic was successfully established—those who resisted any leftward drift in republican politics. This division between left and right
dominated writing about the French Revolution between 1870 and 1989.

The left had an initial advantage in these polemics because it could rely on a strong
university base: in 1886 the Paris city government created a chair of the history of the
French Revolution at the Sorbonne (University of Paris). It was held first by the
ardent republican Alphonse Aulard, then by a succession of talented socialists and
communists, continuing right up to the present. Like most professional historians of

Fig. 6.1   The Marseillaise

A similar emphasis on patriotic unity can be seen in Jean Renoir's film *La Marseillaise* (1938). The movie tells the story of France's national anthem, composed by Rouget de Lisle as a way to rally the troops. The song written for soldiers from Marseilles soon inspired the entire nation.

his time, Aulard focused on political history. His hero was Georges Danton, whom he viewed as the political founder of modern French republicanism. Aulard's successors, in tune with the rise of social history and the influence of Marxism after the Russian Revolution of 1917, turned to the study of social tensions and social classes, including the peasants and the sans-culottes. Aulard's student and successor Albert Mathiez broke with his mentor by preferring Robespierre to Danton, whom he considered a mere opportunist. But Mathiez focused more on material circumstances than on personalities, and he pioneered the study of food shortages and their impact on revolutionary politics.

Mining a similar vein, Mathiez's successor, Georges Lefebvre, produced wide-ranging studies of the peasantry. In 1939, on the 150th anniversary of the French Revolution, just before the outbreak of World War II, Lefebvre published a short celebration of 1789, *The Coming of the French Revolution*. In a call to national unity in a time of danger, Lefebvre insisted that even though the French Revolution ultimately became a bourgeois revolution (as Marx had maintained), all the classes had originally joined in the movement to bring about the French Revolution in 1789 (Fig. 6.1). Lefebvre's combination of narrative skills and analytical studies gave him an unrivaled reputation; even those who object to his Marxist views regard him as the most accomplished academic historian of the Revolution.

The right did not have the same initial foothold within the university system. Hyppolyte Taine (1828–93), for example, wrote his four volumes on the Old Regime and the French Revolution as a general literary and cultural critic, not as a professional historian. (CD-ROM p. 168) He held the post of professor of aesthetics and art history at the École des Beaux-Arts; he was not trained as a historian. Taine's views, though modified and supplemented by later right-wing critics such as Augustin Cochin and Pierre Gaxotte, remained fundamental to the right-wing criticism of the Revolution. Although he could on occasion criticize the monarchical regime, he had little but contempt for "the people" so beloved by Michelet. He frequently likened the lower classes to beasts or insects; at best, they were childish. "In the lower classes," he wrote, "*l'eau de vie* [alcohol spirits] . . . is the literature of the people." The "people" who made the French Revolution at its most crucial moments—the fall of the Bastille, for instance—were a crazed, frenzied rabble. The Revolution was evil because it brought this popular element to the forefront.

Cochin and Gaxotte toned down this more virulent side to Taine's criticism; they viewed the lower classes as the manipulated tools of professional politicians who came to power through the activities of secret societies, such as Masonic lodges. The lodges, salons, and provincial academies of the Enlightenment paved the way for the Jacobin Clubs of the Revolution, and by implication for socialist and communist groups in the nineteenth and twentieth centuries. Gazotte claimed, for example, that the Mountain in 1793–94 stood for "dictatorial communism." In this way, the right took up some of the claims of the left but gave them a negative rather than positive spin. Where Mathiez, for example, celebrated the ways in which the social policies of the Mountain of 1793–94 anticipated those of the socialist revolution of 1917 in Russia, Gaxotte considered this foreshadowing grounds for condemning the French Revolution.

Before the 1970s, the left enjoyed the dominant position in these academic debates, in part because of its strength within the university and in part because the right was associated with losing political positions (absolute monarchy, then constitutional monarchy, antirepublicanism, and, between 1940 and 1944, the Vichy collaborationist regime). The balance began to shift, however, as critics of the Revolution finally accepted the republican form of government and began to exercise more power within the university. This more moderate republican right also got support from a growing body of work produced in the Anglophone countries, especially the United States and the United Kingdom. In the United States, in particular, Marxism had relatively little hold in the universities, so Marxist interpretations coming out of France were bound to come under fire. As the universities expanded and the cost of foreign travel declined in the decades after World War II, American, Canadian, British, and Australian scholars began to produce original work on French history, gathering evidence to test Marxist theses and almost invariably finding that they failed those tests.

The major thesis that came under fire was that of the bourgeois revolution. The critics of the Marxist interpretation argued that the capitalist bourgeoisie had not made the Revolution (first aristocrats and then middle-class officials and lawyers had led it, not manufacturers); that the Revolution had not overthrown feudalism (because feudalism no longer existed); and that the Revolution did not pave the way for capitalism (since industrialization did not take place until the 1840s). On every important point, the critics mounted evidence to demonstrate the weakness of the Marxist interpretation.

In 1978, a former French communist, François Furet (1927–97), published a collection of essays, *Interpreting the French Revolution,* that brought together this new work in a frontal assault on the left-wing, Marxist interpretation of the French Revolution. Taking aim at the communist historian Albert Soboul, who then held the chair of the history of the French Revolution at the Sorbonne, Furet, himself a historian in the École des Hautes Études en Sciences Sociales, denounced the entire tradition of left-wing history of the French Revolution. This "revolutionary catechism," this "Lenino-populist vulgate," he argued, had fundamentally distorted the history of the French Revolution by depicting it as a class struggle that anticipated communism. Furet derided Soboul, the author of a major study of the sans-culottes, as "a perfect illustration" of the kind of teleological history "in which social classes function as metaphysical categories." Furet claimed as his ancestors Tocqueville and Cochin; he did not reject democracy, but wanted to understand why democracy in the French Revolution developed into Terror or totalitarianism. In a particularly striking passage, Furet linked the French and Russian revolutions in ways not unlike those of previous right-wing historians: "Today the Gulag [the Soviet prison camp system] is leading to a rethinking of the Terror precisely because the two undertakings are seen as identical." Marxists such as Soboul could not undertake this rethinking, Furet insisted, because they had become obsessed with the social explanation of the Revolution and ignored its political mechanisms. The social underpinnings of the French Revolution could never explain this skidding out of control into Terror; revolution was "an autonomous political and ideological movement," not the expression of a social class.

Furet's emphasis on the autonomy of politics and ideology led him to focus on the role of language in the French Revolution and, more generally, in the operation of political culture. Rather than referring to class conflict in the Marxist manner (the bourgeoisie overthrowing the aristocracy with the help of peasants and sans-culottes), Furet built up an elaborate network of linguistic and mental terms: the "symbolic system," "an imaginary discourse on power," "the figment of a frenzied occupation with power," "the discourse of equality," and "the mental representations of power." Power resided, it seemed, in words, not social classes. In offering this linguistic or symbolic style of analysis, Furet aligned himself with broader contemporary currents in the social sciences and the humanities, which similarly called attention to the operation of language, signs, symbols, and discourses (called by some, as a result, "the linguistic turn"). He gave a sophisticated linguistic twist to the social evidence uncovered by Anglophone historians.

By 1989, the year of the bicentennial of the French Revolution, Furet's version of the French Revolution had won pride of place in the public eye. Even before the collapse of the Soviet Union, the political balance had shifted, not only in France but almost everywhere else in the Western world as well. Conservatives such as Margaret Thatcher in the United Kingdom and Ronald Reagan in the United States had repeatedly won election by reaffirming the advantages of capitalism. A communist still held the chair of the history of the French Revolution in Paris, but the chairholder in 1989, Michel Vovelle, expounded a much more supple version of Marxism, one that at times hardly even seemed Marxist. Although his political vantage point differed from Furet's, Vovelle had also concentrated on culture, symbols, and mental representations. He made his reputation with a long-term study of "de-Christianization," showing how the revolutionary policies on religion followed from a century-long process of disengagement from Catholic practices, and he particularly encouraged the study of visual imagery. In other words, Marxists too had become more interested in the cultural and linguistic aspects of the French Revolution.

Furet had argued "The French Revolution is over," meaning that everyone in France agreed on the virtues of liberty and equality and of a republican and democratic form of government. What he might have added, if he had written the book ten years later, was that Marxism no longer attracted the same kind of passionate devotion in France, except in increasingly smaller circles. Since the victory of a left coalition of socialists and communists in the French elections in 1981, the communists had steadily lost ground with the voters; they had been able to share power only because their influence was waning. One by-product of the communist electoral decline was a loosening of the hold of left-wing historians on the history of the French Revolution.

Since 1989, as the polemics between French communists and anticommunists have subsided, the work of Anglophone historians has attracted even more attention. Having once served largely as fuel for internal French squabbling, Anglophone studies now offer alternative views of their own. Studies of political language, symbols, and rituals by such historians as Keith Michael Baker and Lynn Hunt reflect the influence of Furet, but they also offer their own, often conflicting, interpretations: Baker traced the Terror to the victory of one kind of political discourse over its competitors, whereas Hunt used engravings, novels, official seals, and voting patterns in elections to argue that democratic republicanism, not Terror, was the most enduring outcome of the Revolution. The contribution of Anglophone historians has been especially prominent in the study of gender relations. Some feminist historians, following the lead of Joan Landes, claim that the Revolution merely extended the masculinist biases of the Enlightenment. The Enlightenment writers—Rousseau was the most

Fig. 6.2   The Solemn Inauguration of the Statue of Liberty in the
United States

This engraving shows a view of New Yorkers celebrating the arrival of the
new Statue of Liberty given by France to the United States. It was finally
put in place in 1886. Symbolic female figures—especially the figure of
Liberty—carried the message of the French Revolution into the nineteenth
and twentieth centuries. Chinese students used a similar Statue of Liberty
in their demonstrations against the Chinese government in 1989.

notorious example—insisted that natural law and reason demonstrated that men
inherently possessed the right to political participation whereas women did not.
Nature and reason justified the exclusion of women from the republic. Other feminist historians have argued, however, that the Revolution opened up new opportunities for women, providing the option of divorce for the first time, ensuring equal
inheritance to girls, and affording women the opportunity to establish political clubs
of their own and to make their voices heard (Fig. 6.2).

No one school, whether left-wing or right-wing, French or Anglophone, now dom-
inates the writing of the history of the French Revolution. Research continues along a
variety of fronts, with new areas, such as the role of religious minorities and the effects
of the Revolution in the colonies, emerging as centers of interest. We have tried to
reflect these new concerns in these pages, even while leaving open the question of the
ultimate meaning of the French Revolution. The French Revolution may be "over" in
the sense that no one now contests the importance of liberty and equality or the virtues
of democratic government. But this does not mean that the interpretive battles have
ended. The rise of feminism and multiculturalism, for example, have inevitably produced new questions for research. Because so many of our modern conceptions of politics and history came out of the experience of the French Revolution, it will always be
a prime candidate for rewriting. In a letter he wrote almost 150 years ago, Tocqueville

expressed his frustration about trying to pin down the French Revolution. "There is something unaccounted for in its spirit and its acts," he said. Historians have labored mightily to lift the veil Tocqueville sensed, yet there will always be something unaccounted for, something left to investigate and puzzle over.

Documents

The Anglo-American Response, from 1789 to the Terror

If the French revolutionaries were expecting support from beyond their borders, they certainly received it, at least early in the Revolution. Although some immediately perceived the French Revolution as a threat to monarchy and other pillars of the Old Regime, favorable reactions to the Enlightenment encouraged Europeans and North Americans to rally on behalf of the Revolution. And no countries should have been more inclined that way than England and America. As demonstrated earlier (Documents 1.11 through 1.16) the Anglo-Americans shared a language of freedom with the French. Many French revolutionaries believed they were, in fact, directly borrowing from American experience.

Yet, amid the early international celebration of the Revolution, the two most celebrated critics were the future American president John Adams and the Anglo-Irish member of Parliament Edmund Burke. Adams's distrust of the common people in America helps explain his resistance to the French Revolution. Burke's negative reaction was less predictable since earlier in his career, he had defended the American cause against his own Parliament. What unified his positions was his belief in British liberties grounded in British history and tradition. He denounced the French notion of "the rights of man," insisting that nothing lasting could be built on such abstract and arid conceptions. Thomas Paine, an English radical who had published *Common Sense* in support of the American Revolution, now rushed into print a rejoinder in favor of the rights of man.

After 1792, opinion in both Britain and the United States began to run against the Revolution. Federalists and Jeffersonians fiercely debated the merits of the French experience. By 1794, however, only a tiny number of Americans continued their support. Even Thomas Jefferson, earlier a strong proponent, eventually changed his mind.

Debate never really ended. Political leaders, scholars, filmmakers, playwrights, and novelists continue to explore this fascinating period. As long as human rights, democracy, military dictatorship, and revolution continue to be issues in the modern world, the French Revolution will arouse passionate feelings and continuing controversy.

Document 6.1: Edmund Burke, Reflections on the Revolution in France *(1790)*

Born in Ireland, Edmund Burke (1729–97) immediately opposed the French Revolution, warning his compatriots against the dangerous abstractions of the French.

He argued the case for tradition, continuity, and gradual reform based on practical experience.

Source: Edmund Burke, *The Works of Edmund Burke,* 3 vols. (New York: Harper & Brothers, 1860), 1:481–83, 488–91.

It is no wonder therefore, that with these ideas of every thing in their constitution and government at home, either in church or state, as illegitimate and usurped, or at best as a vain mockery, they look abroad with an eager and passionate enthusiasm. Whilst they are possessed by these notions, it is vain to talk to them of the practice of their ancestors, the fundamental laws of their country, the fixed form of a constitution, whose merits are confirmed by the solid test of long experience, and an increasing public strength and national prosperity. They despise experience as the wisdom of unlettered men; and as for the rest, they have wrought under-ground a mine that will blow up at one grand explosion all examples of antiquity, all precedents, charters, and acts of parliament. They have "the rights of men." Against these there can be no prescription; against these no argument is binding: these admit no temperament, and no compromise: any thing withheld from their full demand is so much of fraud and injustice.

Against these rights of men let no government look for security in the length of its continuance, or in the justice and lenity of its administration. The objections of these speculatists, if its forms do not quadrate with their theories, are as valid against such an old and beneficent government as against the most violent tyranny or the greenest usurpation. They are always at issue with governments, not on a question of abuse, but a question of competency and a question of title. I have nothing to say to the clumsy subtlety of their political metaphysics. . . .

Far am I from denying in theory, full as far is my heart from withholding in practice (if I were of power to give or to withhold) the real rights of men. In denying their false claims of right, I do not mean to injure those which are real, and are such as their pretended rights would totally destroy. If civil society be made for the advantage of man, all the advantages for which it is made become his right. It is an institution of beneficence; and law itself is only beneficence acting by a rule. Men have a right to live by that rule; they have a right to do justice, as between their fellows, whether their fellows are in public function or in ordinary occupation. They have a right to the fruits of their industry and to the means of making their industry fruitful. They have a right to the acquisitions of their parents, to the nourishment and improvement of their offspring, to instruction in life, and to consolation in death. Whatever each man can separately do, without trespassing upon others, he has a right to do for himself; and he has a right to a fair portion of all which society, with all its combinations of skill and force, can do in his favor. In this partnership all men have equal rights, but not to equal things. He that has but five shillings in the partnership has as good a right to it as he that has five hundred pounds has to his larger proportion. But he has not a right to an equal dividend in the product of the joint stock; and as to the share of power, authority, and direction which each individual ought to have in the management of the state, that I must deny to be amongst the direct original rights of man in civil society; for I have in my contemplation the civil social man, and no other. It is a thing to be settled by convention.

If civil society be the offspring of convention, that convention must be its law. That convention must limit and modify all the descriptions of constitution which are formed under it. Every sort of legislative, judicial, or executory power are its creatures. They can have no being in any other state of things; and how can any man claim under the conventions of civil society rights which do not so much as suppose its existence—rights which are absolutely repugnant to it? One of the first motives to civil society, and which becomes one of its fundamental rules, is that no man should be judge in his own cause. By this each person has at once divested himself of the first fundamental right of uncovenanted man, that is, to judge for himself and to assert his own cause. He abdicates all right to be his own governor. He inclusively, in a great measure, abandons the right of self-defense, the first law of nature. Men cannot enjoy the rights of an uncivil and of a civil state together. That he may obtain justice, he gives up his right of determining what it is in points the most essential to him. That he may secure some liberty, he makes a surrender in trust of the whole of it.

Government is not made in virtue of natural rights, which may and do exist in total independence of it, and exist in much greater clearness and in a much greater degree of abstract perfection; but their abstract perfection is their practical defect. By having a right to everything they want everything. Government is a contrivance of human wisdom to provide for human wants. Men have a right that these wants should be provided for by this wisdom. Among these wants is to be reckoned the want, out of civil society, of a sufficient restraint upon their passions. Society requires not only that the passions of individuals should be subjected, but that even in the mass and body, as well as in the individuals, the inclinations of men should frequently be thwarted, their will controlled, and their passions brought into subjection. This can only be done by a power out of themselves, and not, in the exercise of its function, subject to that will and to those passions which it is its office to bridle and subdue. In this sense the restraints on men, as well as their liberties, are to be reckoned among their rights. But as the liberties and the restrictions vary with times and circumstances and admit to infinite modifications, they cannot be settled upon any abstract rule; and nothing is so foolish as to discuss them upon that principle.

Document 6.2: Thomas Paine, The Rights of Man *(1791)*

Thomas Paine (1737–1809) played a vital role in mobilizing Americans' support for their own independence, and he leapt to support the French revolutionaries when Edmund Burke attacked. Elected deputy to the French National Convention in 1793, Paine nearly lost his head as an associate of the Girondins during the Terror. In his reply to Burke, Paine defended the idea of reform based on reason. He dedicated the work to George Washington with these words: "Sir, I present you with a small treatise in defense of those principles of freedom which your exemplary virtue hath so eminently contributed to establish. That the rights of man may become as universal as your benevolence can wish, and that you may enjoy the happiness of seeing the new world regenerate the old." Paine argued that people now alive should not be bound by what their ancestors did, that tradition and heredity should count for nothing.

Source: Thomas Paine, "Rights of Man: Being an Answer to Mr. Burke's Attack on the French Revolution," in *The Political Works of Thomas Paine* (New York: C. Blanchard, 1860), 6–8, 30, 32–36.

> Not sufficiently content with abusing the National Assembly, a great part of his work is taken up with abusing Dr. Price (one of the best-hearted men that lives) and the two societies in England known by the name of the Revolution Society and the Society for Constitutional Information. Dr. Price had preached a sermon on the 4th of November, 1789, being the anniversary of what is called in England the Revolution, which took place [in] 1688. Mr. Burke, speaking of this sermon, says: "The political Divine proceeds dogmatically to assert, that by the principles of the Revolution, the people of England have acquired three fundamental rights:
>
> 1. To choose our own governors.
> 2. To cashier them for misconduct.
> 3. To frame a government for ourselves."
>
> Dr. Price does not say that the right to do these things exists in this or in that person, or in this or in that description of persons, but that it exists in the whole; that it is a right resident in the nation. Mr. Burke, on the contrary, denies that such a right exists in the nation, either in whole or in part, or that it exists anywhere; and, what is still more strange and marvellous, he says: "that the people of England utterly disclaim such a right,

and that they will resist the practical assertion of it with their lives and fortunes." That men should take up arms and spend their lives and fortunes, not to maintain their rights, but to maintain they have not rights, is an entirely new species of discovery, and suited to the paradoxical genius of Mr. Burke.

The method which Mr. Burke takes to prove that the people of England have no such rights, and that such rights do not now exist in the nation, either in whole or in part, or anywhere at all, is of the same marvellous and monstrous kind with what he has already said; for his arguments are that the persons, or the generation of persons, in whom they did exist, are dead, and with them the right is dead also. To prove this, he quotes a declaration made by Parliament about a hundred years ago, to William and Mary, in these words: "The Lords Spiritual and Temporal, and Commons, do, in the name of the people aforesaid" (meaning the people of England then living) "most humbly and faithfully submit themselves, their heirs and posterities, for Ever."

He quotes a clause of another Act of Parliament made in the same reign, the terms of which he says, "bind us" (meaning the people of their day), "our heirs and our posterity, to them, their heirs and posterity, to the end of time."

Mr. Burke conceives his point sufficiently established by producing those clauses, which he enforces by saying that they exclude the right of the nation for ever. And not yet content with making such declarations, repeated over and over again, he farther says, "that if the people of England possessed such a right before the Revolution" (which he acknowledges to have been the case, not only in England, but throughout Europe, at an early period), "yet that the English Nation did, at the time of the Revolution, most solemnly renounce and abdicate it, for themselves, and for all their posterity, for ever."

As Mr. Burke occasionally applies the poison drawn from his horrid principles, not only to the English nation, but to the French Revolution and the National Assembly, and charges that august, illuminated and illuminating body of men with the epithet of usurpers, I shall, *sans cérémonie*, place another system of principles in opposition to his.

The English Parliament of 1688 did a certain thing, which, for themselves and their constituents, they had a right to do, and which it appeared right should be done. But, in addition to this right, which they possessed by delegation, they set up another right by assumption, that of binding and controlling posterity to the end of time. The case, therefore, divides itself into two parts; the right which they possessed by delegation, and the right which they set up by assumption. The first is admitted; but with respect to the second, I reply there never did, there never will, and there never can, exist a Parliament, or any description of men, or any generation of men, in any country, possessed of the right or the power of binding and controlling posterity to the "end of time," or of commanding for ever how the world shall be governed, or who shall govern it; and therefore all such clauses, acts or declarations by which the makers of them attempt to do what they have neither the right nor the power to do, nor the power to execute, are in themselves null and void. Every age and generation must be as free to act for itself in all cases as the age and generations which preceded it. The vanity and presumption of governing beyond the grave is the most ridiculous and insolent of all tyrannies. Man has no property in man; neither has any generation a property in the generations which are to follow. The Parliament or the people of 1688, or of any other period, had no more right to dispose of the people of the present day, or to bind or to control them in any shape whatever, than the parliament or the people of the present day have to dispose of, bind or control those who are to live a hundred or a thousand years hence. Every generation is, and must be, competent to all the purposes which its occasions require. It is the living, and not the dead, that are to be accommodated. When man ceases to be, his power and his wants cease with him; and having no longer any participation in the concerns of this world, he has no longer any authority in directing who shall be its governors, or how its government shall be organised, or how administered.

I am not contending for nor against any form of government, nor for nor against any party, here or elsewhere. That which a whole nation chooses to do it has a right to do. Mr. Burke says, No. Where, then, does the right exist? I am contending for the rights of the living, and against their being willed away and controlled and contracted for by the manuscript assumed authority of the dead, and Mr. Burke is contending for the authority of the dead over the rights and freedom of the living. There was a time when kings disposed of their crowns by will upon their death-beds, and consigned the people, like beasts of the field, to whatever successor they appointed. This is now so exploded as scarcely to be remembered, and so monstrous as hardly to be believed. But the Parliamentary clauses upon which Mr. Burke builds his political church are of the same nature.

The laws of every country must be analogous to some common principle. In England no parent or master, nor all the authority of Parliament, omnipotent as it has called itself, can bind or control the personal freedom even of an individual beyond the age of twenty-one years. On what ground of right, then, could the Parliament of 1688, or any other Parliament, bind all posterity for ever? . . .

Document 6.3: Thomas Jefferson on the French Revolution

Although deeply sympathetic to the French in general and to the revolutionary cause in particular, Thomas Jefferson (1743–1826) deplored the excesses of violence that took place even before the Terror. Still, he believed that many of the steps taken by the French, such as deposing their king, had been necessary, and he claimed that most North Americans supported the French. The Terror would later make him reconsider still more, though without renouncing the Revolution entirely. Here he explains himself to the secretary he used while working in France.

Source: Thomas Jefferson, "Letter to William Short" (3 January 1793), Thomas Jefferson Papers at the Library of Congress, Series 1, Reel 17.

Philadelphia Jan. 3. 1793

DEAR SIR

The tone of your letters had for some time given me pain, on account of the extreme warmth with which they censured the proceedings of the Jacobins of France. I considered that sect as the same with the Republican patriots, and the Feuillants as the Monarchical patriots, well known in the early part of the Revolution, and but little distant in their views, both having in object the establishment of a free constitution, and differing only on the question whether their chief Executive should be hereditary or not. The Jacobins (as since called) yielded to the Feuillants and tried the experiment of retaining their hereditary Executive. The experiment failed completely, and would have brought on the reestablishment of despotism had it been pursued. The Jacobins saw this, and that the expunging that officer was of absolute necessity, and the Nation was with them in opinion, for however they might have been formerly for the constitution framed by the first assembly, they were come over from their hope in it, and were now generally Jacobins. In the struggle which was necessary, many guilty persons fell without the forms of trial, and with them some innocent. These I deplore as much as any body, and shall deplore some of them to the day of my death. But I deplore them as I should have done had they fallen in battle. It was necessary to use the arm of the people, a machine not quite so blind as balls and bombs, but blind to a certain degree. A few of their cordial friends met at their hands, the fate of enemies. But time and truth will rescue and embalm their memories, while their posterity will be enjoying that very liberty for which they would never have hesitated to offer up their lives. The liberty of the whole earth was depending on the issue of the contest, and was ever such a prize won with so little innocent blood? My own affections have been deeply wounded by some of the martyrs to this cause, but rather than it should have failed, I would have seen half the earth desolated. Were there but an Adam and an Eve left in every country, and left free, it would be better than as it now is. I have expressed to you my sentiments, because they are really those of 99 in an hundred of our citizens. The universal feasts, and rejoicings which have lately been had on account of the successes of the French shewed the genuine effusions of their hearts. You have been wounded by the sufferings of your friends, and have by this circumstance been hurried into a temper of mind which would be extremely disrelished if known to your countrymen. The reserve of *the Pres. of the U.S.* had never permitted me to discover the light in which he viewed it, and as I was more anxious that you should satisfy him than me, I had still avoided explanations with you on the subject. But your [letter] 113 induced him to break silence and to notice the extreme acrimony of your expressions. He added that he had been informed the sentiments you expressed *in your conversations* were equally offensive to our allies, and that you should consider yourself as the representative of your country and that what you say, might be imputed to your constituents. He desired me therefore to write to you on this subject. He added that he considered *France as the sheet anchor of this country and its friendship as a first object.* There are in the U.S. some characters of opposite principles; some of them are high in office, others possessing great wealth, and all of them hostile to France and fondly looking to England as the staff of their hope. These I named to you on a former occasion. Their prospects have certainly not brightened. Excepting them, this country is entirely republican, friends to the constitution, anxious to preserve it and to have it administered according to it's [*sic*] own republican principles. The little party above mentioned have espoused it only as a stepping stone to monarchy, and have endeavored to approximate it to that in it's [*sic*] administration, in order to render it's [*sic*] final transition more easy. The successes of republicanism in France have given the coup de grace to their prospects, and I hope to their projects.— I have developed to you faithfully the sentiments of your country, that you may govern yourself accordingly. I know your republicanism to be pure, and that it is no decay of that which has embittered you against it's [*sic*] votaries in France, but too great a sensibility at the partial evil by which it's [*sic*] object has been accomplished there.

Document 6.4: Alexander Hamilton on the French Revolution

Alexander Hamilton (1755–1804) shared the Federalist Party perspective on events in France. He, and they, supported the moderate phase of the Revolution, which they understood to be about United States–style liberty, but detested the attacks on security and property that took place during the Terror. In particular, Hamilton distrusted the popular masses. However, even he concedes the importance of the French Revolution.

Source: Alexander Hamilton Papers at the Library of Congress, Container 25, Reel 22.

[Philadelphia, 1794]

In the early periods of the French Revolution, a warm zeal for its success was in this Country *a sentiment truly universal.* The love of Liberty is here the ruling passion *of the Citizens of the United States* pervading every class animating every bosom. As long therefore as the Revolution of France bore the marks of being the cause of liberty it united all hearts and centered all opinions. But this unanimity of approbation has been for a considerable time decreasing. The excesses which have constantly multiplied, with greater and greater aggravations have successively though slowly detached reflecting men from their partiality for an object which has appeared less and less to merit their regard. Their reluctance to abandon it has however been proportioned to the ardor and fondness with which they embraced it. They were willing to overlook many faults—to apologise for some enormities—to hope that better justifications existed than were seen—to look forward to more calm and greater moderation, after the first shocks of the political earthquake had subsided. But instead of this, they have been witnesses to one volcano succeeding another, the last still more dreadful than the former, spreading ruin and devastation far and wide—subverting the foundations of right security and property, of order, morality and religion sparing neither sex nor age, confounding innocence with guilt, involving the old and the young, the sage and the madman, the long tried friend of virtue and his country and the upstart pretender to purity and patriotism—the bold projector of new treasons with the obscure in indiscriminate and profuse destruction. They have found themselves driven to the painful alternative of renouncing an object dear to their wishes or of becoming by the continuance of their affection for it accomplices with Vice Anarchy Despotism and Impiety.

But though an afflicting experience has materially lessened the number of the admirers of the French Revolution among us and has served to chill the ardor of many more, who profess still to retain their attachment to it, from what they suppose to be its ultimate tendency; yet the effect of Experience has been thus far much less than could reasonably have been expected. The predilection for it still continues extensive and ardent. And what is extraordinary it continues to comprehend men who are able to form a just estimate of the information which destroys its title to their favour.

It is not among the least perplexing phenomena of the present times, that a people like that of the United States—exemplary for humanity and moderation surpassed by no other in the love of order and a knowledge of the true principles of liberty, distinguished for purity of morals and a just reverence for Religion should so long persevere in partiality for a state of things the most cruel, sanguinary, and violent that ever stained the annals of mankind, a state of things which annihilates the foundations of social order and true liberty, confounds all moral distinctions and *substitutes to* the mild & beneficent religion of the Gospel a gloomy, persecuting and desolating atheism. To the eye of a wise man, this partiality is the most inauspicious circumstance, that has appeared in the affairs of this country. It leads involuntarily and irresistibly to apprehensions concerning the soundness of our principles and the stability of our welfare. It is natural to fear that the transition may not be difficult from the approbation of bad things to the imitation of them; a fear which can only be mitigated by a careful estimate of the extraneous causes that have served to mislead the public judgment.

But though we may find in these causes a solution of the fact calculated to abate our solicitude for the consequences; yet we cannot consider the public happiness as out of the reach of danger so long as our principles continue to be exposed to the debauching influence of admiration for an example which, it will not be too strong to say, presents the caricature of human depravity. And the pride of national character at least can find no alleviation for the wound which must be inflicted by so ill-judged so unfortunate a partiality.

If there be anything solid in virtue—the time must come when it will have been a disgrace to have advocated the Revolution of France in its late stages.

This is a language to which the ears of the people of this country have not been accustomed. Every thing has hitherto conspired to confirm the pernicious fascination by which they are enchained. There has been a positive and a negative conspiracy against the truth which has served to shut out its enlightening ray. Those who always float with the popular gale perceiving the prepossession of the people have administered to it by all the acts in their power—endeavoring to recommend themselves by an exaggerated zeal for a favorite object. Others through timidity caution or an ill-judged policy unwilling to expose themselves to the odium of resisting the general current of feeling have betrayed by silence that Truth which they were unable not to perceive. Others, whose sentiments have weight in the community have been themselves the sincere dupes of ————. [*sic*] Hence the voice of reason has been stifled and the Nation has been left unadmonished to travel on in one of the most degrading delusions that ever disparaged the understandings of an enlightened people.

To recall them from this dangerous error—to engage them to dismiss their prejudices & consult dispassionately their own good sense—to lead them to an appeal from their own enthusiasm to their reason and humanity would be the most important service that could be rendered to the United States at the present juncture. The error entertained is not on a mere speculative question. The French Revolution is a political convulsion that in a great or less degree shakes the whole civilized world and it is of real consequence to the principles and of course to the happiness of a Nation to estimate it rightly.

SUGGESTIONS FOR FURTHER READING

Readers will find that historians have produced a wealth of excellent studies on the French Revolution. Provided here are a group of books, mainly produced of late, that those interested can use to move beyond the survey into more specialized studies. Although we tried to select roughly the same number of works for each chapter, the number suggested varies a bit—a reflection of different levels of current scholarly attention. The readings for Chapter 6 are particularly numerous because the subject matter—the revolutionary legacy—brings into focus the writings of scholars, critics, and intellectuals. We therefore listed some of the major works that have appeared during the last two centuries, instead of only a few recent books that introduce important subjects.

Chapter 1: France on the Eve of 1789

Bell, David A. *Lawyers and Citizens: The Making of a Political Elite in Old-Regime France*. New York: Oxford University Press, 1994.

Bouton, Cynthia A. *The Flour War: Gender, Class, and Community in Late Ancien Régime French Society*. University Park: The Pennsylvania State University Press, 1993.

Censer, Jack R. *The French Press in the Age of Enlightenment*. New York: Routledge, 1994.

Chartier, Roger. *The Cultural Origins of the French Revolution*. Translated by Lydia G. Cochrane. Durham, N.C.: Duke University Press, 1991.

Darnton, Robert. *The Forbidden Best-Sellers of Pre-Revolutionary France*. New York: W. W. Norton, 1995.

Goodman, Dena. *The Republic of Letters: A Cultural History of the French Enlightenment*. Ithaca, N.Y.: Cornell University Press, 1994.

Maza, Sarah. *Private Lives and Public Affairs: The Causes Célèbres of Prerevolutionary France*. Berkeley and Los Angeles: University of California Press, 1993.

Roche, Daniel. *France in the Enlightenment*. Translated by Arthur Goldhammer. Cambridge, Mass.: Harvard University Press, 1998.

Van Kley, Dale K. *The Religious Origins of the French Revolution: From Calvin to the Civil Constitution, 1560–1791*. New Haven, Conn.: Yale University Press, 1996.

Chapter 2: From Constitutional to Democratic Revolution

Desan, Suzanne. *Reclaiming the Sacred: Lay Religion and Popular Politics in Revolutionary France.* Ithaca, N.Y.: Cornell University Press, 1990.

Hanson, Paul R. *Provincial Politics in the French Revolution: Caen and Limoges, 1789–1794.* Baton Rouge: Louisiana State University Press, 1989.

Hunt, Lynn. *The Family Romance of the French Revolution.* Berkeley and Los Angeles: University of California Press, 1992.

Jordan, David P. *The King's Trial: Louis XVI vs. the French Revolution.* Berkeley and Los Angeles: University of California Press, 1979.

Tackett, Timothy. *Becoming a Revolutionary: The Deputies of the French National Assembly and the Emergence of a Revolutionary Culture, 1789–1790.* Princeton, N.J.: Princeton University Press, 1996.

Chapter 3: Terror, War, and Resistance

Arasse, Daniel. *The Guillotine and the Terror.* Translated by Christopher Miller. London: A. Lane, 1989.

Godineau, Dominique. *The Women of Paris and Their French Revolution.* Translated by Katherine Streip. Berkeley and Los Angeles: University of California Press, 1998.

Hufton, Olwen H. *Women and the Limits of Citizenship in the French Revolution.* Toronto: University of Toronto Press, 1992.

Ozouf, Mona. *Festivals and the French Revolution.* Translated by Alan Sheridan. Cambridge, Mass.: Harvard University Press, 1988.

Sutherland, Donald M. G. *The Chouans: The Social Origins of Popular Counter-Revolution in Upper Brittany, 1770–1796.* New York: Oxford University Press, 1982.

Chapter 4: The Revolution in the Colonies

Blackburn, Robin. *The Overthrow of Colonial Slavery, 1776–1848.* London: Verso, 1988.

Garrigus, John C. "'Sons of the Same Father': Gender, Race, and Citizenship in French Saint-Domingue, 1760–1792." In *Visions and Revisions of Eighteenth-Century France,* ed. Christine Adams, Jack R. Censer, and Lisa Jane Graham. University Park: The Pennsylvania State University Press, 1997.

Gaspar, David Barry, and David Patrick Geggus, eds. *A Turbulent Time: The French Revolution and the Greater Caribbean.* Bloomington: Indiana University Press, 1997.

Geggus, David Patrick. *Slavery, War, and Revolution: The British Occupation of Saint Domingue, 1793–1798.* New York: Oxford University Press, 1982.

James, C. L. R. *The Black Jacobins: Toussaint L'Ouverture and the San Domingo Revolution.* Second edition. New York: Vintage Books, 1989.

Chapter 5: The Rise and Fall of Napoleon Bonaparte

Bergeron, Louis. *France Under Napoleon.* Translated by R. R. Palmer. Princeton, N.J.: Princeton University Press, 1981.

Blanning, T. C. W. *The French Revolutionary Wars, 1787–1802.* New York: Arnold, 1996.

Connelly, Owen. *Napoleon's Satellite Kingdoms.* New York: Free Press, 1965.

Lyons, Martyn. *France Under the Directory.* Cambridge: Cambridge University Press, 1975.

————. *Napoleon Bonaparte and the Legacy of the French Revolution.* New York: St. Martin's Press, 1994.

Popkin, Jeremy D. *The Right-Wing Press in France, 1792–1800.* Chapel Hill: University of North Carolina Press, 1980.

Woloch, Isser. *The New Regime: Transformations of the French Civic Order, 1789–1820s.* New York: W. W. Norton, 1994.

Chapter 6: Legacies and Interpretations

Political Legacies

Buonarroti, Filippo (Philippe). *Buonarroti's History of Babeuf's Conspiracy for Equality.* Translated by Bronterre. London: H. Hetherington, 1836.

Burke, Edmund. *Reflections on the Revolution in France.* London: J. Dodsley, 1790.

Chateaubriand, François-René. *An Historical, Political, and Moral Essay on Revolutions, Ancient and Modern.* English translation by anonymous translator. London: H. Colburn, 1815.

Maistre, Joseph de. *Considerations on France.* Translated and edited by Richard A. Lebrun. Montreal: McGill-Queen's University Press, 1974.

Marx, Karl, and Friedrich Engels. *The Communist Manifesto: With Related Documents.* Introduction by John E. Toews. Boston: Bedford/St. Martin's, 1999.

Paine, Thomas. *The Rights of Man: Being an Answer to Mr. Burke's Attack on the French Revolution.* 2 vols. London: J. S. Jordon, 1791.

Staël, Germaine de. *Madame de Staël on Politics, Literature, and National Character.* Translated, edited, and with an introduction by Morroe Berger. Garden City, N.Y.: Doubleday, 1964.

Scholarly Interpretations

Aulard, Alphonse. *The French Revolution: A Political History, 1789–1804.* 4 vols. Translated by Bernard Miall. New York: Scribner, 1910.

Baker, Keith Michael. *Inventing the French Revolution: Essays on French Political Culture in the Eighteenth Century.* Cambridge: Cambridge University Press, 1990.

Furet, François. *Interpreting the French Revolution.* Translated by Elborg Forster. Cambridge: Cambridge University Press, 1981.

Gaxotte, Pierre. *The French Revolution.* Translated and with an introduction by Walter Alison Phillips. London: C. Scribner's Sons, 1932.

Hunt, Lynn. *Politics, Culture, and Class in the French Revolution.* Berkeley and Los Angeles: University of California Press, 1984.

Landes, Joan B. *Women and the Public Sphere in the Age of the French Revolution.* Ithaca, N.Y.: Cornell University Press, 1988.

Lefebvre, Georges. *The Coming of the French Revolution.* Translated by R. R. Palmer. Princeton, N.J.: Princeton University Press, 1979.

Mathiez, Albert. *The French Revolution.* Translated by Catherine Alison Phillips. New York: A. A. Knopf, 1929.

Michelet, Jules. *Historical View of the French Revolution.* Translated by C. Cocks. London: H. C. Bohn, 1848.

Mignet, François-Auguste. *History of the French Revolution.* Anonymous English translation. London: G. Bell and Sons, 1902.

Soboul, Albert. *The Parisian Sans-Culottes and the French Revolution, 1793–1794.* Translated by Gwynne Lewis. Oxford: Clarendon Press, 1964.

Taine, Hippolyte. *The Origins of Contemporary France: The Ancient Regime, the Revolution, the Modern Regime: Selected Chapters.* Edited and with an introduction by Edward T. Gargan. Chicago: University of Chicago Press, 1974.

Thiers, Adolphe. *The History of the French Revolution.* 5 vols. Translated by Frederick Shoberl. London: Richard Bentley, 1838.

Tocqueville, Alexis de. *The Old Régime and the French Revolution.* Translated by Stuart Gilbert. Garden City, N.Y.: Doubleday, 1955.

Vovelle, Michel. *The Revolution Against the Church: From Reason to the Supreme Being.* Translated by Alan José. Columbus: Ohio State University Press, 1991.

INDEX

CREDITS FOR IMAGES

The following images are courtesy of the Museum of the French Revolution, Vizelle, France, and are used by permission: 1.3, 2.1, 2.2, 2.3, 2.4, 2.5, 3.1, 3.2, 3.3, 3.6, 5.1, 5.2, 6.1. Color Images 2, 3, 5, 6, 8, and 9 are also courtesy of the Museum of the French Revolution.

The following images are courtesy of the Cornell University Division of Rare Books and Manuscript Collections, Ithaca, New York, and are used by permission: 1.2, 3.4, 3.5, 5.3, 6.2. Color Images: 1, 4, and 7 are also courtesy of the Cornell University Division of Rare Books and Manuscript Collections.

Figure 1.1 is courtesy of the Prints and Photos Division of the Library of Congress and is used by permission.

Figures 4.1 and 4.2 are from Marcus Rainsford, *An Historical Account of the Black Empire of Hayti* (London: J. Cundee, 1805), 241.

Maps by Andrea Ades Vasquez.

INSTALLATION FOR *LIBERTY, EQUALITY, FRATERNITY* CD-ROM

FOR WINDOWS USERS: Quit all open applications and save your work before beginning the installation. Insert *Liberty* CD-ROM into CD-ROM drive. Double click on My Computer. Double click the *Liberty* icon to open the disk. Double click on the "TK3_Reader_Setup.exe" icon on the CD and follow the on-screen instructions. (TK3 Reader is the software that "reads" the Liberty book; a shortcut to the Reader software will be placed on your desktop. That shortcut allows you to open *Liberty* or any other book built with TK3.)

If you do not already have QuickTime 4.0 or higher, you need to install it. Double click on the QuickTime installer and follow the on-screen instructions. (If you already have a newer version of QuickTime, it will tell you and you do not have to reinstall.) Although the instructions imply that it will download QuickTime from the Web, the disk contains the full QuickTime program and you do not need an Internet connection to proceed. If you install QuickTime, you will be asked to restart your computer.

Once TK3 (and QuickTime) is installed, double click on the LIBERTY book icon on the CD. (You can locate the CD by double clicking on My Computer. After the book is open, you can choose "Getting Started" from the Table of Contents page for some tips on using it. (You can also open the book by launching the TK3 reader and then choosing "open book" from the file menu.)

FOR MAC USERS: Quit all open applications and save your work before beginning the installation. Insert *Liberty* CD-ROM into CD-ROM drive. Double click the *Liberty* icon (the stylized FR) to open the disk. Double click on the "TK3 Reader Installer" icon on the CD and follow the on-screen instructions. (TK3 Reader is the software that "reads" the *Liberty* book; an alias to the Reader software will be placed on your desktop. That shortcut allows you to open *Liberty* or any other book built with TK3.)

If you do not already have QuickTime 4.0 or higher, you need to install it. Double click on the QuickTime installer and follow the on-screen instructions. (If you already have a newer version of QuickTime, it will tell you and you do not have to reinstall.) Although the instructions imply that it will download QuickTime from the Web, the disk contains the full QuickTime program and you do not need an Internet connection to proceed. If you install QuickTime, you will be asked to restart your computer.

Once TK3 (and QuickTime) is installed, double click on the "LIBERTY.tk3" icon on the CD. After the book is open, you can choose "Getting Started" from the Table of Contents page for some tips on using it. (You can also open the book by launching the TK3 reader and then choosing "open book" from the file menu.)

The *Liberty, Equality, Fraternity* CD-ROM was produced by Pennee Bender, Joshua Brown, and Roy Rosenzweig at the Center for History and New Media (George Mason University) and the American Social History Project (City University of New York).